I0114561

# POLITICAL AND SOCIAL CHANGE

Edited by Martin Bak Jørgensen and Óscar García Agustín

## VOLUME 10

*Zu Qualitätssicherung und Peer Review der vorliegenden Publikation*

Die Qualität der in dieser Reihe erscheinenden Arbeiten wird vor der Publikation durch einen Herausgeber der Reihe sowie durch einen externen, von der Herausgeberschaft ernannten Gutachter im Blind-Verfahren geprüft. Dabei ist der Autor der Arbeit dem Gutachter während der Prüfung namentlich nicht bekannt.

*Notes on the quality assurance and peer review of this publication*

Prior to publication, the quality of the work published in this series is reviewed by one of the editors of the series and blind reviewed by an external referee appointed by the editorship. The referee is not aware of the author's name when performing the review.

Rieke Schröder / Anabel Soriano Oliva / Steffen Jensen (eds.)

# Situating Displacement

## Explorations of Global (Im)Mobility

PETER LANG

**Bibliographic Information published by the Deutsche Nationalbibliothek**
The Deutsche Nationalbibliothek lists this publication in the Deutsche Nationalbibliografie; detailed bibliographic data is available in the internet at http://dnb.d-nb.de.

**Library of Congress Cataloging-in-Publication Data**
A CIP catalog record for this book has been applied for at the Library of Congress.

Cover Image: Colourbox

This book was funded by the Department of Politics and Society,
Aalborg University

ISSN 2198-8595
ISBN 978-3-631-84760-2 (Print)
E-ISBN 978-3-631-87215-4 (E-PDF)
E-ISBN 978-3-631-87216-1 (EPUB)
DOI 10.3726/b19375



Peter Lang – Berlin · Bern · Bruxelles · New York ·
Oxford · Warszawa · Wien



This publication has been peer reviewed.

www.peterlang.com

# Table of Contents

Rieke Schröder, Anabel Soriano Oliva, and Steffen Jensen

# Situating Displacement

Displacement and forced mobility have become perennial issues of our time (Hakovirta, 1993; Malkki, 1995). According to the United Nations High Commissioner for Refugees (UNHCR), there were 82.4 million forcibly displaced people worldwide at the end of 2020 (UNHCR, 2021: n.p.) demonstrating the large scale of this issue. Especially in the wake of the so-called migration and refugee crisis in 2015–2016, in electoral campaigns all over Europe and the United States, the issues of displacement, refugees and migrants are omnipresent and objects of intense political attention and anxieties. Increasingly restrictive policies and national solutions are *en vogue*. Border controls and walls are becoming a choice solution for many governments especially in the global North in the hope that if enough borders are closed and fences and walls are put up, people will not be able to enter the country at hand, and thus will not be an issue of concern for that state. For this reason, Norbert Cyrus (2017) for instance proposes to use the term 'refugee protection crisis' instead.

Whether he is right or not, Cyrus' text testifies to the academic and policy focus on displacement and enforced mobility. In a recent agenda setting piece Alexander Betts and Paul Collier (2017), for instance, explore ways to mend a broken refugee system. In this way, it is the legal and interventionist approach to displacement that takes centre stage. We do not aim to critique or review the specific approaches. Rather, we agree with Amanda Hammar (2014: 3–4) in her analysis of *Displacement Economies* that displacement cannot be reduced to an often legalistic discussion of refugees. As she notes, refugee studies tend to ignore or downplay the importance of for instance political economy. She continues to suggest that mobility studies sometimes, but not always, downplay the element of force and violence and that the work on war economies often downplay the effects of displacement. Hence, she identifies a need to locate displacement in 'enforced changes in interweaving spatial, social and symbolic conditions and relations' in which displaced lives are produced (ibid.: 9). Hammar's analysis makes clear that displacement always relates to some level and kind of force. However, what constitutes force is seldom clear-cut, as Bjarnesen and Turner (2020) point out in their succinct analysis of invisibility and displacement in Africa. Economic as well as environmental, subjective and political drivers may force people to leave. What do we make of Ghanaian fishermen who leave their coastal villages that have been depleted of fish stock by Chinese and European fishing vessels to brave the Sahara, the Mediterranean Sea and the rough informality of the Italian labour market as in Hans Lucht's remarkable book *Darkness before Daybreak* (Lucht, 2011)? Have they been forced and if by what and by whom? Finally, displacement does not always entail that people are forced to leave. As Jefferson, Turner and Jensen (2019) argue, stuckness is the conceptual twin of displacement as both concepts focus on the element of force – to put people on the move or to impede their movement. As Stephen Lubkemann (2008, 2010) implicitly suggests in his analysis of war in Mozambique, sometimes the world and opportunities move, leaving people displaced of the relations that sustained them. These and other studies of displacement and forced mobility have been central in our understanding of displacement. In this volume, we want to make two contributions to the discussion, one conceptual and one empirical or geographical.

Conceptually, we suggest that it is useful to privilege interdisciplinary understandings even further. Displacement studies are per definition interdisciplinary, involving law, political science, anthropology, historical and a host of other humanities, public health and social science disciplines. Notwithstanding this interdisciplinary framing, and at the danger of crudifying a complex and varied literature, forced mobility and displacement studies tend to foreground the processes and structures of mobility and displacement as well as the actions of the people on the move. While such focus sounds evident and as the logical analytical approach, we think it might be useful to de-centre displacement slightly, not to do away with it but to situate it in a larger body of literature beyond explorations of systems of and around displacement and the actions of the displaced. In this volume, we look at displacement and forced mobility from urban studies, queer, gender and race studies, conflict studies, human rights and development, labour market studies, architecture, governance studies and studies of mineral extraction. Displacement and forced mobility have roles to play in all the contributions. For instance, mineral extraction, as in Raftopoulous' contribution, produces displacement but does not have to be reduced to displacement. Rather to understand the element of displacement, we need to understand the complicated relations between mineral extraction and human rights for instance. Displacement is also absolutely central for understanding how conflicts move in place and time as in Kublitz' contribution. However, if we only privileged displacement we would lose sight of the complex intersections between urban life, history and conflicts that she describes.

The multi-disciplinary nature of this anthology offers a fresh look at the theme of forced mobility and displacement. Through case studies that do not necessarily, or exclusively, fit the mould of these disciplines, and with analytical perspectives from other academic fields, we broaden the scope of thinking about displacement. By bringing well-established ideas from migration, mobility, and refugee research into conversation with other disciplines and approaches, we aim to open up new reflections, relevant across several disciplinary fields. The aim of this exercise is not to downplay the importance of displacement. That would be ill-advised for a book that has displacement in the title. Rather, by situating displacement and bringing it into dialogue with other themes, we hope to understand displacement as well as the theme at hand better. For instance, we cannot understand displacement in Cape Town as explored by Steffen Jensen, without understanding urban politics in its own right. At the same time, by introducing displacement in the analysis of urban politics we also learn something about the latter, which is that urban politics historically have been constituted by layers or sedimentations of multiple and diverse processes of displacement. It also allows us to see that those people that are normally constituted as 'host populations' cannot be understood without understanding internal, historical processes of displacement. By situating, not foregrounding displacement, we understand both displacement and urban politics better.

Empirically, we insist on the global nature of displacement and mobility. This may also sound like an obvious point. However, we would suggest that much attention, especially in discussions related to present-day migration and displacement foreground an assumed directionality of cross-border displacement and forced mobility from the global South to the global North. To engage with a global perspective entails a deconstruction of the oppositional binary interpretation of peoples' displacement, in which people on the move are oftentimes categorized within the binaries of North/South, legal/illegal, mobile/immobile, temporary/permanent, voluntary/forced etc. These binaries represent the phenomena of migration and displacement as a linear movement from 'poorer' to 'richer' areas, or solely from the global South to the global North that animate much research on mobility (Glick-Schiller and Çağlar, 2016; Xiang and Lindquist, 2014). Such binaries run the risk of obscuring lived realities, as it disallows reflections of the multifaceted nature of the movement of people, in this way neglecting the complexity of displaced lives. This suggests that instead of only looking at the country of arrival or country of origin, we must be interested in all the stages of displacement and mobility; people come from some place, via routes and roads, to somewhere. Again, this is what Hans Lucht (2011) does as he follows Ghanaian fishermen forced to migrate due to overfishing and depletion of natural resources on their way through the desert and across the sea to end up as illegal migrants in Naples. However, while we need to understand such routes from the South to the North, this understanding of people's displacement is complicated by the different contributions. Tamirace Fakhoury's and Ahlam Chemlali's contributions suggest that the transit areas may become end stations as EU border agencies work hard to keep migrants out of EU in North Africa and the Middle East. Furthermore, as Morten Lynge Madsen and Brigitte Dragsted illustrate in their analyses of urban Nairobi, much displacement takes the form of intra-city and rural-urban migration in the global South. Finally, Magnus Andersen, Marlene Spanger and Sophia Dørffer Hvalkof explore Danish labour markets and Eastern European migration through the lens of precarity unsettling easy reduction to North and South. Hence, the book situates displacement in the global south, in transit as well as in the global North.

## Organizing the argument

The anthology has emerged out of ongoing conversations between scholars and students in Global Refugee Studies at the department of Politics and Society, Aalborg University. With contributions from different disciplines such as political science, anthropology, sociology, media studies, history and philosophy, the anthology questions and explores flight, migration and conflict from rather different perspectives and methods as well as across the global North and South. All chapters are based on primary research, many of them on long-term fieldwork. Following the conversational origins of the volume, we have tried to keep chapters short, at times in an essayistic style to enable debate. In this way, we hope that the anthology can be an invitation to grapple with the broad scope of mobility and displacement from perhaps surprising angles outside but speaking to the literature on displacement and mobility.

Chapters 1 through 5 home in on issues of displacement and forced mobility in the global North. In the first chapter, 'In and Out and in and Out the Closet: Queer Refugees and Epistemic Furniture' Rieke Schröder writes from a queer studies perspective. She invites us to think in new ways about integration beyond service delivery and legal frameworks to begin thinking about the dilemmas of cultural integration. She explores how queer refugees navigate the closet and coming out of it during their asylum process in Denmark. In order to become intelligible for the Western lens, queer refugees have to integrate themselves into Western ideas of how to be queer – what Lisa Duggan (2002) has termed homonormativity. As their pre-asylum accommodation is often queer hostile, queer refugees have to juggle a closetedness in their homes and an expected 'out and proudness' during their asylum processes. In this way, Schröder provides an intersectional analysis to refugee studies in which issues of race and nationality frequently dominate.

Furthermore, her analysis homes in on one of the cultural fault lines at which queer people often find themselves as the West celebrates particular forms of queerness in contrast to perceived Muslim antagonism.

In Chapter 2, Anabel Soriano Oliva takes on the issue of the selling of sex in surprising ways from a philosophical perspective. In 'Discussing Pateman Through Khamis' Exhibition *Black Birds*' Soriano explores how the different ontological consideration of those involved in the sex-money exchange generates different frames of its epistemological understanding. Her chapter is a philosophical deconstruction of Carol Pateman's seminal contribution to sex work, *What's Wrong with Prostitution?* (Pateman, 1999). Soriano first confronts Pateman argument with Khamis' exhibition Black Birds (Hodal, 2020). The exhibition *materializes* the case of some Afghans and Iranian asylum seekers that while identifying as heterosexual men, sell homosexual sex in Tiergarten, Berlin. The materialization of this case points out the urgency of not only reconsidering the selling of sex from an intersectional gaze but also from non-essentialist location. As refugee studies are frequently overly empirical, Soriano's philosophically inspired analysis illustrates the potential of combining rigid philosophical thinking and method with empirical data about displacement. Taking her empirical point of departure in an exhibition, Soriano's analysis illustrates the potentiality in finding new sources of empirical material beyond interviews and policies that are able to enrich global studies of displacement.

In the third chapter of the collection, Anja Kublitz writes from a perspective of anthropology of conflict. In 'Conflicts on the Move: Passing on the Palestinian Conflict', Kublitz explores how conflicts move across space and time, more specifically how the Palestinian conflict moves from the Middle East to Denmark and from parents to children. Based on eighteen months of fieldwork between 2005 and 2008 among Palestinian families in Danish housing projects, Kublitz argues that the Palestinian conflict is transmitted not only through stories of the past but first and foremost through forgetting and silences. Taking her point of departure in the extended case of a young Palestinian, Yassin, and his family, Kublitz examines how the silences (of a country, relatives, a past) are very loud and present. Kublitz suggests that what the parents do not wish to speak of, and what the youngsters do not want to hear, constitutes a gap that enables the conflict to be re-created and transformed. Apart from being a succinct analysis of integration processes in Denmark and their failures, Kublitz' chapter also highlights how conflicts do not stop when the war is over but continue to affect the lives of refugees for generations.

In Chapter 4, 'Living a Precarious Life as Migrant Worker in the Danish Labour Market', Magnus Andersen, Marlene Spanger and Sophia Dørffer

Hvalkof foreground labour market structures and social inequality. They explore how the Danish labour market system, also called the 'Danish model', becomes the vehicle for the exploitation of migrant workers in Denmark. Based on the migrants' experiences, they pay attention to the theoretical concept of precarity as an analytical tool allowing them to analyse how the Danish system legitimizes practices that exploit the migrants' work. In particular, they focus on precarious dimensions such as working situations, the relationship to the employer and the difficulties in navigating the Danish system. They ask, 'How can we understand the precarious experiences of migrant workers in Denmark?' In this way, the chapter contributes to the emerging discussions of the particular links between displacement and precarity. While the migrants explored in the chapter, who mostly come from Eastern and Central Europe, are not displaced in the same manner as a refugee from Syria, force is nonetheless a central concern at both ends of a highly precarious journey.

In Chapter 5, Asta Smedegaard Nielsen focuses on media representations of race and displacement. In her chapter, 'What Makes an Innocent Child? Exploring Innocence and Whiteness in a European Context', she explores how certain identities are contested while others are favoured. Nielsen explores how mediated representation allows bodies to take up time and space in particular ways, and thus how they become racialized and gendered (Ahmed, 2006). Empirically, Nielsen looks at representations of children positioned in an out-of-place-ness that works to constitute them as objects of public emotional investment. The chapter focuses on the case of Maria, a white girl who was found in a Romani neighbourhood in Greece in 2013. The media reporting on the case caused an affective intervention (Smedegaard Nielsen & Myong, 2019) from the public aimed at moving her from her locality of living to address her being out-of-place. The chapter highlights the importance of understanding children, affect and racialized forms of politics that dominate much debate about migration and displacement in Europe today.

In the following two chapters, a more classical understanding of displacement as something merely spatial is challenged by introducing its temporal consideration. In 'Chronotopes of Displacement in a Cape Town Squatter Camp', Steffen Jensen explores temporalities of displacement. Locating his analysis in a Cape Town Squatter Camp, Jensen writes from within urban studies focusing on how the space of the squatter camp is traversed by numerous movements across time. He demonstrates how contemporary displacement relates – but is not reducible – to different instantiations of (post)-coloniality in Cape Town. He presents the different forms of displacement co-existing in Overcome Heights by adapting Bakhtin's concept of chronotopes to understand the simultaneous temporality and spatiality of displacement. Jensen closes the contribution with a discussion of what these different forms of displacement reveal about the colonial instantiations in present-day Cape Town. In this way, the chapter contributes to the emerging postcolonial turn in displacement studies by foregrounding colonialism rather than seeing it as the context of displacement.

In Chapter 7, Brigitte Dragsted explores how dreams shape forms of social, bodily and existential mobility among illegal hawkers in central Nairobi. 'Dreams: Mobile Bodies and Troubled Temporal Unfolding in Nairobi' shows how the unsettlement experienced by the hawkers who constantly have to run from law enforcement officers in central Nairobi is not only a bodily kind of unsettlement, but also a temporal one. Hawkers feel an urge to move from their current situation in life. This finds expression in the widespread dream of opening their own shop. However, better-off Nairobians see the presence of hawkers who become too permanent in the city's streets as a danger of derailing urban development – of temporal regression of their metropole. Middle class Nairobians' fear that their dreams of development is under threat allows for the violent policing of hawkers, further denying hawkers the possibility of settling on the streets in which they work. The situation of hawkers illustrates how rural-urban migration and displacement do not end with migrants settling in cities, but how migrant status becomes a mark attached to bodies, and an occasion for continued violation.

Chapters 8 and 9 explore the relation between human rights, violence and displacement. In 'Extractivism, Territorialization, and Displacement in Latin America', Malayna Raftopoulos helps us understand the relations between extraction and displacement. She explores how the impositions of resource extractionist activities in Latin America have given birth to several spill-over effects framed in a logic of territorialization-reterritorialization. In this sense, the extractivism territorializes the land and those who inhabit it by producing the displacement of the population and forms of production. At the same time, it has redefined land disputes in the regions pitting poor and marginalized populations against major economic players. Finally, Raftopoulos investigates how the state responds to those who oppose such activities, and how they have been criminalized under authoritarian actions. Resource extraction is central in many contexts of displacement globally and is part of wider discussions around limited resources that extends, as well, to displacement in relation to climate change. Raftopoulos' contribution illustrates just how complex such questions of resources are and how they are always tied into struggles of power.

On a slightly different note, Morten Lynge Madsen takes Nairobi as a field to study human rights and humanitarianism in 'Do Human Rights Matter When you are Stuck in an Urban Informal Settlement?' Through a case study of two young men, both around 20 years of age, who have grown up in Mathare, an informal settlement in Nairobi, Lynge explores the relationship between urban violence and men's encounters with authority. Lynge foregrounds the relevance and limitations of Human Rights Based Approaches in a context where young men are more often than not killable subjects, where immobility is not so much a physical but a social factor, and where violence constitutes a primary repertoire of action for the young men and the state. Lynge illustrates that while human rights and legal frameworks are and should be central in our advocacy and research, there are limits to how much we can rely on them – especially at the bottom of the global, social pile.

Chapters 10, 11 and 12 take us into the borderlands in ways that complement traditional studies of borders in migration and displacement studies. In her chapter, Ahlam Chemlali looks at the externalized borders from Europe in Northern Africa, and in what ways the 'border violence' there is a gendered phenomenon. 'Understanding "Gendered Border Violence": The Case of Libya' demonstrates how European policymakers, media and humanitarian actors frame migrant women as a specific victim group, a 'pure' victim in need of rescue. Chemlali asks how gender and constructions of victimhood play part in contexts of border control and externalization in new spaces of transit.

In her contribution, 'Governing displacement: A Polycentric Perspective' Tamirace Fakhoury draws on illustrative cases from scholarship on the politics of displacement in the Middle East and explores how refugee governance manifests itself empirically. She investigates how the study of refugee spaces, experiences and voices are able to enrich our understanding of the ways through which trans-scalar authority materializes across time and space. This analysis complements the analytical privileging of the actions of migrants and host countries in migration and displacement studies.

Finally, in Chapter 12, Michael Alexander Ulfstjerne explores borders as material and symbolic phenomena. However, rather than exploring borders solely as obstacles to migration and cause of migrant suffering, Ulfstjerne proposes a more ambiguous reading of the border. In 'Ode to Wall', he discusses the borders as intense sites of imaginations and contestation beyond its use as a technology of power. Following this, thinking along other kinds of territorial markers as walls, murals and private hedges, the social function of physical boundaries is discussed through the case of refugee housing design. This approach moves us beyond simple dichotomous discussions of borders as inherently good or bad. While such issues of border security, externalization of borders, violence and violence caused by border politics are important, the border cannot be reduced to effects of the national order of things.

## Bibliography

Ahmed, S. (2006) *Queer Phenomenology. Orientations, Objects, Others*. Durham and London: Duke University Press.

Betts, A. & Collier, P. (2017) *Refuge: Transforming a Broken Refugee System*. London: Allen Lane.

Bjarnesen, J. & Turner, S. (eds.) (2020) *Invisibility in African Displacements. From Structural Marginalization to Strategies of Avoidance*. London: Zed Books.

Cyrus, N. (2017) "Die Flüchtlinge und ihr Status. Praktische Implikationen einer defizitären Rechtsstellung." In T. Eppenstein, and C. Ghaderi (eds.), *Flüchtlinge. Multiperspektivische Zugänge*. Wiesbaden: Springer VS: 113–127.

Duggan, L. (2002) 'The New Homonormativity: The Sexual Politics of Neoliberalism'. In R. Castronovo, and D. D. Nelson (eds.), *Materializing Democracy: Toward a Revitalized Cultural Politics*. Durham: Duke University Press: 175–196.

Glick Schiller, N. & Çağlar, A. (2016) "Displacement, Emplacement and Migrant Newcomers: Rethinking Urban Sociabilities within Multiscalar Power." *Identities*, 23(1): 17–34.

Hakovirta, H. (1993) "The Global Refugee Problem: A Model and Its Application." *International Political Science Review / Revue Internationale De Science Politique*, 14(1): 35–57.

Hammar, A. (2014) "Introduction: Displacement Economies – Paradoxes of Crisis and Creativity." In Hammar, A. (ed.), *Displacement Economies – Paradoxes of Crisis and Creativity*. London: Zed Books: 3–32.

Hodar, K (2020) "A Step Away from Hell: The Young Male Refugees Selling Sex to Survive." *The Guardian*. https://www.theguardian.com/global-development/2020/feb/21/a-step-away-from-hell-the-young-male-refugees-selling-sex-to-survive-berlin-tiergarten.

Jefferson, A., Turner, S. & Jensen, S. (2019) "Introduction: On Stuckness and Sites of Confinement." *Ethnos*, 84(1): 1–13. DOI 10.1080/00141844.2018.1544917

Lubkemann, S. C. (2008) *Culture in Chaos. An Anthropology of the Social Condition in War*. Chicago: The University of Chicago Press.

Lubkemann, S. C. (2010) "Past Directions and Future Possibilities in the Study of African Displacement." Unpublished Scoping Study. Stockholm: Nordic Afrika Institute.

Lucht, H. (2011) *Darkness Before Daybreak*. Berkeley University of California Press.

Malkki, L (1995) "Refugees and Exile: From 'Refugee Studies' to the National Order of Things." *Annual Review of Anthropology*, 24(1): 495–523.

Pateman, C. (1999) "What's Wrong with Prostitution?" *Women's Studies Quarterly*, 27(1/2): 53–64.

Smedegaard Nielsen, A. & Myong, L. (2019) "White Danish Love as Affective Intervention: Studying Media Representations of Family Reunification Involving Children." *Nordic Journal of Migration Research*, 9(4): 497–514. DOI: http://doi.org/10.2478/njmr-2019-0038.

UNHCR (June 2021) "Figures at a Glance." [Online data] Available from <https://www.unhcr.org/figures-at-a-glance.html> [Accessed 24 September 2021].

Xiang, B. and Lindquist, J. (2014) "Migration Infrastructure." *IMR*, 48(1): 122–148.

Rieke Schröder

# In and Out and in and Out of the Closet: Queer Refugees and Epistemic Furniture

## Introduction

*'So we are out of the closet, but into what?' – Judith Butler (1993: 309)*

Political discourse surrounding the integration of refugees[1] often calls for an assimilation of perceived 'Western'[2] ways of living from the side of the refugees. In much discourse, Western societies are supposed to value gender equality and freedom in expressing sexual orientation or gender identity. Because (most) member states of the European Union are proclaiming themselves LGBTQ+ [3] friendly,[4] these countries should be a safe haven for people who are fearing persecution in their country of origin on grounds of their non-cis-heterosexual sexual orientation or gender identity, on grounds of being queer.[5]

In Denmark, which is often described as one of the most LGBTQ+ friendly places in the world (Rainbow Europe, n.d.), the majority of inhabitants are in favour of legal same-sex marriage (Sahgal, 2018). Even though Denmark has a rather restrictive asylum regime (Kreichauf, 2019), it is possible to apply for asylum on grounds of being queer. However, questions remain regarding in what ways and to what extent queer refugees have to follow Nordic notions of how to be queer, in order to become intelligible for the Danish asylum authorities. This,

1 Refugees here is not used as a legal term but refers to people who are legally recognized as refugees, as well as people waiting for their asylum case to be settled.

2 Western here is 'relating to countries in the west part of the world, especially North America and countries in the west of Europe' (Cambridge Dictionary, n.d.), which also includes Denmark (see e.g. Sahgal, 2018).

3 LGBTQ+ is short for Lesbian, Gay, Bisexual, Transgender or Transsexual, Queer or Questioning. The plus signifies the inclusion of other sexual orientations or gender identities, such as non-binary or genderqueer.

4 One exception is Poland, who has recently declared over half of its territory 'LGBT-free zones' (Ciobanu, 2020).

5 Queer is an umbrella term that covers non-cis-heterosexual sexual orientation and gender identities, which could be, but are not limited to, people identifying as lesbian, gay, bisexual, transsexual, transgender, intersex, asexual, non-binary and genderqueer.

queer refugees must archive to enhance their chance of being granted asylum on the grounds of being queer. Here, it becomes evident that the complexity of refugees' and queers' lives is sometimes neglected, a point already made in the introduction of this anthology. Often, queer refugees are asked to conform to 'queer ideals' (Schippert, 2011: 77), such as expectations on how queers supposedly behave, look, act and have sex.

In their country of origin, queer refugees frequently face discrimination or criminalization due to their queerness, which results in them concealing their non-cis-heterosexual sexual orientation or gender identity. From a Western point of view, these non-visible queer practices are often termed as closeted. Still, queer refugees do not necessarily articulate their queerness or gender identity in this way and would therefore not perceive themselves as closeted – as the idiom of the closet does not exist in every vocabulary. Telling someone in German 'das du aus dem Kleiderschrank gekommen bist' might lead to ideas of owning a walk-in closet, but no one would connect this statement to a disclosure of a queer sexual orientation or gender identity. In Denmark however, it is possible to use 'komme ud af skabet' as an idiom connected to coming out.

This chapter will use the idiom of the closet as discussed by Eve Kosofsky Sedgwick (1990) in order to visualize how queer refugees are expected to integrate themselves in the Western discourse of hetero- and homosexuality – something that according to Sedgwick (1990) has affected the whole Western culture in itself. Even though they might not perceive themselves as closeted, queer refugees' identities and lives are being shaped by the closet. If they want to claim asylum on grounds of their queerness, they are asked to come out of the closet and prove their sexual orientation or gender identity. Therefore, I pose the following question: How are queer refugees navigating the closet and coming out of it during their asylum-seeking process in Denmark? I will argue that queer refugees come out of the closet into a society that forces them to adhere to Western ideas of how to be queer. In particular, in this chapter I argue that coming out is a process and not a singular event.

Methodologically, the article is based on secondary empirical material produced by Marie Lunau (2019) presented in the article The trouble with 'truth'. On the politics of life and death in the assessment of queer asylum seekers and the report LGBT Asylum Applicants in Denmark. Applying for asylum on grounds of sexual orientation and gender identity from LGBT Asylum (2015), a support group for queer refugees and asylum seekers in Denmark. In both sources, the data are anonymized. Lunau analyses how refugees in Denmark perform and/ or hide queer identities. Unlike Lunau, I re-analyse the empirical material in the context of the closet. This metaphor is relevant if we want to understand the asylum process from queer refugees' perspectives, because it visualizes the importance and simultaneity of in- and out-ness during their lives in Denmark. The individuals have to switch between different expressions of their identity, going back and forth, in and out of the closet. This confusing process makes them 'come out' in a certain way, thereby still forcing them to hide part of themselves.

The chapter first offers a brief explanation of important theoretical concepts, setting the heteronormative scene in which queer refugees have to navigate themselves – back in their country of origin and in Denmark. The Danish state is still influenced by ideas surrounding the closet and coming out of it, using this discourse as a way to position itself as queer friendly, opposed to 'other', 'underdeveloped' countries with a 'backward' approach to sexual attraction and gender identity – a logic that has been termed 'homonationalism' (Puar, 2017). After describing what role the closet plays during the asylum process of queer refugees, I demonstrate that their living conditions might force them to juggle an 'out and proud' queerness during their asylum process, and a closetedness in their private lives by using their accommodation as an example. The chapter thus concludes that queer refugees have to come in and out, and in and out of the closet.

## The closet in heteronormative societies

To underline the importance of the closet for queer refugees, this subsection presents the main queer theoretical concepts that aim to deconstruct the mainstream view on sexual attraction and gender identity. Judith Butler's (1999) heterosexual matrix describes the 'grid of cultural intelligibility through which bodies, genders, and desires are naturalized' (Butler, 1999: 7). Read through a heterosexual matrix, people are expected to have a fixed sex – male or female – according to which they are then building a stable gender – masculine or feminine. This stable gender identity constitutes their desire towards either the opposite or the same sex (Barker & Scheele, 2016). Peoples' sexual orientation and gender identity is read through this matrix, but Butler (1999) calls for the need of destabilizing it, arguing that there exists no 'natural' determination from sex to gender to desire.

The concept of heteronormativity describes the 'privilege, power, and normative status invested in heterosexuality – of the dominant society' (Cohen, 1997: 455). The 'normal' and 'natural' attraction is described as the one between one man and one woman, whereby the two of them embody the conventional gender roles and norms for each of their sexes/genders (Barker & Scheele, 2016). This is also described as 'compulsory heterosexuality' (Rich, 1980), and even though it seems to be 'natural', Butler (1999) stresses the performative character of any doing of gender or sexuality. Queer refugees have to navigate within this normative setting, a heteronormative scene.

Sedgwick (1990) detects this performative character also inside the act of coming out of the closet. Compulsory heterosexuality (Rich, 1980) and its 'deadly elasticity' (Sedgwick, 1990: 68) are constructing the closet in the first place. If heteronormativity would cease to exist, there would not be the need for anyone to come out of the closet. The closet as a piece of epistemic furniture – where epistemic here stresses the imaginative character of the closet – would not have been built had it not been for the heteronormative ideals. It is only 'built' and kept alive as an idiom to describe a person's out- or closetedness concerning their queerness by perpetually validating the assumed knowledge about hetero- and homosexuality, the hegemonic thought that heterosexuality inhabits the 'natural' hierarchical position.

In Epistemology of the Closet, Sedgwick (1990) points to the apparent contradiction that the closet as such was only created once people started to come out of it post the Stonewall riots.[6] Looking at queer refugees' countries of origin with a Western lens therefore leads to a perception of places filled with epistemic furniture: unintended purchases of shelters to cover up parts one one's identity. These closets are therefore often described as safe spaces in hostile environments. Coming out of the closet is described by Sedgwick as 'a publicly intelligible signifier for gay-related epistemological issues' (Sedgwick, 1990: 14). Thus, it is an idiom that is understood and used by many individuals of a society when discussing if someone is not cis-heterosexual – and if that person has already disclosed this information or not. In current debates around queer theory, much has been said about the dispensability of the concept of coming out. Where do you come out from, and where are you transcending to? Scholars like Diana Fuss (1991) even go so far as to argue that with pursuing the expected coming out, one actually ends up securing the hierarchical position of heterosexuality, as one acknowledges it as the 'natural' sexual orientation. Because queer refugees are asked to perform such a coming out during their asylum processes, they are asked to be part of securing heterosexuality as dominant.

6 In 1969, queer people sparked a riot in the Stonewall Inn, a gay bar in Manhatten, as a response to ongoingly being targeted by the police. These riots are depicted as the start of the LGBTQ+ rights movement (Frizzell, 2013).

## Scandinavian design – the closet in Denmark

In this section, I present Denmark as the fieldsite for the analysis, especially focusing on the ways in which heteronormativity is influencing the society. As I stressed in the introduction, Denmark is one of the most open countries in the world when it comes to LGBTQ+ rights and protection and is using this to brand itself.[7] Yet, the logic connected to the epistemic furniture of the closet has not been abolished and is still an unintended purchase queers have to live with(in). Even though Denmark is argued to be a safe place for people to come out of the closet, queer people still face discrimination on a daily basis (Lev Og Lad Leve, n.d.). In the newly launched campaign Lev og lad leve (Eng.: Live and let live), Danish queers are trying to sensitize Danish citizens and the country's politicians to the fact that hate crimes and discrimination against LGBTQ+ people are daily and constant (ibid.). The campaign started with the protest Kjoler mod hadforbrydelser (Eng.: Dresses against hate crimes), initiated by Elijah Kashmir Ali and Mizz Privileze. After the Danish actor Ali Sivandi harassed Aleksander Aarstad, who was walking the streets of Copenhagen in a dress, high heels and a full beard, this protest aimed to show that anyone can wear a dress and should feel safe while doing so (Gammelgaard, 2020).

In this incident, the notion of heteronormativity intersects with homonormativity. Heteronormativity dictates that dresses are for women only, and as a perceived male, you should not wear them. Homonormativity, as coined by Lisa Duggan (2002), describes an emerging homosexual normative position that is distancing itself from 'queerer' others; stereotypes connected to being queer in a 'proper' way. In general, lesbians and gays are accepted in Denmark – as long as they are conforming to and not contesting hetero- and homonormativity. This makes visible that there are normative rules that structure membership and power, even within marginalized groups (Cohen, 1997).

Here, the concept of intersectionality, as coined by Kimberlé Crenshaw (1989), is of importance. The situation of queer refugees differs from the ones of queer 'Danes', as they belong to more than one 'category of difference' (Davis, 2008). The intersections of categories, both between and within groups, are structured by power relations (Atewologun, 2018), influencing individual lives, social practices, institutional arrangements, and cultural ideologies. For Danish queers, the Nordic idea of how to be queer is the one they grew up with, which

7 VisitDenmark is for example advertising: 'Experience one of the world's most LGBTQ-friendly destinations', see: <https://www.visitdenmark.com/denmark/things-do/lgbtq-travel>, accessed 23 October 2020.

makes it more natural for them to live up to those ideas. Queer refugees, on the other hand, grew up with very different hegemonic understandings about gender and sexual attraction. They therefore potentially find it hard to know how they should perform their queerness in front of the Danish state. Thus, queer refugees have to navigate the closet differently to queer 'Danes'.

## Homonationalism – the closet of the nation in the nation of the closet

In order to visualize the obstacles queer refugees meet in their lives in the country of asylum – in this case Denmark – this section demonstrates how these different understandings of gender and sexual attraction are used by nation states as a way to portray themselves as progressive, in comparison to other 'less developed' countries. For this, Jasbir K. Puar (2017 [2007]) introduces the concept of homonationalism. In the book Terrorist Assemblages. Homonationalism in Queer Times Puar demonstrates how discourses on race, class and gender are being related to the nation-state. Writing from a US context, Puar (2017) makes visible how the LGBTQ+ rights movement there is used to paint 'other' cultures as less developed and backwords. Puar stresses how 'rights [protecting LGBTQ+ populations] within modes of global governmentality as a marker of civilized states, and as a frame for understanding why and how "homophobia" and its liberal counterpart, tolerance, are used to laud populations with certain attributes at some moments and then vilify other (racialized) populations for these same attributions' (Puar, 2017: 224). This discourse is idealizing the situation of queer people in 'the West', neglecting the fact that only very narrow ways of being queer and out of the closet are accepted there, and people who choose to stay in the closet are not accepted equally to 'out and proud' queers (ibid.).

For the argument of this chapter, it is important to see how the concept of homonationalism has been situated in Denmark. Michael Nebeling Petersen (2016) discusses the downsides of including lesbian and gay (not queer) people in the Danish laws, e.g., through allowing them to marry. This might benefit some individuals but is at the same time constructing a new 'normal', which in turn produces hierarchies between the people that are living up to this normality, and the people who are not (Nebeling Petersen, 2016). The politics in Denmark are inscribing and validating the privileged position of white, liberal queer subjects over non-white, progressive queers, exactly what Puar (2017) is describing within the concept of homonationalism. This points again to the different experiences queer refugees have when coming out of the closet, compared to queer 'Danes' experiences, and the relevance of the perspective of intersectionality in this context. Within the category of 'refugee' it needs to be said that experiences of gender norms differ significantly within this category, not only because of the different situation for cis and trans applicants, but also depending on the race and/or ethnicity of the applicant.

## The closet in the asylum process in Denmark[8]

This section looks specifically at the closet's role during the asylum processes from queer refugees, in order to zoom in on the research question. During their asylum process, queer refugees are not only asked to prove their need for protection, but also their belonging to 'the queers', them having a non-heteronormative sexual orientation or gender identity. The Danish Immigration Service is drawing on homonormative exclusion and inclusion criteria that it applies to decide whether someone is really queer – or not. But how does one prove to be credibly queer? Queer refugees are expected to live up to Westernized 'queer ideals' (Schippert, 2011: 77). One homonormative expectation in Denmark is that queer people will be 'out and proud' and participate in the annual pride parades for instance. A participation in these parades is used as a signifier for being actually queer by the Danish Immigration Service, as well as the Refugee Appeals Board (EDAL, n.d. a, b). As they only become intelligible as queer to the Danish Immigration Service once they perform according to homonormative expectations, queer refugees are asked to conform to homonationalism.

The Western discourse on sexual orientation and gender identity is defined by 'narrow norms of white queerness' (Lunau, 2019: 21), which have to be performed by queer refugees when they come out of the closet during their asylum process. Nina Held and Moira Dustin (2018) argue that this Westernized expectation of being queer 'presumes clear boundaries between hetero and homosexuality and requires public expression of private and sexual behaviour' (Dustin & Held, 2018: 80). These Western homonormative frames of identities are largely foreign to queer refugees claiming asylum, and while they may not personally adhere to labels such as lesbian, gay, or trans, they are forced to publicly identify with them in order to become legible through the European lens.

Edward Ou Jin Lee and Shari Brotman (2011) state 'that sexual minority refugee conceptualizations of their sexual and gender identity shifts and change over time and do not always align with Western notions of a linear and essentialized

8 Because of a lack of space, the Danish asylum process will not be fleshed out here. For a detailed presentation, see 'LGBT+ rights in Denmark' <https://lgbtasylum.dk/in-english/legislation/> accessed 3 November 2020.

sexual identity trajectory' (Lee & Brotman, 2011: 262). Even though the general understanding of sexuality is growing more and more towards understanding it as fluid and changing, this comprehension has not reached the asylum system yet. In order to enhance their chances of being granted asylum, 'queer refugee applicants repeat essentialist notions of identity in order to fit the "immutability of character," the criterion that qualifies gays, lesbians, and trans people as refugees' (Shakhsari, 2014: 1002).

Feminist scholar Sima Shakshsari (2014) states that there exists a call for '[f]ixed identities in progressive time' (ibid.: 1001), in which the queer refugees are expected to move forward when it comes to rights and freedom that they are now able to access in the 'first world'. At the same time, there is the need for them to keep to their fixed 'timeless and immutable identities that legitimate their claims for refuge' (ibid.: 999). In depicting their country of origin as backwards, adding on 'third world' narratives, their chances of being granted asylum increase (ibid.). The Danish asylum regime is reproducing the pre-existing 'distinction between "Danishness", liberalism and gay rights on the one side and "non-Danishness", non-liberalism and homophobia on the other' (Lunau, 2019: 17).

But how can anyone credibly perform their sexual orientation and gender identity, if, like Butler (1999) states, there exists no authentic way of doing so, and each 'doing of gender' is defined by its performative character? In extension hereof, Butler questions the need to distinguish between act, practice and identity and argues that sexual orientation could qualify as an involuntary social characteristic, deserving of protection against discrimination under the law, and thus should remain 'unchosen' (Athanasiou & Butler, 2013: 47).

During their interview with the Danish Immigration Service, queer refugees go so far as to consider how to look queer enough to be granted asylum. One queer refugee said: 'I show them, I bring my make-up, so they can see (...) If you are gay, you know you are gay, because it is my way – the way I talk, wear make-up and remove all my hair, all this is the proof' (Lunau, 2019: 16). This queer refugee does not seem to have an issue with the apparent homonormative stereotypes that they are asked to live up to. Contrary to this, another queer refugee said: 'The people who are doing the interviews, they expect you to look and act like a women [sic], if you are a gay man. But everybody has a style. I look very straight, and if you appear straight, they think you are lying. But being gay does not have to mean that you should appear feminine' (LGBT Asylum, 2015: 5). This quote shows how some queer refugees are indeed feeling uncomfortable with having to ascribe themselves to the Western way of coming out of the closet to become a homonormative, stereotyped queer.

The task of determining if someone is indeed queer seems to be insoluble, as 'there are no universal characteristics or qualities that typify LGBTI [lesbian, gay, bisexual, transgender and intersex] individuals, any more than there are for heterosexual individuals' (UNHCR, 2013: 71). The willingness of Denmark to grant asylum on these grounds – even though the Danish asylum system is getting more and more restricted (Kreichauf, 2019) – can be traced to homonationalism, which is allowing Denmark to depict itself as more developed than the countries from which the queer refugees are fleeing from.

Held (2019) states that as of 2019, there has been no case of a bisexual person claiming asylum in Germany (Held, 2019) – even though it seems highly unlikely that no bisexual has ever applied for asylum. An explanation could be that a bisexual refugee fears to be sent back to their country of origin, and into the closet, with the attraction towards people of the same sex, and just focus on / live out the attraction for people of the 'opposite' sex. Even though EU law has ruled out the possibility of going back into the closet as a reason to reject an asylum claim (EU, 2014), the claim of having a lesbian or gay sexual orientation seems to be the 'safer' way. Oftentimes bisexuals are understood as half straight and half homosexual – which could lead to the understanding of having less of a good claim for asylum on the grounds of persecution because of a non-cis-heterosexual sexual orientation or gender identity.

There exists an inherent contradiction in the need to prove what the queer refugees have tried to hide as best as they could during their lives back in their country of origin. Due to them being closeted, it might be very difficult to gather anything that could be used as proof for their queerness. The authorities in the country of potential asylum could therefore be convinced that the queer refugees are not fearing any persecution, as the closet has been their safe space for so long. One queer refugee tells about his experience with the Danish Immigration Service: 'Sometimes they don't accept certain things. For example, if you have children, the authorities don't understand or believe you are LGBT. When you come from a place, where it is taboo to be LGBT, you try to change your behaviour, pretend you are not LGBT, and it can be hard for authorities to accept you have been forced to live in the closet' (LGBT Asylum, 2015: 5). Even though queer refugees might have distinctively chosen to stick to a closeted sexual or gender practice in their country of origin, the Western narrative perceives closeted practices as backwards, and thus queer refugees are understood as captives of a repressive understanding of queerness (Manalansan, 1995).

## Back in the closet outside the asylum procedure

In this final section before concluding, I want to point towards the other side of the closet in the lives of queer refugees. While they are forced to come out of it during their asylum processes, they might distinctively go back into the closet in their private lives. This is because it can be difficult for queer refugees to immediately live up to the expectation of an 'out and proud' sexual orientation or gender identity once they reach Denmark, as many of them tried to conceal their queerness to the best of their ability for years. Due to this, 'shame might remain as a permanent, structuring feeling of [their] sexuality – even in Denmark' (Lunau, 2019: 16). Therefore, many queer refugees choose to go back into the closet outside of their asylum interviews or spaces that are specifically queer friendly, such as group meetings with supportive non-governmental organizations like LGBT Asylum. One queer refugee says: 'In and out of the asylum centre, I still have not picked the guts to talk about myself and my sexuality as a lesbian to other people. I feel the stigma, which is somehow unexplainable. I only feel safe to behave and feel as LGBT when I am close to those who understand it – for example, when I attend LGBT meetings. That is my safe zone' (LGBT Asylum, 2015: 14). This experience of staying consciously closeted about one's own queerness towards certain people or in certain places is not only limited to queer refuges, but also described by other people with a non-cis-heterosexual sexual orientation or gender identity (Sedgwick, 1990).

Thomas Wimark (2019) demonstrates how the lives and safety of queer refugees are impacted by the way that housing and accommodations are structured in Sweden. Wimark states that these homes are built onto an assumed heterosexuality and are therefore placing queer refugees as outcasts, leaving them in a feeling of non-belonging (Wimark, 2019). It can be argued that this is not limited to Sweden, because Denmark is – as demonstrated earlier – also a country in which heterosexuality is still always assumed, until proven otherwise. Another queer refugee in Denmark says: 'The problem is in the camps: you cannot be yourself, you must hide and be careful how you move and speak. I have to act macho and try not to be myself. No one in the camp even knows my name or my nationality. I try to avoid other Arabs. I don't dare to put in my earrings. I live with three guys I don't know. They might stab me in the middle of the night. All this would end if there was a LGBT camp' (LGBT Asylum, 2015: 12).

Such an LGBT camp was introduced in several bigger cities in Germany (Laugstien, 2016). Still, queer refugees are put into heteronormative accommodations first, and then have to apply for a place in a queer shelter. Therefore, they are put into the closet again, and can decide to go out of the closet to receive better and more fitting housing. Living inside such a queer shelter is a direct outing, a dragging of the queer refugees out of the closets. Even though they are aware of this when applying for accommodation in a specifically queer shelter, they might be seen by others while entering or leaving their home which is then an involuntary outing. Not all queer refugees might feel ready to take this risk, so these forms of accommodation cannot be the only measure. This example visualizes the fundamental contradictions in the lives of queer refugees.

## Conclusion

In this chapter I have discussed the ways in which queer refugees have to follow the Nordic idea of how to be queer, in order to become intelligible for the Danish asylum authorities and to enhance their chance of being granted asylum on the ground of it. This I did with using the metaphor of the closet and coming out of it, demonstrating how this is framing queer refugees' experiences. This epistemic furniture is staying with the queer refugees while they navigate the multiple stations until getting granted asylum. I mentioned the closet that queer refugees had to stay in back in their country of origin, which they are then asked to come out of during their asylum process (but only in a way that makes their queerness readable for the Danish authorities) only to be forced back into it e.g., because of security issues during their stay in the refugee camps. Even though Denmark deems itself to be an open society, the idea of coming out of the closet has not been abolished yet – people are building closets that they can put others into, so that they then have to come out. Compulsory heterosexuality is an (almost) uncontested reality, and even though sexual orientation and gender identity are more and more understood as being fluid and not fixed, this understanding has not yet reached the asylum procedures, which makes it complicated for queer refugees to claim asylum on the grounds of them being part of the queer community. In order to enhance their chances, they are forced to integrate themselves into the Western narrative around sexual orientation and gender identity. To conclude, queer refugees' lives are shaped by hetero- and homonormativity, which are putting them in the closet and dictating the way they should come out of it.

## Bibliography

Atewologun, D. (2018). 'Intersectionality Theory and Practice', Oxford Research Encyclopedia, Business and Management, <https://doi.org/10.1093/acrefore/9780190224851.013.48>, accessed 17 December 2020.

Athanasiou, A. and Butler, J. (2013). Dispossession: The Performative in the Political – Conversations with Athena Athanasiou. Cambridge: Polity Press.

Barker, M.-J. and Scheele, J. (2016). Queer. A Graphic History. London: Icon Books.

Butler, J. (1993). 'Imitation and Gender Insubordination'. In H. Abelove, M. A. Barale, and D. M. Halperin (eds.), The Lesbian and Gay Studies Reader, pp. 307–320. New York, London: Routledge.

Butler, J. (1999). Gender Trouble. New York, London: Routledge.

Cambridge Dictionary (n.d.). Western https://dictionary.cambridge.org/de/worterbuch/englisch/western> accessed 24 November 2020.

Ciobanu, C. (2020). 'A Third of Poland Declared "LGBT-Free Zone"', Balkan Insight, 25 February, <https://balkaninsight.com/2020/02/25/a-third-of-poland-declared-lgbt-free-zone/> accessed 30 November 2020.

Cohen, J. C. (1997). 'Punks, Bulldaggers and Welfare Queens: The Radical Potential of Queer Politics?', GLQ: A Journal of Lesbian and Gay Studies, 3, 437–462.

Crenshaw, K. W. (1991). 'Mapping the Margins: Intersectionality, Identity Politics, and Violence against Women of Color', Stanford Law Review, 42(6), 1241–1299.

Davis, K. (2008). 'Intersectionality as Buzzword: A Sociology of Science Perspective of What Makes a Feminist Theory Successful', Feminist Theory, 9(1), 67–85.

Duggan, L. (2002). 'The New Homonormativity: The Sexual Politics of Neoliberalism'. In R. Castronovo, and D. D. Nelson (eds.), Materializing Democracy: Toward a Revitalized Cultural Politics, pp. 175–196, Durham: Duke University Press.

Dustin, M. and Held, N. (2018). 'In or Out? A Queer Intersectional Approach to "Particular Social Group" Membership and Credibility in SOGI Asylum Claims in Germany and the UK', Genius, 2, 74–87.

EDAL (European Database of Asylum Law) (n.d. a). Denmark – Refugee Appeals Board's Decision of 6 March 2018, <https://www.asylumlawdatabase.eu/en/case-law/denmark-refugee-appeals-board's-decision-6-march-2018> accessed 23 October 2020.

EDAL (European Database of Asylum Law) (n.d. b). Denmark – the Refugee Appeals Board's Decision of 17 May 2018, <https://www.asylumlawdatabase.eu/cs/case-law/denmark-refugee-appeals-board's-decision-17-may-2018> accessed 23 October 2020.

EU (2014) Judgment of the Court (Grand Chamber). 2 December 2014., <https://curia.europa.eu/juris/document/document.jsf;jsessionid=4DAD23B51DC8845294DD927278FDB472?text=&docid=160244&pageIndex=0&doclang=EN&mode=lst&dir=&occ=first&part=1&cid=702353> accessed 23 October 2020

Frizzell, N. (2013). 'Feature: How the Stonewall Riots Started the LGBT Rights-Movement', Pink News UK, 19 August, <https://www.pinknews.co.uk/2013/06/28/feature-how-the-stonewall-riots-started-the-gay-rights-movement/> accessed 30 November 2020.

Fuss, D. (1991). 'Inside/Out'. In D. Fuss (ed.), Inside/Out. Lesbian Theories, Gay Theories, pp. 1–10, New York: Routledge.

Gammelgaard, A. V. (2020). 'Flere hundrede i aktion mod hadforbrydelser: Slut med tilråb for at gå i kjole', DR, 2nd June, <https://www.dr.dk/nyheder/indland/flere-hundrede-i-aktion-mod-hadforbrydelser-slut-med-tilraab-gaa-i-kjole>, accessed 15 October 2020.

Held, N. (2019). 'Sexual Orientation and Gender Identity. Claims of Asylum in Germany. Intersectional Legal, Social and Methodological Challenges'. In C. Küppers and Bundesstiftung Magnus Hirschfeld (eds.), Refugees & Queers. Forschung und Bildung an der Schnittstelle von LSBTTIQ, Fluchtmigration und Emanzipationspolitiken, pp. 53–76. Bielefeld: transcript Verlag.

Kreichauf, R. (2019). 'Legal Paradigm Shifts and Their Impacts on the Socio-Spatial Exclusion of Asylum Seekers in Denmark'. In B. Glorius and J. Doomernik (eds.), Geographies of Asylum in Europe and the Role of European Localities, pp. 45–67. IMISCOE Research Series, Cham: Springer Nature.

Laugstien, F. (2016). 'Neue Unterkunft für queere Geflüchtete. Coming out of the Heim', Taz, 17 February, <https://taz.de/Neue-Unterkunft-fuer-queere-Gefluechtete/!5276160/> accessed 4 November 2020.

Lee, E. U. J. and Brotman, S. (2011). 'Identity, Refugeeness, Belonging: Experiences of Sexual Minority Refugees in Canada', Canadian Review of Sociology/Revue canadienne de sociologie, CRS/RCS, 48(3), 243–263.

Lev Og Lad Leve (n.d.). Om. EN BEVÆGELSE MOD HADFORBRYDELSER, <https://www.levogladleve.com/hvem-er-vi>, accessed 9 October 2020.

LGBT Asylum (2015). LGBT Asylum Applicants in Denmark. Applying for Asylum on Grounds of Sexual Orientation and Gender Identity, <https://lgbtasylum.dk/website/wp-content/uploads/2019/09/Rapport-engelsk.pdf>, accessed 23 October 2020.

Lunau, M. (2019). 'The Trouble with "Truth". On the Politics of Life and Death in the Assessment of Queer Asylum Seekers', WOMEN, GENDER & RESEARCH, 3–4, 12–23.

Manalansan, M.F. (1995). 'In the Shadows of Stonewall: Examining Gay Transnational Politics and the Diasporic Dilemma', GLQ: A Journal of Lesbian and Gay Studies, 2(4), 425–438.

Petersen, M. N. (2016). 'These are queer times indeed. En introduktion til homonationalisme i en dansk kontekst', Kvinder, Køn & Forskning, 25(4): 55–66. https://doi.org/10.7146/kkf.v25i4.104399.

Puar, J. K. (2017). Terrorist Assemblages: Homonationalism in Queer Times. Durham, London: Duke University Press.

Rainbow Europe (n.d.). Country ranking, <https://rainbow-europe.org/country-ranking>, accessed 23 October 2020.

Rich, A. (1980). 'Compulsory Heterosexuality and Lesbian Existence', Signs, 5(4), 631–660.

Sahgal, N. (2018). 'Ten Key Findings about Religion in Western Europe', Pew Research Center, 29 May, <https://www.pewresearch.org/fact-tank/2018/05/29/10-key-findings-about-religion-in-western-europe/>, accessed 24 November 2020.

Schippert, C. (2011). 'Implications of Queer Theory for the Study of Religion and Gender: Entering the Third Decade', Religion and Gender, 1(1), 66–84.

Sedgwick, E. K. (1990). Epistemology of the Closets Berkeley and Los Angeles: University of California Press.

Shakhsari, S. (2014). 'The Queer Time of Death: Temporality, Geopolitics, and Refugee Rights', Sexualities, 17(8), 998–1015.

UNHCR (2013). Beyond Proof. Credibility Assessment in EU Asylum Systems, <https://www.unhcr.org/51a8a08a9.pdf>, accessed 23 October 2020

Wimark, T. (2019). 'Homemaking and Perpetual Liminality among Queer Refugees', Social & Cultural Geogr

Anabel Soriano Oliva

# Discussing Pateman's Understanding of Prostitution Through Khamis' Exhibition *Black Birds*

Nowadays, the debate about prostitution, sex work, or sex for sale is an arena for strong disagreement within contemporary strains of feminisms. Taking these debates as my point of departure, I aim in this article to go beyond more classical understandings of the Prostitute as a universal category. I will move past the understanding of 'the prostitute' as an identity in itself, that is, an identity with a universal essence that, regardless of context and circumstance, is subjugated to the same logics. From a philosophical point of view, I argue that in order to embrace the theoretical complexity of the selling of sex, it is necessary to attend to the differences between positionalities. Its universalization homogenizes different experiences, making other existences who sell sex invisible.

To illustrate such essentialist understandings of the Prostitute, I will critically explore the potentialities and limitations of Carole Pateman's work What's Wrong with Prostitution? (1999) and the implications of The Sexual Contract (1988, 1999). I will put her argument into conversation with Heba Khamis' exhibition Black Birds (2018) which, in a series of photographs and interviews, captures the sexual services provided by young Afghan and Iranian men in Tiergarten park in Berlin, Germany. Using this exhibition as an empirical point of departure for the philosophical discussion, I will explore the following questions: Under which circumstances do these asylum seekers start selling gay sex? Why do they sell gay sex if they self-identify as heterosexuals? Does this practice emancipate them from their previous precarious condition, or subject them to increased precarity? Upon exploring these questions, I identify a tension between the Tiergarten case and Pateman's gender-binary understanding of prostitution, dissolving the hierarchical logic of binarism. It is in such a clash where we can begin confronting Pateman's ideas and begin to challenge her essentialist premises. By using the empirical case I am able to raise (but not answer) questions about Pateman's theoretical pre-conditions and perhaps begin to examine how different types of subjectivities intersect in those who sell sex.

I will begin with an exploration of the Black Birds (Khamis, 2020), a photo project in which some Afghan and Iranian asylum seekers who sell sex are portrayed in Tiergarten park, to initiate the philosophical discussion. Second, taking the photo exhibition as a case study and following Pateman's argument on the institution of prostitution, I will challenge her assumptions. Finally, I will explore new paths for understanding the role of heterosexual men who sell sex through Judith Butler's performative theory (1990, 1997, 2010) and the intersectional frame (Davis, 2014) to challenge essentialist points of view. The ultimate goal is not to explore the problematics presented by Khamis, but rather to challenge Pateman's argument of Prostitution through the exhibition. I think that in the friction and discord of Pateman's theory with the present empirical example, new, intersectional ways of understanding the sale of sex and the role of heterosexual men may take shape. Following Butler's arguments, I believe that the intersectional reconsideration, both ontological and epistemological, of heterosexual men in relation to the sale of sex may open a space for the redefinition of their political legitimacy. In this way, my aim in the chapter is to contribute to the wide range of intersectional feminist literature that challenges the calcified identitarian positions of some feminist literature.

## Exhibition: Black Birds

Between 2017 and 2018, the Egyptian photographer Heba Khamis captured the circumstances experienced by some Afghan and Iranian asylum seekers in Tiergarten park in Berlin in a series of photographs. The exhibition was named Black Birds[1] (Khamis, 2018) and was composed of 26 photos. Among the photos we find landscapes/sections of the northern area of Tiergarten (which is a well-known area for the sale of male homosexual sex) and 13 half-naked bodies. Both tell a common story narrated throughout the exhibition. The exhibition is a collection of naked torsos (some of them clothed by scarves, others untouched even by age), hidden spots between the bushes, a ground covered by flowers and used condoms, hidden sleeping bags, tennis tables, a tent, and a map of the park. Not a single face is portrayed; though in a single photo, one eye peeks through the branches and stares at the viewer. Khamis plays with shadows and the cover of branches to illustrate the reality of some young Afghan and Iranian men, selling gay sex while self-identifying as heterosexual men in Tiergarten in the wait for refugee asylum acceptance.

Through the use of bodies without faces, Khami's exhibition opens the doors to a reality that exists in the covered, the shadows, and, for most people, the unknown. However, despite faceless bodies, the photos do not lose potentiality.

1 To see more: https://archive.noorimages.com/?1051153305422153594O&EVENT=WEBSHOP_SEARCH&MEDIAGROUP_SCOPE=10&MEDIANUMBER=00083851&SEARCHMODE=SERIES&SHOWSERIES=1.1588.

I understand the exhibition as a performative space. A space where the bodies become materialized, or in other words, become epistemologically visible/intelligible. In How Bodies Come to Matter: An Interview with Judith Butler (Meijer & Prins, 1998) Butler discusses her interpretation of the concept of abjection. She explores abjection in the context of the body.[2] Before explaining what abject bodies are, it is important to clarify the social aspect of the body. What Butler proposes is an ontology of the social body (Butler, 2010:15). For Butler, the being of the body is not something individualized and disconnected from the others (i.e. the social), but rather it is a body that by being exposed/vulnerable 'is a being that is always given to others: to rules, to social and political organizations that have developed historically in order to maximize the precarity for some and minimize it for others'[3] (ibid.). Based on this, the abject bodies are those which are neither epistemologically nor politically recognized by others. In Butler's words, 'to live as such a body in the world is to live in the shadowy regions of ontology' (Coster & Prins, 1998: 277). The exhibition is the condition under which these bodies come into being, but it does not mean that it constitutes the bodies entirely. Following Foucault, Butler affirms that the materiality is not accessible 'without the means of discourse' (ibid.: 278). But at the same time, 'no discourses can ever capture that prior materiality (…) there is a limit to constructedness' (ibid.).

By accessing Khamis' exhibition one in turn accesses a discourse under which certain bodies become materialized, thereby coming into existence and becoming epistemologically intelligible. The intelligibility of the bodies – that is, their epistemological materialization – is the prior condition for their legitimate existence, for them to matter, politically speaking. The exhibition is a means through which I will work with two different feminists' understandings of the role of heterosexual men in prostitution/the selling of sex.

---

2 The ontological consideration of the body is the result of the XX century critic to the history of the fleshleed body. This critique overcome the historical interpretation of the dualism body-soul(mind) heritance from the long history of philosophy. In this currency we can find authors as Michael Foucault and feminist theories of the xx century such as J. Butler, D. Haraway or R. Braidotti (Oliva, 2015).

3 Self-translated: ' es un ser que siempre está entregado a otros: a normas, a organizaciones sociales y políticas que se han desarrollado históricamente con el fin de maximizar la precariedad para unos y de minimizarla para otros' (Butler, 2010: 15).

## Pateman's blindness in essences: The intersection between prostitution and national identity

Since prostitution has been legal in Germany since 2002, The Prostitution Act (referred to as The Act in the following) aims 'neither to abolish prostitution nor to enhance its status. Rather (...) to improve the legal and social situation of prostitutes' (European Commission, 2007: 9). In doing so, this act aspires to move away from moralistic interpretations of prostitution. However, based on the Report by the Federal Government on the Impact of the Act Regulating the Legal Situation of Prostitutes (Prostitution act) of 2007: 'the Prostitution Act by and large disregarded the legal and social situation of immigrants without a valid residence permit, the situation of minors engaged in prostitution and drug-related prostitution' (ibid.). The Act left unanswered the social and economic vulnerabilities that force irregular migrants into prostitution practices.

As Khamis explains, 'prostitution in Germany is legal for consenting adults since 2002 but for undocumented refugees, it comes from a lack of choice' (2017: n.p.). In Germany, it is not legal to work, study or attend a language course while waiting for an asylum application to be accepted or denied (AIDA & ECRE, n.d.). Additionally, even though the asylum process usually takes between three and six months on paper, between 2017 and 2018 the waiting time was between six to ten months (ibid.). Among the factors that impacted the waiting time was the nationality of the asylum seekers, with priority given to those coming from countries with an on-going conflict (Bathke, 2019: n.p.). Under these circumstances, the interviewed asylum seekers came to Germany without any knowledge of the German language, so they associate with people who share their mother tongue and become familiar with Tiergarten park.

What at first glance was merely a place to kill time is by closer inspection a central location for a precarious set of economic exchanges. As Khamis narrates, 'they spend days surrounded by the people doing drugs and rich men offering money for sex (...). They use drugs to forget about their situation (...). To afford the drugs, they start prostitution and continue using drugs to forget about the shameful feeling they have after prostituting themselves' (2017: n.p.). All of the men interviewed self-identified as heterosexual men while selling homosexual sex, having wives or girlfriends in their country of origin where homosexuality is legally and socially punished, even with the death penalty.

In this section, I will analyse Khamis narrative to examinate why they enter into the money-sex relationship undertaking homosexual rather than heterosexual practices, and how by doing so they reproduce the already patriarchal logics of the capitalist system, where certain bodies are demanded for consumption while others consume them. To do so, I will explore the Sexual Contract by Carole Pateman (Pateman, 1989, 1999; Boucher, 2003). This investigation is carried out through the men-women binary distinction. According to Pateman, in the institution of prostitution heterosexual woman and homosexual men occupy the same role within Sexual Contract Theory (Pateman, 1999).

Carole Pateman is one of the important figures of contemporary feminist political theory. One of her important contributions has been the feminist critique of modern contractual theories and its heirs (Pateman, 1988, 1999). Classical contractarians based the legitimacy of the original contract – which is already patriarchal – on three assumptions: the law of male sex-right, the illusion of consent, and the fictional property in the person. According to Pateman, classical social contractarians have obscured the transformation of the modern patriarchy from a paternal right to a fraternal pact. As Boucher explains, it 'signals the victory of brothers over the father's right to rule' (Boucher, 2003: 24). The fraternal pact is a binding contract of the domination of men together over women and thereby consolidates 'the law of male sex-right' (ibid.). ensuring in that way men's accessibility to women's bodies. In that sense, through contract theory the modern patriarchy is established (ibid.: 24). Having the sexual contract prior to the social contract, makes possible the implementation of a patriarchal social contract, which creates the sexual division of society into two spheres: the private/natural and the public/political. Women belong to the first one and men to second one (ibid.: 25). Therefore, women remain pre-political while men enter civil society practising civil freedom. Thus, 'civil freedom is a masculine attribute and depends upon patriarchal right' (Pateman, 1988: 2) and not a universal quality of citizenship.

This sexual differentiation is the pre-condition for a subordinate role for women, or, said differently, subjecting women to the social contract results in their subordination. Therefore, by individual consent we literally talk about his consent. In this sense, how the contract serves to produce inequal social structures is masked by the supposed voluntary nature of contractual relationships (Patmen, 1988: 6). Freedom is no more than a label that covers civil subordination and blurs the interdependence between civil freedom and patriarchal right. It is the masking of the patriarchal relationship in the contract's origin, what allows to take for granted that the contract is always constituting free relations, while in fact it is creating relations of subordination. The sexual contract establishes the a priori unequal conditions in which 'free choices' are already subjected to the patriarchal interests. Thus, the social contract rests upon the illusion of freedom and consent.

The illusion of consent coexists in deep relationship with the fiction of property in the person. The fiction is built on the belief that under capitalist conditions it is possible to separate agency and labour-power from the body. This is especially noticeable in the case of prostitution. Pateman criticizes the belief that sexual services are disembodied; that is, she claims that where there is a service, there is always a body that performs it. She notes, 'the property of the person (…) cannot be separated from its owner' (Pateman, 1999: 59). Thereby, in prostitution what is for sale is not a service, but a body: the unilateral sexual access to the female body (ibid.: 57).

Moreover, for Pateman, 'the body' is not only conceived as a set of organs, but is indeed the very location of the self. Pateman affirms, 'the body and the self are not identical, but selves are inseparable from the bodies' (ibid.: 60). Ontologically, humans, and so the prostitute, are embodied selves. Taking into consideration that Pateman defines prostitution as 'the unilateral use of a woman's body by a man in exchange for money,' (ibid.: 57) what the man obtains in return for his money is also a self. Pateman explains the relationship as a relationship between the master and his subordinate. Both are embodied selves sexually differentiated. She explicitly states, 'the self is a masculine or feminine self' (ibid.: 60, emphasis added). The sexual master is 'he', and the subordinated is 'she'. Through her subordination and use of her body 'men affirm their manhood' (ibid.), which is their fraternal relation.[4] Prostitution is one of the consequences of the aforementioned male-sex right, in which by reproducing its logics the fraternal pact also re-affirm itself.

As Marilyn Fyre (1983) has noticed, the fraternal relationship is sustained by a sort of 'incest taboo'.[5] This taboo is necessary within the fraternity, as 'there is always a temptation to make the relation more than a fellowship' (ibid.: 56). However, if the body that they consume is one among the fraternity, the competition could destabilize the foundations of the original contract. Therefore, the sexual contract is a story about heterosexual relations. It is a story of how the

4 It is important to consider that Pateman is attempting to displace the focus of the feminist debate about prostitution. For her it is urgent to understand why there is such a demand for male and female bodies in the global capital market (Pateman, 1999: 63). This changes the focus from the selling in the capitalist market (why women prostitute?) to the demand (why is there such a demand for women and gay men in the market?).

5 'Where men are confined together and prevented from obtaining access to women (as in prison), the "taboo" is not observed; masculinity is then exhibited by using other men, usually young men, as if they were women.' (Pateman, 1999: 56)

few (white hetero men) exclude the Others (racialized men/women, women, homosexuals) from the social contract, and from equal conditions of freedom. This is the case, for instance, in homosexual prostitution where 'from the start point of the contract, they are no different from female prostitution' (ibid.: 55).

If we now consider the case of the undocumented Afghan and Iranian refugees, we can deduce several things. Following Pateman's logic, we see how even the men who self-identified as heterosexual entered the market of prostitution as gay man, such that the commodification of their embodied selves matches the logic of mastery (freedom)/subordinate (subjection). In this sense, their prostitution is translated into a repetition of the same; it is the implementation of the male-sex right over those who do not conform to fraternity. However, Pateman does not give us the conceptual tools to understand that their exclusion from civil freedom is not based solely on the patriarchal logic.

From an intersectional perspective, it can be argued that it is their exclusion from the enjoyment of civil rights such as working or studying (that is, the lack of options) that drives them to search for alternatives, one of which is prostitution. Then their sexuality, as heterosexual men, is not a reason to reproduce neither the modern patriarchy, nor the subordinate position – their sexuality is not the prior condition of their subjection. Rather, it is another othering logic which excludes them from the fraternal community. In this case, the most obvious differentiating factor, but not the only one, is their national identity,[6] since they are in Berlin on irregular conditions. In an attempt to escape such subjection, they conform to the logics of the hetero-normative fraternity. Trying to escape their precarious situation, they engage in the sexual market as gay men, their bodies becoming a source of productive value in the capitalist system. By taking the role of the subjugated body in the patriarchal logic, their bodies can be productively commercialized under the capitalist system. This reproduction of the fraternal patriarchy reinforces their stagnation: in their attempts to escape their subjugated position in the system they fall into another structure which traps them again subordination. In summary, their position in the patriarchal system does not correct their previous position in the national sphere, and they remain

---

6 It should be noted that national identity is one of multiple othering logics that excludes them from full citizenship at a macropolitical level. Categories such as gender and race intersect with nation. As Spanger explains 'the category of the nation is a kind of tool to distinguish between who belongs and who does not belong: us versus them' (Spanger, 2010: 61).

confined in their pre-existing precarity. Rather than escape the subjugating logics they reproduce them.

## Displacing normativity

Despite the fact that Pateman's argument allows us to shed light on patriarchal mechanisms, its lack of intersectional considerations and universal understanding of women/men and heterosexuals/homosexuals causes several analytical limitations. The first limitation is its understanding of prostitution as a consequence only of sexuality (Scoular, 2004: 345), or in other words, understanding the sex-money exchange exclusively through the lens of sexuality. In the case under study, even though the asylum seekers intelligibility as commodified subjects have to be performed in patriarchal terms (providing homosexual sex), the oppressive force which has driven them there is not their sexuality, but rather the enactment of policies creating precarious migration (refugee) conditions, which consequently segregate different peoples (citizens vs. migrants) into different types of labour and labour conditions. Scoular explains that 'gender and sexuality clearly play important structuring roles in prostitution, but it is a phenomenon that cannot be reduced to either gender or sexuality' (ibid.).

The second limitation is the essentialization of the self in binary terms. Pateman explicitly says 'the self is a masculine or feminine self' (1988: 60). Essentialization defines the universal experience of what it means to be a woman and what it means to be a heterosexual or homosexual man (Smiraglia, 2017: 43). This ontological position not only generates a universal understanding of humankind in binary terms, but also exemplifies what Butler called the heterosexual matrix (Butler, 1990). Pateman does this by taking for granted that sex practices are preceded and determined by the sexes, genders, and sexual desires of those involved. It is true that Pateman contemplates sexual orientations other than heterosexuality. However, her essentialist understanding of men and women already situates them in an immutable hierarchical relationship regardless of the time and space where they are located.

If we consider the positionality (the spatial and temporal location) of the subject, can a self not be both at the same time the dominant and the submissive? The refugees constitute subjected selves in Berlin's capitalist market, but would their selves change in another context? How can different spaces re-ascribe the social position of the subject within the gender relationship? In other words, must the subordinate role be an unchanging identity? For instance, following the two points mentioned above, it can be asked whether this double identity (the hetero and gay man) plays both roles in the patriarchy: the dominant (in relation to those that are the same national identity) and the submissive (among those who are the others, those who do not belong to their fraternity). The fact that asylum seekers do not belong to the national fraternity (as citizens) does not mean that on the basis of national identity another fraternity cannot be formed. Based on their statements, they only sell homosexual sex to others, that is, to Germans or tourists. But among them the incest taboo may exist, and, if it does, it may be that they are masters through the lens of their national identity, in this case regarding women's bodies.

Finally, in her interpretation, the power in sexual relationships is embodied in two subjects. Explicitly personified, the male orders the subordination of the female gender. Nancy Fraser (1997) criticizes that the model master-subject is not adequate to analyse contemporary societies. Fraser proposes that "gender inequality is being transformed through the passage of dyadic relations of dominance and subjection to impersonal structural mechanisms that they are lived through more fluid cultural forms" (1993:180). Judith Butler´s conception of the heterosexual matrix also destabilized Pateman understanding of the pre-existence of the self in two sexes and genders. In contrast, Butler's category of performance allows us to study the implications of men who self-identify as heterosexual selling homosexual sex.

Butler suggests the category of heterosexual matrix, and with it problematizes Pateman's binary essentialization of the Body and the Self. Contrary to Pateman, Butler defends an ontology of becoming. The subject's existence is something that is in a continuous process of doing; it is 'already there and yet-to-come' (Butler, 1997: 18). The being of the selves and the selves of the bodies are consequently something in the making, in a never-ending process. Such ontological openness is the foundation of their subjection to unchosen logics, which constitutes them, but at the same is the foundation for their freedom. Hence, on the one hand, 'external power makes the subject's becoming possible' (Spanger, 2010: 24) and the internal power 'enable the subject´s own acting' (ibid.). Subjects are because they are produced by and under the interests of power relations. The reproduction and compulsion of such power are 'constituted by the heterosexual discourse that simultaneously constitutes and dissolves the very same subject' (Spanger, 2013: 41). The heterosexual matrix has literally created the existence of two opposite sexes that respectively correspond to a body, a gender, a sexual practice, and a sexual desire. The correlation of these four categories is achieved by the correct performance, which is based on the normative division of: woman/femininity and man/masculinity (ibid.: 40). Within the heterosexual matrix, those who do not match one of the possibilities are not systematically expulsed, but differentially included, ordering them hierarchically in relation to their dissimilarity.

In the previous section, I examined how the commercialization of the male body, if it is to be on the sex market, should be under homosexual practices in the patriarchal system, following Pateman's rationale. However, if we follow Spanger's reading of Butler, it could be argued that such a practice not only reproduces Pateman's understanding of the patriarchal logics of prostitution (and consequently of sex and sexuality), but simultaneously displaces them, that is, deconstructs them. This deconstruction is the result of the mismatching between what a hetero man desires and what his sexual practice is. By self-identifying as heterosexual, men disconnect the link between sex and sexuality, and between practice and identity. This not only challenges the heterosexual matrix but also the normative relationship between practice and identity. Consequently, even accepting the patriarchal essentialisation of the institution of prostitution and the normative demands of certain bodies (and not others), the case of the Afghan and Iranian asylum seekers problematizes the relationship between the sexual identities and practices of those involved. This leads to the conception of identity as something always in the making, depending on the power rationalities that influences it. The bodies of the asylum seekers exist within the heterosexual matrix, and are thereby conditioned (and shaped) by it.

## Conclusion

Understanding prostitution as an institution in universal terms, where Men and Women fulfil certain roles, regardless of time, space, and the forces that constrain their identities and practices blurs the complexity of the sex-money exchange. In this paper I have problematized Pateman's understanding of prostitution first through Khamis exhibition and second through Butlers performative theory. The mismatch between sexual desire and sexual practices challenges the essentialistic understanding of both heterosexual and homosexual men. Khamis' exhibition illustrates how the vulnerability of the asylum seekers is primarily produced by refugee policies that generates uncertainty. What constrains them to their vulnerable positions is not the sale of sex in itself, but the conditions under which that activity is carried out. The primary conditions defined by a lack of choices – since they cannot work or study while they go through the asylum process – and the precarious environments where they sell sex (in a park, in bushes, and mostly under the influence of drugs).

As I pointed out at the beginning of this paper the materialization of the bodies precedes them starting to matter. The abjected bodies are those that are not materialized and thereby not matter. Those who are in the margin of ontology are in the margin of the things that are, exists, and then matter. Consequently, the ontological understanding of the bodies is what will materialize their existence and delimit their political importance or problematics. This empirical case in particularly demands an intersectional analysis where the irregular status of asylum seekers is the reason for their vulnerable circumstances. Thereby, an understanding of the bodies as always in between relations (with other people with other things and within power logics) uncovers a realm of nuances where the same event (the sale of sex) should be analysed contextually rather than universally undifferentiated.

## Bibliography

AIDA & ECRE. (2020). Regular Procedure Germany. Report. https://asylumineurope.org/reports/country/germany/asylum-procedure/procedures/regular-procedure/.

Bathke, B. (2019/02/11). Germany Reduces Time of Asylum Process But Still Misses Three-Month Target. Info Migrants. https://www.infomigrants.net/en/post/15086/germany-reduces-time-of-asylum-process-but-still-misses-three-month-target.

Boucher, J. (2003). Male Power and Contract Theory: Hobbes and Locke in Carole Pateman's "The Sexual Contract". Canadian Journal of Political Science / Revue Canadienne De Science Politique, 36(1), 23–38. Retrieved February 19, 2021, from http://www.jstor.org/stable/3233344.

Butler, J. (1990). Gender Trouble: Feminism and the Subversion of Identity. New York: Routledge, 33.

Butler, J. (1997). The Psychic Life of Power: Theories in Subjection. Stanford, CA: Stanford University Press.

Butler, J., (2010): Marcos de guerra: las vidas lloradas. Barcelona, Paidós. La primera edición en inglés fue publicada en Londres, Verso, 2008.

Costera, I., and Baujke, P. (1998). How Bodies Come to Matter: An Interview with Judith Butler. Signs, 23(2), 275–286.

Davis, K. E. (2014). Intersectionality as Critical Methodology. In N. Lykke (Ed.), Writing Academic Texts Differently: Intersectional Feminist Methodologies and the Playful Art of Writing (pp. 17–29). (Advances in Feminist Studies and Intersectionality). Routledge.

European Commission. (2007). Report by the Federal Government on the Impact of the Act Regulating the Legal Situation of Prostitution. https://ec.europa.eu/antitrafficking/sites/antitrafficking/files/federal_government_report_of_the_impact_of_the_act_regulating_the_legal_situation_of_prostitutes_2007_en_1.pdf.

Fraser, N. (1993). Beyond the master/subject model: Reflections on Carole Pateman's Sexual Contract. Social Text 37: 173–81.

Frye. (1983). The Politics of Reality: Essays in Feminist Theory. Trumansburg, NY: Crossing Press, 1983, 143.

Khamis, H. (2018). Black Birds, in Noor (2020). https://archive.noorimages.com/?10511533054221535940&EVENT=WEBSHOP_SEARCH&MEDIAGROUP_SCOPE=10&MEDIANUMBER=00083851&SEARCHMODE=SERIES&SHOWSERIES=1.1588.

Meijer, I. C., & Prins, B. (1998). How Bodies Come to Matter: An Interview with Judith Butler. Signs, 23(2), 275–286. http://www.jstor.org/stable/3175091

Oliva, P. (2015). Hacia una Ontología Social del Cuerpo en Butler: Análisis y Límites. Instituto de Investigaciones Feministas de la U.C.M.

Pateman, C. (1999). What's Wrong with Prostitution? Women's Studies Quarterly, 27(1/2), 53–64. Retrieved December 7, 2020, from http://www.jstor.org/stable/40003398.

Pateman, C. (1988). The Sexual Contract. Stanford, CA: Stanford University Press.

Scoular, J. (2004). The 'Subject' of Prostitution: Interpreting the Discursive, Symbolic and Material Position of Sex/Work in Feminist Theory. Feminist Theory, 5(3), 343–355. Doi:10.1177/1464700104046983

Smiraglia, R. (2017). Feminismo y Liberalismo: Una revisión crítica sobre El Contrato Sexual de Carole Pateman. Leviathan (São Paulo), (11), 33–55. https://doi.org/10.11606/issn.2237-4485.lev.2015.132379

Spanger. (2013). Gender Performances as Spatial Acts: (fe)male Thai Migrant Sex Workers in Denmark. Gender, Place & Culture, 20(1), 37–52, DOI: 10.1080/0966369X.2011.625079

Spanger, M. (2010). Destabilising Sex Work and Intimacy?: Gender Performances of Female Thai Migrants Selling Sex in Denmark. Roskilde Universitet.

Spanger, M. and Skilbrei, M. (2017). Prostitution Research in Context: Methodology, Representation and Power. New York: Routledge.

Anja Kublitz

# Conflicts on the Move: Passing on the Palestinian Conflict

## Introduction

Based on ongoing fieldwork since 2005 among Palestinian refugees in Danish housing projects, this chapter explores how the Palestinian conflict moves from the Middle East to Denmark and from parents to children.

The majority of Palestinians in Denmark have followed a route from villages in Palestine, via refugee camps in Lebanon to housing projects in Denmark. Spending time with Palestinians' families in Denmark, it is hard not to notice the constant references to the parents' experiences of growing up in Lebanon. These might be made through direct comparisons between political events in Denmark and past events in the Middle East, but also in connection with more mundane activities like dining out, relationships with neighbours or playing paintball. Most of these memories are related to war. The constant evoking of my interlocutors' multi-facetted and rich experiences with war does not only reflect their violent past but also the fact that in many ways the wars never ended but continues in the Middle East as well as in Denmark although in a different form. Whereas the parents grew up during the Days of the Revolution in Lebanon that were dominated by the secular ideologies of the Palestinian Liberation Organisation, today their children grow up in the shadow of the War on Terror and with an understanding of the Palestinian conflict as a religious conflict between Muslims and 'the West'.

My ethnography attests to that such changes in global politics cannot be distilled or isolated from the intimate sphere of family relations. Global politics do not exist outside of the mundane practices of everyday life but are enacted through social relations such as the bonds between parents and children. My specific concern in this chapter is how the transmission of the Palestinian-Israeli conflict within Palestinian families in Denmark enables its reproduction as well as transformation. Within the singular household the conflict is transmitted not only through stories of the past but first and foremost through forgetting and silences. Based on the extended case of Yassin and his family, I examine how these silences are very loud and present. I suggest that what the parents do not wish to speak of, and what the youngsters do not want to hear, constitutes a gap that enables the conflict to transmute and be created anew. I argue that it is exactly this gap that lends the conflict its plasticity and allows it to travel from Lebanon to Denmark and from secular ideologies to Islam. The chapter highlights that mobility is not reserved for humans, conflicts are on the move too, and just as humans both adapt to new contexts and change them, conflicts simultaneously adapt to new contexts and transform them.

## From secular ideologies to Islam

The parental generation of my interlocutors grew up during the Lebanese Civil War that lasted from 1975 to 1990 (Peteet, 2005: 8). The civil war covered a range of sub-wars, several of them targeting the Palestinian refugees in Lebanon. Most prominent was the Israeli invasion of Lebanon in 1982, especially the massacre in the Palestinian refugee camps of Sabra and Shatila, and the 'War of the Camps' that comprised a series of sieges and attacks on Palestinian refugee camps by the Syrian-backed Amal militias between 1985 and 1987 (Peteet, 2005: 151). The wars in Lebanon are among the interlocutors considered a continuity of the catastrophe of 1948, al-Nakba, when the present generation of grandparents were expelled from their villages in Palestine by the newly-established state of Israel (Kublitz, 2015). Whereas those grandparents fled from Palestine to the neighbouring Arab countries such as Lebanon, this time some of the parents fled to Europe. By chance, and because the asylum law was then more liberal, many of them ended up in Denmark (Kublitz, 2016).

My fieldwork observations attest to how changes in global power relations have informed the Palestinian conflict. The parental generation of my interlocutors grew up in refugee camps in Lebanon in the seventies and eighties during the Cold War between the Soviet Union and the USA. The camps were controlled by the Palestinian Liberation Organisation, which relied on the former Soviet Union for political, economical and military support (Cobban, 1984: 221–228). The PLO was preoccupied with left-wing ideologies and the Palestinian conflict was conceptualised as a conflict concerning territory and political rights. Since the beginning of this century, the Palestinian conflict has become a symbol of and an epicentre for the antagonistic relationship between Muslims and the West and the War on Terror and has been reconceptualised as a religious conflict. In Palestine the political failure of the PLO and the peace process paved the way for religious parties like Hamas, who in January 2006 won the election to the Palestinian parliament.

Among Palestinians in Denmark this development has been reinforced by the development of national Danish politics. In 2001 a right-wing government came to power in Denmark. The government was supported by the Danish People's Party, which is primarily known for agitating for a strict policy against immigrants and refugees. Since then, issues relating to Muslims have been centre stage of public debate, peaking with the infamous printing of the twelve cartoons of the Prophet Mohammed in the biggest Danish daily newspaper in 2005 (Højer et al., 2018; Kublitz, 2010). Simultaneously, Denmark has taken an active part in the War on Terror since 2001, both militarily, by participating in the wars in Afghanistan, Iraq and Syria, and legally, by passing three packages of legislation and policies targeting terrorism (Kublitz, 2021). To sum up, whereas the majority of the parental generation of my interlocutors during their youth in Lebanon were identified as well as identifying with the secular left wing, today they and their children in Denmark are being identified as well as identifying with Islam (Kublitz, 2016).

## Passing on the conflict: Three ways of forgetting

Professor Lila Abu-Lughod, a Palestinian herself, recalls how during her childhood in the United States her father told her stories about his boyhood in Palestine. She refers to Marianne Hirsch's concept of post-memory, which designates the 'experience of having one's everyday reality overshadowed by the memory of a much more significant past that one's parents lived through' (Abu-Lughod, 2007: 79). According to Abu-Lughod one way the transfer of traumatic memory across generations takes place is through narratives of the past transmitted from one generation to the next (Abu-Lughod, 2007: 79). In this chapter I wish to highlight other aspects of these trans-generational processes. Like Abu-Lughod, I argue that the past indeed is very much present but in an extremely fragmented way (Kublitz, 2011). Furthermore, I suggest that the fragments do not consist only of memories or spoken words but also of forgetting and silences. Paul Connerton identifies seven different types of forgetting in the body of anthropological literature (Connerton, 2008). Three of them seem particularly relevant for understanding how the Palestinian conflict is reproduced and transformed across generations: 'Humiliated silence', 'Forgetting that is constitutive in the formation of a new identity' and 'Structural amnesia'. The reason that I emphasize forgetting and silences in this chapter is to highlight that the events we choose not to pass on to our children are passed on anyway. After spending time with Palestinian families, I have come to think of the silences and forgetting as the backbones of what is going on within these intimate relations. As far as I see it, the love and concern between parents and children are moulded by these silences.

Below I will describe Yassin's family through the silences and forgetting that prevail within it. Yassin lives in a housing project on the outskirts of the centre of Copenhagen. His mother suffers from anxiety attacks and is afraid to leave the house on her own, while his father suffers from recurring depressions. In other words, what is not talked about is extremely manifest and present. In a sense, words are not necessary. The events that are actively forgotten are just as tangible as if they were written on the wall next to the Islamic creed or the embroidery of Palestine that are part of the interior decoration. In the following I will spell out the most important forgetting in the family.

## Forgetting one: Humiliated silence

In 2005 I visited Yassin's parents Mariam and Hassan for the first time and asked them for an interview, Hassan responded straight away by asking what good it would do them to talk to me. 'If I tell you about my years in a Syrian prison, I will only start feeling bad and nothing will come of it'. Since I had no idea that he had been in prison and had no intention of interviewing him on the subject, his outburst left me speechless, and we spent the afternoon drinking coffee while he entertained me with the deficiencies of the Danish welfare system.

According to Connerton, 'some acts of silence may be an attempt to bury things beyond expression and the reach of memory' (Connerton, 2008: 67). He writes that, faced with terror, some people are unable to find appropriate words (Connerton, 2008: 6.). Having been confronted with Hassan's statement above and similar statements made by others during my fieldwork, I have come to believe that the issue at stake is not so much the insufficiency of words but rather that recalling resembles reliving. Originally, Lawrence Langer used the term 'humiliated memory' to refer to the testimonies of Holocaust survivors (Langer, 1991). He writes that humiliated memory is a form of recall without compensation. 'Instead of restoring a sense of power or control over a disabling past, it achieves the reverse, re-animating the governing impotence of the worst moment in a distinctly non-therapeutic way' (Langer, 1991: 84). This way of framing it seems closer to my experiences during fieldwork.

During the month of Ramadan in 2007, I spent most of my evenings at Yassin's home with his mother Mariam watching Bab Al Hara, a popular Ramadan serial. During the commercial breaks, Mariam and I would chat about our husbands, children, parents and other concerns and pleasures of everyday life. After I had known the family for more than a year, Mariam told me about her life before she met Yassin's father. The tale lasted several hours and included, among other events, the attacks on and invasion of South Lebanon by Israel and, as it turned out, a previous marriage, including two other children. The following is one excerpt from her story:

'When I was young, I was very beautiful', Mariam stated. Several men approached her parents asking to marry her, and when she turned fifteen her parents accepted an offer. Mariam and her husband had two children. Her husband worked for the PLO and they hid weapons in their house, which was frequently searched by the Lebanese army. When the conflict broke out between Syria and the PLO, Amal started searching the house as well and in 1985 the family fled to Denmark. After they were granted asylum, the family settled on a small island. Mariam's husband was unemployed, and the small family spent the days together. Her husband's bad temper soon turned to violence, and he would often beat Mariam and their children. The following are Mariam's words as I wrote them down later that night:

> I remember one evening. It was dark outside. Amr [the five-year-old son] had done something and Bilal [her husband] threw him out of the house and locked the door. It was cold outside, and Amr was standing in the dark crying and calling out, 'Mummy, I'm afraid', Bilal said he would beat us both up if I let him back in. Amr was afraid of the dark and I spent the entire evening next to the door trying to comfort him, repeating, 'Don't be afraid, mummy is here', I remember everything. [Mariam starts crying].

While her children were still young, Mariam divorced her husband. The only way her husband would let her go was if she left the children with him. And so, she did. Mariam did not see her children for several years; as grown-ups they now visit her once or twice a year and they sometimes talk on the phone.

When Hassan proclaims that he will not talk about his experience in jail, or when Mariam does not refer to her own childhood or her two other children, it is because they do not want to recall but prefer to stay silent to try to avoid the pain. Furthermore, it is important to note that both parents and children contribute to the 'humiliated silence' because of their concern for each other. The parents do not wish to be a burden to their children, and the children do not wish to cause their parents further trouble, an issue Yassin raised several times. The silent agreement between children and parents implies that even though Yassin is painfully aware that his parents grew up during a war, that his father has been in prison and that his mother has abandoned two other children (he has met his half-siblings twice), he knows nothing about the specifics, and he does not ask.[1]

---

1 The observant reader may have noticed that Mariam did, in fact, tell me the story in detail. During our fifteen years of friendship, she has told it to me only once, and I am quite certain that she has never shared the details with Yassin or Hassan. I believe she shared it with me for the following three reasons. First, the story is humiliating for

## Forgetting two: Forgetting that is constitutive in the formation of a new identity

During one conversation, Yassin proudly told me that his father had been imprisoned by the Syrian military because he held a prominent position within a Muslim organisation: 'It was like Hizb ut-Tahrir', he said. I was rather taken aback by this statement since I already knew that Hassan had been a member of The Popular Front for the Liberation of Palestine (PFLP), which is known for its radical left-wing ideologies, quite unlike Hizb ut-Tahrir's Islamic objectives. When Hassan did talk about the war in Lebanon, he would always specify – as other Palestinians from his generation – that it was the War of the Camps, and that it was Syrian-backed Amal militias that besieged the camps and imprisoned and killed people. This version indirectly (and often directly) indicated that the conflict was between the PLO and Syria, and that it was about power and control in Lebanon rather than about religious differences.

Connerton suggests that forgetting should not only be perceived in terms of loss; it can also be understood as a gain (Connerton, 2008: 63). He writes that many small acts of forgetting are not random but patterned and have a negative significance by allowing other images to come to the fore. 'What is allowed to be forgotten provides living space for present projects' (Connerton, 2008: 63). When Yassin relates the imprisonment of his father to a war between religious groups, it indicates that he is part of a new historical generation that perceive the Palestinian conflict as a religious conflict (Kublitz 2016). In a different context, Carsten writes that to forget is part of an active process of creating a new and shared identity (Carsten, 1995: 317). By choosing to ignore his parents' secular interpretation of the Palestinian conflict, and by turning a deaf ear to the boring details of the factional politics of the PLO, Syria and Lebanon, Yassin and

---

Mariam, primarily because it questions her ability as a mother. As a trusted friend but not a member of her family, she could more easily share it with me than with her son or husband. Second, since an ongoing theme in my conversations with Mariam is our challenges with marriage and motherhood, she trusted that I knew that she had weighed the pros and cons for years before she finally left her husband. And that I knew that these pros and cons, of course, would never outweigh the pain that remains. Finally, I do not believe that sharing her story with me was a way for her to regain her human agency in the face of disempowering circumstances as Michael Jackson suggests (Jackson, 2002), but I do believe that for a moment, we carried the weight of her pain together and that she told me because she knew I would.

his generation pave the way for a religious re-interpretation of the Palestinian conflict.

In a sense, the two types of forgetting mirror each other. 'Humiliated silence' addresses what the parents do not wish to recount, whereas 'Forgetting that is constitutive in the formation of a new identity' addresses what the children do not want to hear. However, even though no words are spoken, and Yassin does his best to avoid the details of his parents' youth, the silences are still very much present and create a gap that enables the conflict to be not only transmitted but simultaneously transformed. The last type of forgetting highlights how the conflict is transmitted without being explicitly told.

## Forgetting three: Structural amnesia

Connerton relates the concept of 'structural amnesia' to the history of cooking. Referring to Jack Goody, he writes that 'the attraction of regional cooking [...] is tied to what grandmother did, and the methods of country cuisine are acquired by observation rather than by reading. In these circumstances recipes are systematically forgotten' (Connerton, 2008: 64). Even though there are no recipes for conflicts, I still find the concept of 'structural amnesia' apt to describe the gap that is created by what the parents do not wish to recount and what the children do not wish to hear. Structural amnesia in this context implies that the specifics of the Palestinian conflict are lost, but the plot remains. The 'who,' 'when' and 'where' are forgotten, but the wrongdoing and the concept of Palestinians as victims and fighters is remembered. Furthermore, the idea that you learn how to cook not by reading a recipe but simply by growing up in the kitchen of your mother or grandmother struck me as being similar to how the Palestinian conflict is transmitted across generations. Even if your mother or grandmother do not explicitly teach you how to cook, you still grow up knowing how to use pots and pans, being capable of distinguishing different sorts of food, and with a feel for when the potatoes are done. First and foremost, you grow up with the embodied knowledge that food is a vital part of everyday life. In a similar vein, growing up surrounded by silences and forgetting that all relate to a conflict creates an acute sense of being part of this conflict no matter how diffuse the conflict itself seems. One evening during the Israeli invasion of Gaza in January 2008, I was watching Al Jazeera together with Mariam. Witnessing the horrible pictures of dead and wounded children in Gaza, I asked Mariam how Yassin reacted to all of this. Mariam told me he was frustrated and blamed her and Hassan for just watching television and doing nothing. Mariam said she was concerned, but at the same time ... She struggled for words before she said, 'Anja, to be frank with you, I want Yassin to eat like he hates Israelis'. After a short pause she added, 'It's not … I want Yassin to have an education and all that … and I tell him so but, you know, it's really difficult'. Mariam is caught in a dilemma: she wants what is best for Yassin, but simultaneously she wants him to become a Palestinian ('to eat like he hates Israelis'). Even though she wants to spare him the details of her own past, she acknowledges that he is reared into the conflict. And Yassin is becoming a Palestinian, although a slightly different one from the one Mariam envisions.

## The creative potential of forgetting

In her book Partial Connections, Marilyn Strathern distinguishes between loss of knowledge and loss of information (Strathern, 2004: 97). She suggests that knowledge that is lost is not lost knowledge but knowledge about forgetting and about an unrecoverable background (Strathern, 2004: 98). The important thing for people is not to fill in these gaps, an impossible task anyway, but rather to preserve the gaps 'as if they knew that by insisting on that absence they create their own creativity' (Strathern, 2004: 98). In relation to the Palestinians, the children enhance their parents' silences by not listening, rather than diminish them by probing them. Strathern twists Claude Lévi-Strauss's concept of bricolage and points out that rather than simply fill in the gaps with the knowledge that already is to hand, people have to make what is to hand (Strathern, 2004: 98). In the case of Yassin and other young Palestinians growing up in Danish housing projects, this entails buying into a discourse on the hostile relationship between the Danish state and 'second generation immigrants,' and a discourse on the antagonistic relationship between Muslims and the West. In the following I hope to show that Yassin is simultaneously transforming the conflict and reproducing it in accordance with his own experiences as he goes along.

Yassin is seventeen and until recently he was known as a good kid who did well in school, respected his parents and other adults, and stayed out of trouble. He has recently started at a vocational school, training to become a mechanic, and is a loyal, hardworking employee at his spare-time job in the local supermarket. Yassin is growing up as an only child, and his mother has kept him under strict and affectionate surveillance to prevent him getting involved with the local groups of boys who hang out in small clusters around the housing estate. She has encouraged his healthy interest in football, forbidden him to stay out late in the evenings, and in the school vacations she has sent him to her brother in Sweden to keep him away from the neighbourhood.

Yassin, however, is not simply growing up; with his skin colour, he is also growing into a specific category of potential troublemaker in relation to the

Danish police. Due to many episodes of shooting, the police have classified several neighbourhoods in Copenhagen 'visitation zones,' which allows them to randomly search people to confiscate knives and other weapons. Several of the shooting episodes have been related to clashes between the biker group Hells Angels and gangs of immigrant youngsters, and Yassin complains that he is often stopped and searched by the police when he strolls down the local high street with his friend. Yassin finds these public searches extremely embarrassing and interprets them as discriminatory actions, both by the police and ultimately by the Danish state. After a local incident where the Danish police had pushed an elderly immigrant, riots broke out in the neighbourhood, and in housing projects all over Denmark (Kublitz, 2013). One evening when Yassin was sitting with his friends on a bench next to the housing project, the police suddenly arrived and forced the group of youngsters to lie down on the concrete, tied them up with strips and told them that they were under arrest. Yassin had managed to text Mariam before he was handcuffed, and his parents came running and asked the police why they were arresting their son. They were told that he was under suspicion and that he would be taken to the police station. At the station, Yassin was locked in a small cell until five o'clock in the morning when he was released, still without being interrogated or being told why he had been arrested. The next day Yassin was in an extremely bad mood, unwilling to communicate with his parents or me, only repeating that he hated the cops – and Denmark for that matter. Mariam was very upset; smoking one cigarette after another while she alternately blamed herself and her son for the incident.

A few months later, loud knocking on the front door awoke Mariam and Hassan in the middle of the night. It was the police. Before they understood what was going on, the police had entered Yassin's room, dragged him out of bed and started searching his room. Finally, they declared that Yassin was under arrest and took him to the police station. As on the previous occasion, it was unclear to Mariam and Hassan why their son had been arrested and what he had been charged with. It turned out that the police had found two guns beneath some bushes next to the housing estate. They suspected one boy from the housing estate and had furthermore arrested three other young people whom the suspect had texted from his mobile phone. As the police wanted to run DNA tests, they were all detained for fourteen days. Due to lack of space in the prisons for young people, Yassin was placed in an ordinary adult prison. Mariam nearly went out of her mind picturing her son among hardened criminals. After two weeks Yassin was released, and the charges were dropped.

Back at the vocational school, Yassin was told that he had to repeat a course due to his absence. Yassin refused and chose to drop out of school instead. A few days later, I overheard the following argument between Yassin and his father:

**Yassin:** You don't know a thing about what it is like growing up around here. When I grow up, I will leave this country. I will move to an Arab country.

**Hassan:** Yassin, you don't know how the Arab countries treat Palestinians. If you think you are being discriminated here, you just wait and see what it would be like in an Arab country.

**Yassin:** It can't be worse than here. They hate Muslims, they'll never accept us.

**Hassan:** Trust me, it can be worse. They won't even accept you as an Arab in an Arab country. You don't speak Arabic; they will always consider you Danish.

**Yassin:** I'll learn Arabic. (Addressing me:) You know, it's not only Denmark, it's the entire West. The other day I saw this video on YouTube. It showed how the entire 9/11 was a scam thought out by the CIA, a conspiracy to make people hate Muslims.

**Hassan:** You should not believe everything you see on the Internet ...

Yassin has become a target not only for the police but also for local religious groups, including Hizb ut-Tahrir. He has told me that he has been approached several times by religious adolescents in the housing project who ask him why he does not attend mosque and encourage him to study pamphlets about the Prophet.

When the invasion of Gaza took place in December 2008, Yassin was extremely frustrated with what he perceived as his parents' passiveness. 'You are just watching Al Jazeera', he accused them; 'why don't you do something?' Furthermore, he started to take an interest in family history. 'Why did we leave Palestine, anyway?' he would ask them. Not satisfied with his parents' rather complicated answers, Yassin decided to act on his own.

The following Friday, one of the religious Palestinian associations arranged an official demonstration in the centre of Copenhagen. In the square in front of the Danish parliament, a group of young males, including Yassin, attracted media attention by burning an Israeli flag while they shouted, 'Allahu aqbar' [God is great]. This time Yassin was not arrested. However, after the demonstration the police chose to escort the group of young people away from the center of the city and back to the housing project. And maybe we should just leave Yassin here: in the middle of a Danish high street with a Palestinian flag in his hand under surveillance by the Danish police while local pedestrians look at the procession in astonishment and bewilderment.

The above case highlights that, although Yassin considers himself Palestinian, it is another kind of Palestinian from that his parents fought for in Lebanon.

Whereas they were involved in secular politics, today Yassin reinterprets the Palestinian conflict as part of a larger conflict between Muslims and the West. Yassin finds himself in repeated confrontations with the Danish police. However, he interprets the injustice he experiences as similar to the injustice he believes that the West inflicts on Muslims all over the world, including through the invasion of Gaza by Israel in 2008.

Strathern elaborates on her idea that people make what is to hand. She writes that this 'includes seeing an unrecoverable background in the present artefacts, for there are only these artefacts to contain it' (Strathern, 2004: 98). For Yassin, this entails seeing the Palestinian conflict encapsulated in the conflict between Muslims and the West and, on a smaller scale, in the conflict between the Danish police and young immigrants. According to Strathern, 'everything is in place: sociality, values, relationships. But what must be constantly made and remade, invented afresh, are the forms in which such things are to appear' (Strathern, 2004: 98). The gap of information between parents and children ensures that the young people can reinvent the meaning of being Palestinian in accordance with the present. By ignoring secular interpretations of the Palestinian conflict, Yassin, along with many other Palestinians, makes the one available form – a conflict between Muslims and the West – do multiple work.

## Mobile conflicts: The reproduction and transformation of global conflicts

The case of Yassin and his parents demonstrates that it is impossible to separate the intimate sphere of family relations from the global sphere of politics. Global conflicts are an intrinsic part of everyday life and I suggest that political conflicts are passed on from one generation to the next, not just through the conscious upbringing of children but also through forgetting and silences. I argue that what the parents do not wish to speak of and what the children do not want to hear constitutes a gap that enables the conflict to be transformed and re-created. In this sense, the processes of social forgetting are not so much a matter of oblivion as a source of potential creativity.

If we accept Strathern's premise that all social relations are already in place, then it is by cutting relations, in this case by actively forgetting some, that others can achieve prominence. Strathern writes that 'in making connections visible people assert their ever-present capacity to act upon them' (Strathern, 2004: 102). By using the demonstration in front of the Danish parliament arranged by a religious organisation, Yassin simultaneously protested the Israeli invasion of Gaza and challenged the Danish police.

I will add that it is the silences and the forgetting that make the conflict transmutable. It is because of the gaps, the active forgetting of the specifics, the 'who', 'when' and 'where', that the conflict achieves its plasticity and thereby its relevance for Yassin. It does not make sense for Yassin to 'eat like he hates Israelis', but it does make sense to confront the inequalities he faces in his everyday life. In this sense, I will argue that it is exactly because the conflict is convertible that it can be reproduced across generations. As Yassin pointed out, his parents' experiences in Lebanon or Syria are of no use to him, but what he can and does use is a contemporary interpretation of the Palestinian conflict as a conflict between Muslims and the West.

## Bibliography

Abu-Lughod, L. (2007). 'Return to Half-Ruins: Memory, Postmemory, and Living History in Palestine'. In A. H. Sa'di and L. Abu-Lughod (eds.), Nakba: Palestine, 1948, and the Claims of Memory, pp. 77–106. New York: Colombia University Press.

Carsten, J. (1995). 'The Politics of Forgetting: Migration, Kinship and Memory on the Periphery of the Southeast Asian State', Journal of the Royal Anthropological Institute, 1 (2), 317–335.

Cobban, H. (1984). The Palestinian Liberation Organisation: People, Power and Politics. Cambridge: Cambridge University Press.

Connerton, P. (2008). 'Seven Types of Forgetting', Memory Studies, 1 (1), 59–71.

Højer, L., A. Kublitz, S. S. Puri and A. Bandak. (2018). 'Escalations: Theorizing Sudden Accelerating Change', Anthropological Theory, 18 (1), 36–58.

Jackson, M. (2002). The Politics of Storytelling. Violence, Transgression and Intersubjectivity. Narayana Press, Gylling: Museum Tusculanum Press.

Kublitz, A. (2021). 'Omar is dead: Aphasia and the escalating anti-radicalization business', History and Anthropology, 32 (1), 64-77.

Kublitz, A. (2016). 'From Revolutionaries to Muslims: Liminal Becomings across Palestinian Generations in Denmark', International Journal of Middle East Studies, 48, 67–86.

Kublitz, A. (2015). 'The Ongoing Catastrophe: Erosion of Life in the Danish Camps', Journal of Refugee Studies, 29 (2), 229–249.

Kublitz, A. (2013). 'Seizing Catastrophes: The Temporality of Nakba among Palestinians in Denmark'. In M. Holbraad and M.A. Pedersen (eds.), Times of Security: Ethnographies of Fear, Protest and the Future, pp. 103–121. London and New York: Routledge.

Kublitz, A. (2011). 'The Sound of Silence: The Reproduction and Transformation of Global Conflicts within Palestinian Families in Denmark'. In M. Rytter and K.F. Olwig (eds.), Mobile Bodies, Mobile Souls: Family, Religion, Migration in a Global World, pp. 161–180. Aarhus: Aarhus University Press.

Kublitz, A. (2010). 'The Cartoon Controversy: Creating Muslims in a Danish Setting', Social Analysis, 54 (3), 107–125.

Langer, L. (1991). Holocaust Testimonies: The Ruins of Memory. New Haven: Yale University Press.

Lybarger, L. D. (2007). Identity and Religion in Palestine: The Struggle between Islamism and Secularism in the Occupied Territories. Princeton: Princeton University Press.

Peteet, J. (2005). Landscape of Hope and Despair: Palestinian Refugee Camps. Philadelphia: University of Pennsylvania Press.

Strathern, M. (2004 [1991]). Partial Connections. Oxford: Altamira Press.

Magnus Andersen, Marlene Spanger, and Sophia Dörffer Hvalkof

# Living a Precarious Life as Migrant Worker in the Danish Labour Market

This chapter explores the precarious lives of migrants who work on temporary contracts in the construction or the service industry in Denmark. Thinking through the theoretical concept of precarity, we analyse the (im)mobility of migrant workers and their experiences of how the arrangement of the Danish labour market legitimises exploitative practices of migrant labour. In the following, we argue that the (im)mobility is shaped by their particular precarious working situation, which is enhanced by the reliant relationship to their employer and the difficulties in navigating the Danish labour market.

In Denmark, precarity is generally perceived as an exception rather than a norm (e.g. Rasmussen et al., 2017). However, inspired by the cultural studies scholars Brett Neilson and Ned Rossiter (2008) we reverse this relationship arguing that the Danish state apparatus is the exception and precarity is the norm. In the following, we demonstrate how such an approach produces a more nuanced perspective on the migrant workers' precarious situations when they encounter the structures of the Danish labour market. We ask: How can we understand the precarious experiences of migrant workers in Denmark?

Historically, migrant workers have played an important role within several sectors in the Danish labour market with relatively stable working conditions. Recently, however, there has been an increase in short-term, temporary and flexible work within low-skilled and low-paid sectors where many migrants work (Doellgast et al., 2018). The EU expansion in 2004 and 2007 increased the number of migrants travelling from East and Central Europe to Denmark (Andersen & Felbo-Kolding, 2013; Arnholtz & Andersen, 2016; Arnholtz & Hansen, 2009; Refslund, 2016; Spanger & Hvalkof, 2020b). This has posed new challenges in the Danish labour market. Denmark is known for the 'Danish model', a state apparatus that divides the responsibility of regulating the conditions, such as salary and working conditions within the labour market between three parties; the government, the employer's organisations and the labour organisations (Høgedahl & Jørgensen, 2017). Despite a highly regulated labour market encompassing collective agreements, 'flexicurity' (flexibility with security) and tripartite agreements between labour market stakeholders, research demonstrates how migrant workers in Denmark experience insecure working conditions (lack of contracts, extra working hours without pay etc.). This is in particular evident within the industries of construction, cleaning, agriculture and horticulture (Friberg et al., 2014; Korsby, 2011; Lisborg, 2012; Refslund, 2018; Skvirskaja, 2015; Spanger & Hvalkof, 2020b, 2020a). These labour market characteristics have reconfigured the previously stable working conditions within these industries, as employment within these industries are more often than not short-term, flexible and informal (Anderson, 2010; Paret & Gleeson, 2016).

To highlight the precarious situation of migrant workers on the otherwise imagined stable labour market, the chapter takes its point of departure in two settings: the stories of Stefan and David.[1] These two migrant workers are both from Romania, and work within the service and construction industry in Denmark respectively. Focusing on the particularities of the different situations that Stefan and David found themselves in while living in Denmark, the two stories reveal how the schism between life and work is appropriated through the 'Danish model'. This schism produces a space for employers to take advantage of the migrant workers' insecurity and lack of knowledge on a foreign labour market, leading to specific subjective precarious experiences that are intrinsically tied to their entire livelihood.

We first provide an introduction to the concept of precarity, before we move on to analyze the stories of Stefan and David. In the case of Stefan, we show how migrant workers have difficulties navigating in the Danish state apparatus and as a result, employers take exploits migrants' personal information registered in the Danish state apparatus to their own benefits, leaving the migrant displaced in Denmark. In the case of David, we show how migrant workers are moved from site to site, and how the employment contract is merely symbolic when the Danish authorities conduct inspection visits. The story of David shows how migrants at the same time are highly mobile but also immobile. Finally, the chapter concludes.

1 This chapter draws on the qualitative research project *Human Trafficking and Forced Labour Migration* (META) carried out from 2016–2019 investigating exploitation of migrant labour and human trafficking. The research is based on 72 interviews with migrants, 19 interviews with enterprises, agencies, and educational institutions, 20 interviews with public authorities, trade unions and NGOs (see Spanger & Hvalkof, 2020b). All quotes in the following are translated from Danish to English by the authors. David and Stefan are not their real names.

## Precarity as a norm

The last four decades, neoliberalism has expanded ideas of market liberalisation, free trade, and a minimisation of the role of the state in the regulation of enterprises to support a more competitive market (Harvey, 2007). Together, these societal changes seek to promote flexible working relations through entrepreneurship and innovation (Boltanski & Chiapello, 2007). This logic changes the way in which the labour market is structured, which in Denmark is reflected in the increasing focus on 'optimistic rhetoric' and 'active subjects' (Hansen, 2019; Nielsen, 2019). In turn, this produces working situations that are increasingly precarious due to the heightened focus on flexibility, entrepreneurship, innovation and competition which manifest itself through weakening of employment security in general.

Workers are no longer bound to the relative stable conditions of working in large-scale industrial places, such as factories, that characterises the historical period of that has come to be known as Fordism. Rather, labour has increasingly been substituted by precarious work characterised by elements of instability, lack of protection, insecurity and social or economic vulnerability (Risager, 2015). This is most evident in the way that full time positions are substituted for temporary ones often in the disguise of the creative entrepreneurial knowledge worker.

In recent years various kinds of studies explore precarity by stressing how the concept is constituted by the experience of a fundamental lack of secure employment in terms of length of employment, fixed salary, and career development (Jørgensen & Schierup, 2018; Paret & Gleeson, 2016; Standing, 2011; Woolfson et al., 2012). Another branch of literature focuses on the nexus of migration and precarity by emphasising time and space. The focus here is the position of the worker in the labour market and how the different configurations of precarious employment positions are affected by race, ethnicity, gender, nationality etc. (Anderson, 2010, 2013; Lewis & Waite, 2015; McDowell et al., 2009). Overall, these branches of literature discuss whether the concept of precarity ought to be understood as a process wherein people are not in a constant state of being precarious, but rather as an on-going process of becoming precarious both in relation to the work and, more importantly, life in general (e.g. Butler, 2004; Hirslund et al., 2020). In this chapter, we understand precarity as a process of becoming by focusing on the migrant worker's ongoing negotiation of their experience on a highly regulated foreign labour market.

Thus, we do not only understand the concept of precarity through the migrant workers' position in the receiving society. In line with Neilson and Rossiter (2005, 2008), we stress how 'precarity strays across any number of labour practices, rendering their relations precisely precarious – which is to say, given to no essential connection but perpetually open to temporary and contingent relations' (Neilson & Rossiter, 2005, p. 11). In short, precarity traverse the spectrum of the labour market and refers to the general experiences in the intersection between work and life. Therefore, the concept of precarity is both tied to the ontological experiences of the migrants as well as to the particular labour conditions (Lewis et al., 2014, 2015; Munck, 2013). Following Neilson and Rossiter, we thus need to understand that precarity is an 'irregular phenomenon only when set against Fordist or Keynesian norm' (Neilson & Rossiter, 2008, p. 54). Instead, the ideal labour market under Fordism, constituted by stable working conditions and employment structures, is rather the exception. Thus, instability and insecurity related to precarious labour becomes the norm.

In the following two sections, we outline and analyse the two stories of Stefan and David as they move from place to place relying on their unstable networks. The two stories of David and Stefan are applied to illustrate how precarity does not only define their position on the labour market, but their entire existence.

## Stefan's story

Stefan migrated from Romania to Denmark to find work. In Romania, his income was based on what he and his parents could earn by selling vegetables from their private allotment. Many men from Stefan's village had already, or were working in Denmark. Based on their experiences and stories, Stefan decided to migrate.

At first, Stefan temporarily moved to his uncle's flat in the capital of Denmark, Copenhagen. His first job was as a cleaner, but he quickly took up a different job in a corner shop, offered through the network of his uncle. Shortly after he was hired, another employee in the corner shop was fired. As a result, Stefan was put in charge of the shop.

After he was put in charge of the corner shop, Stefan left his uncle's flat and moved into an attic where ten other people were clustered together. They were all working for the same employer but in different corner shops around Copenhagen. The employer offered to help Stefan with registering him online in the Danish civil registration system. Hence, the employer gained access to all Stefan's personal information by taking charge of the online registration process, and by registering his address at the employers. In this way, the employer gained access to his physical mail, NemID and CPR number.[2]

2 NemID is an online ID login to use for online banking, public services etc. in Denmark. CPR number (civil registration number) is a personal identification number given to people with a residence permit in Denmark.

Stefan worked in the corner shop for three years. His salary was first payed into his bank account, but later on he was payed cash-in-hand as the employer changed his mind. During the three years in the corner shop, Stefan was never allowed a day off and worked almost 24/7 from seven to ten every day. Under the pressure of such an immense workload, a friend of Stefan expressed his concerns about his health and working conditions. Doing so, the friend convinced Stefan to reach out to the municipality to make sure that he was registered correctly, and to get himself a new 'NemID'. With the help of the trade union, he initiated a meeting with the municipality. At this meeting with the municipality, Stefan was made aware of that an enterprise was registered in his name. During an interview with Marlene and Stefan tells how he found out that the employer had stolen his Danish ID[3]:

| | |
|---|---|
| **Stefan:** | We tried an old ID … it didn't work. The day after I went to the library, and I got a new ID: NemID. I went again the day after at 9 am and [3F employee] checked and told me, you have a firm, you have this and that. I said no, I was shocked. No it is not true. But yes, it is true. |
| **Interviewer:** | You have a firm? |
| **Stefan:** | Yes, they set up a firm and everything. |
| **Interviewer:** | In your name? |
| **Stefan:** | Yes, I don't know how they did that. |
| **Trade union employee:** | They did it when they set up the residency permit. |
| **Interviewer:** | Yes, then they also set up a CVR number.[4] |
| **Stefan:** | Yes, yes. |
| **Trade union employee:** | No, they did it [set up the firm] when they got access to all of Stefan's papers [NemID, CPR number]. |
| **Stefan:** | I have written all my dates down. Everything … it is only him that knows all my dates because every time they visit me in the shop, they say "here you go, here is a new contact" because I do not read Danish. I sign these papers because I trust him like I trust my family; like my dad or … |

While Stefan initially worried about the working conditions in the corner shop, he instead – and to his surprise – found out that his employer had set-up a firm

3 For the research interview, Stefan had taken a trade union employee with him.

4 A CVR number (central enterprise register) consists of eight digits and it is your company identification number. It can be compared with the CPR number (civil registration number) which is a personal identification number given to people with a residence permit in Denmark.

in his name through the personal information that he had gained access to three years prior.

| | |
|---|---|
| **Trade union employee:** | I don't know if you have heard of a warehouse in Ballerup where they found two young people who were working with repacking candy? |
| **Stefan:** | Yes exactly, and they say I am the boss there. They said that it was [Stefan's] … and those people who were there said that they worked for me. The only thing is that I know nothing about that place. |
| **Trade union employee:** | The employer had another middleman who is called [name] that owns the space in the location where they found these two young people who did not have access to anything, not food, not water, toilet. And [name] said that it was Stefan's warehouse. |
| **Stefan:** | It makes no sense. |
| **Trade union employee:** | And these two young people had been in there for a long time. |
| **Interviewer:** | Do you know these two young people? |
| **Stefan:** | No, I do not know them. |

Stefan's story shows how he occupies an already insecure position in the labour market. However, Stefan is not only exploited through labour practices as such. Rather, the exploitation transverses the practices that are found in the nexus of their unstable employment and the compulsory registration of migrant workers in relation to obtaining a residence and work permit in Denmark. As such, Stefan's employer takes advantages of the Danish state apparatus in order to not only exploit the labour-power of Stefan, but also his entire life by gaining access to his personal data issued by the Danish public authorities. In this way, the precarious situation that Stefan finds himself in takes place through the very relation between him and his employer facilitated by the digitalised state apparatus. The relationship is rendered by Stefan's immediate trust to his employer perceiving the employer as a family member. Yet, in reality, Stefan hands over his identity that is then used by the employer to exploit other migrant workers.

The employer gained access to all of Stefan's mail, both physically and virtually, including Stefan's CPR number and NemID. Facilitated by the state apparatus, the employer gained the opportunity to create a seemingly legal enterprise in the name of Stefan. This not only shows how the state apparatus facilitates the exploitation but also how migrant workers in Denmark faces an apparatus that is complex and difficult to navigate. On the surface, the Danish state apparatus seems to secure the labour and social rights of the migrant workers. However, as Stefan's story illustrates this state apparatus is an exception that can be subverted by the employers, as the migrant worker is subjected to the various ways of exploitation legitimised by the formal structures; in this case the 'Danish model'. In other words, the impersonal virtual space of the codes, numbers and data on each citizen in Denmark further intensifies the already precarious situation of migrant workers such as Stefan, reducing them to a body among many that encompasses an exploitation of their entire life.

## David's story

Stefan's story illustrates how the Danish digitalised state apparatus allows for the exploitation of personal information. This form of exploitation is not tied to the labour, but also the sphere of an already insecure, yet stuck life. Differently, David's story grants another perspective on how the Danish state apparatus legitimises the exploitation of migrant workers through constant mobility.

David migrated to Denmark in 2015 after being offered a job through a Romanian friend who already worked in Denmark. Shortly after starting work, his employer was arrested based on theft charges, which left David without a salary for the month he had worked. Left in no man's land, David decided to look for a new job in Viborg – a city with around 40.000 inhabitants located in the middle of Jutland. David found a new job through a network of other migrants working in Denmark. He was hired at a construction company shortly after his arrival to the city.

Upon hiring him, the employer told him that they would take care of the necessary registrations including the creation of a bank account. The company also found housing for David in an apartment with two other Romanians. David worked eleven hours per day from Monday to Saturday. After a while, however, he realised that he was not paid enough for the hours he was working. Before he was able to raise the problem with his employer, David was fired without notice together with the other Romanians. They were told that they had twelve hours to leave the apartment that the firm had found for them. The Danish police showed up, and when David tried to explain his current working situation, he was told that they could not help him. Following the loss of his second job in a short period of time, David yet again found himself in no man's land without a place to stay and without work. During that time, he earned money by collecting bottles with two other Romanians while drifting around in the streets of Viborg.

Fortunately, a new employer contacted David through a Facebook group for Romanians living in Denmark, and offered him a job in the Southern part of Zealand. When he arrived in Copenhagen, David was picked up and escorted to a house in the suburbs where the employer had offered him a place to stay. There were fourteen Romanians living in the house that, according to David, was in dire shape; there was no hot water and they had to cook and take baths by using the fireplace. Like the previous one, the new employer told David that they would take care of registering him with a CPR number, NemID and bank account; just as in the case of Stefan.

The new employer was in charge of a nearby construction site. One day all the employees were informed that there would be an official inspection of the construction site where David allegedly worked:

> Then we were informed that there would be an inspection at the building site … I don't know who is in charge of the inspection but police cars arrived. Then, we were told to meet in front of the shed and we were given an employment contract, and when I saw mine, I could see that the salary was set to 125 – 140 kroner per hour. The signature, it was not my signature. Everything was false. For all the Romanians [at the building site]. Then a police officer came over to me. He asked to see my employment contract, and asked for how long I had worked and what my living conditions were like, and then he took a picture of the contract and left. After the inspection, our contracts were taken away from us again.

As David reflects, he had never seen the specific employment contract before. He noticed that the salary written in the contract was far higher than what he really received. He was always payed cash-in-hand and never – like Stefan in the beginning – received his salary via a personal bank account.

What is more, David was not actually working at this construction site. Instead, he was moved around to different private sites, renovating apartments and houses without any protective gear or adequate tools. Often he received less payment for the work he did at private addresses. Sometimes David did not receive any payment at all. Instead, the employer told him that he would pay him later: "I only received 1500kr [from employer] while in that house … in that period. Maximum a month in that house. When I asked about the money, he always said 'tomorrow, tomorrow, tomorrow'."

To save money on transportation, David often slept in the places where he worked, together with other employees. During a renovation, the owner of the house offered David and his colleagues some food and a radiator to keep them warm. The owner told David to contact the police if he did not receive his salary for the work he was doing for them. At the end of his employment, David and a colleague thus started to put pressure on the employer to pay them their missing salaries, but the employer threatened them when they said they would contact the Danish tax authorities to get information about their payments.

From the perspective of the authorities, David is legally allowed to stay and work in Denmark as an EU citizen from Romania. So, why should the Danish authorities worry? What is more, the statement by David also illustrates how a thorough regulated Danish labour market has placed an immense trust in the structures already put into place. The Danish authorities does not even question the authenticity of the employment contract. In this way, the so-called trust in the 'Danish model', we argue, is turned into a tool hiding the actual exploitation of migrant workers.

Contrary to Stefan's story, David's precarity is constituted by the way his employer moves him around from one working site to another. The relevant point that aligns the two stories is therefore not that they are precarious migrant workers, but rather how their precarity is produced in relation to their entire sphere of life. In the case of David, his housing situation is never stable. As already demonstrated, he cannot afford the transportation between the working site and the housing he was offered by the employer. Thus, David constantly is forced to sleep over at the same place where he works. Not knowing where he will work, and being forced to sleep at the working site, shows, on the one hand, how the spheres of work and life become merged and, on the other hand, how David is at one time stuck but mobile.

While Stefan finds himself stuck working in the same place for three years, David faces the constant shifting working sites in Denmark even though his 'official' employment contract states that he works at one particular construction site. Thus, David's story also illustrates how the Danish state apparatus underpins the precarious life of David, as the employer is able to display a contract that is consistent with the collective agreements, but does not reflect how the work of David is organised in practice. Instead of the collective agreements secure the David's working rights, the collective agreements is (mis)used by the employer as a cover for exploiting Davids' labour.

## Conclusion

Together, the stories of Stefan and David reflect the complexity of the migrant workers' precarious lives in Denmark. Drawing attention to the perspective of the migrant workers through the two stories, we show how the 'Danish model' enables and legitimises the production of precarious lives among migrant workers. The experiences of Stefan and David are paradigmatic examples of how precarity, following Neilson and Rossiter (2008), is a norm rather than an exception shaped through the experiences of (im)mobility.

On the one hand, Stefan's story illustrates how the Danish digitalised state apparatus allows the exploitation of personal information affecting not only the labour but also his already insecure life situation. David's story, on the other hand, shows how a similarly insecure position of the migrant workers in

Denmark is reproduced through the Danish model as the Danish authorities perform controls that ends up eclipsing the exploitation.

On the surface, the Danish labour market gives the impression of a secure and well-regulated environment for workers. However, as our analysis demonstrates, the Danish state apparatus rather legitimatises the very practices (of exploitation) that it seeks to prevent. In other words, before the employer is able to exploit the migrant worker, the employer needs to abuse the regulatory apparatuses of the Danish labour market (e.g. the collective agreements, tax fraud, and identity theft). Thus, precarity is not solely produced through the exploitative relation between the migrant worker and the employer. Rather, the Danish state apparatus conditions the precarious life of the migrant workers, as shown through the stories of Stefan and David.

The establishment of precarious lives is further intensified by the migrants' lack of knowledge of the state apparatus in Denmark. Besides crossing territorial borders, they are also forced to cross the cognitive borders that make them unable to navigate in the state apparatus of Denmark. Having difficulties to navigate in this apparatus, they are dependent on their network, which is rather unstable, left to nothing than a lucky spin on the wheel of fortune in their search for work and a better life in Denmark. In other words, they are defined by the constant process of becoming precarious on a labour market that has to be perceived as a historical exception.

## Bibliography

Anderson, B. (2010). Migration, Immigration Controls, and the Fashioning of Precarious Workers. Work, Employment and Society, 24(2), 300–317.

Anderson, B. (2013). Us and Them? The Dangerous Politics of Immigration Control. Oxford University Press.

Andersen, S. K., & Felbo-Kolding, J. (2013). Danske virksomheders brug af østeuropæisk arbejdskraft. Museum Tusculanums Forlag.

Arnholtz, J., & Andersen, S. K. (2016). Udenlandske virksomheder og udstationerede arbejdstagere i bygge- og anlægsbranchen. FAOS, Institut for Sociologi, Københavns Universitet.

Arnholtz, J., & Hansen, N. W. (2009). Polonia i København. Et studie af polske arbejdsmigranters løn-, arbejds- og levevilkår i Storkøbenhavn. FAOS, Institut for Sociologi, Københavns Universitet.

Boltanski, L., & Chiapello, E. (2007). The New Spirit of Capitalism. Verso.

Butler, J. (2004). Precarious Life: The Powers of Mourning and Violence. Verso.

Doellgast, V., Lillie, N., & Pulignano, V. (Eds.). (2018). Reconstructing Solidarity: Labour Unions, Precarious Work, and the Politics of Institutional Change in Europe. Oxford University Press.

Friberg, J. H., Arnholtz, J., Eldring, L., Hansen, N. W., & Thorarins, F. (2014). Nordic Labour Market Institutions and New Migrant Workers: Polish Migrants in Oslo, Copenhagen and Reykjavik. European Journal of Industrial Relations, 20(1), 37–53.

Hansen, M. P. (2019). The Moral Economy of Activation: Ideas, Politics and Policies. Policy Press.

Harvey, D. (2007). A Brief History of Neoliberalism. Verso.

Hirslund, D., Møller, J. R., & Salamon, K. L. (Eds.). (2020). Prekarisering uden grænser. U Press.

Høgedahl, L. K., & Jørgensen, H. (2017). Udviklingen i regulering af løn- og arbejdsvilkår set i et lønsmodtagerperspektiv. Samfundsøkonomen, 1, 18–24.

Jørgensen, M. B., & Schierup, C.-U. (Eds.). (2018). Politics of Precarity: Migrant Conditions, Struggles and Experiences. Haymarket Books.

Korsby, T. M. (2011). Menneskehandel i rengøringsbranchen? En kvalitativ undersøgelse af migrations- og arbejdsvilkårene for en gruppe migrantarbejdere i Danmark. Servicestyrelsen.

Lewis, H., Dwyer, P., Hodkinson, S., & Waite, L. (2014). Precarious Lives: Forced Labour, Exploitation and Asylum. Bristol University Press.

Lewis, H., Dwyer, P., Hodkinson, S., & Waite, L. (2015). Hyper-precarious Lives: Migrants, Work and Forced Labour in the Global North. Progress in Human Geography, 39(5), 580–600.

Lewis, H., & Waite, L. (2015). Asylum, Immigration Restrictions and Exploitation: Hyperprecarity as a Lens for Understanding the Tackling Forced Labour. Anti-Trafficking Review, 5, 49–67.

Lisborg, A. (2012). Human Trafficking for Forced Labour in Denmark? Servicestyrelsen.

McDowell, L., Batnitzky, A., & Dyer, S. (2009). Precarious Work and Economic Migration: Emerging Immigrant Divisions of Labour in Greater London's Service Sector. International Journal of Urban and Regional Research, 33(1), 3–25.

Munck, R. (2013). The Precariat: A View from the South. Third World Quarterly, 34(5), 747–762.

Neilson, B., & Rossiter, N. (2005). From Precarity to Precariousness and Back Again: Labour, Life and Unstable Networks. Fibreculture Journal, 5, 10–13.

Neilson, B., & Rossiter, N. (2008). Precarity as a Political Concept, or, Fordism as Exception. Theory, Culture & Society, 25(7–8), 51–72.

Nielsen, M. H. (2019). Optimismens politik: Skabelsen af uværdigt trængende borgere. Frydenlund Academic.

Paret, M., & Gleeson, S. (2016). Precarity and Agency through a Migration Lens. Citizenship Studies, 20(3–4), 277–294.

Rasmussen, S., Larsen, T. P., & Andersen, P. T. (2017). Det prekære arbejdsliv. Tidsskrift for Arbejdsliv, 19(1), 5–9. https://doi.org/10.7146/tfa.v19i1.109074

Refslund, B. (2016). Intra-European Labour Migration and Deteriorating Employment Relations in Danish Cleaning and Agriculture: Industrial Relations under Pressure from EU8/2 Labour Inflows? Economic and Industrial Democracy, 37(4), 597–621.

Refslund, B. (2018). When Strong Unions Meet Precarious Migrants: Building Trustful Relations to Unionise Labour Migrants in High Union Density. Economic and Industrial Democracy, 34(3), 401–422.

Risager, B. S. (2015). Prekæritet og prekariat – Sociologisk diskussion og politisk aktivisme. Slagmark – Tidsskrift for Idéhistorie, 71, 45–60.

Skvirskaja, V. (2015). Converting Experiences in 'Communities of Practice': 'Educational' Migration in Denmark and Achievements of Ukrainian Agricultural Apprentices. Identities: Global Studies in Culture and Power, 22(3), 347–361.

Spanger, M., & Hvalkof, S. D. (2020a). Danmark er ikke bedre end USA eller Sydeuropa – også her udnyttes migranters arbejdskraft. Dagbladet Information.

Spanger, M., & Hvalkof, S. D. (2020b). Migranters mobilitet: Mellem kriminalisering, menneskehandel og udnyttelse på det danske arbejdsmarked. Aalborg Universitetsforlag.

Standing, G. (2011). The Precariat: The New Dangerous Class. Bloomsbury Academic.

Woolfson, C., Herzfeld Olsson, P., & Thörnqvist, C. (2012). Forced Labour and Migrant Berry Pickers in Sweden. International Journal of Comparative Labour Law & Industrial Relations, 28(2), 147–176.

Asta Smedegaard Nielsen

# What Makes an Innocent Child? Exploring Innocence and Whiteness in a European Context

## Introduction

In this chapter, I engage with the topic of intensely contested identities through the phenomenon of 'child innocence' and its entanglement with the racialized structuring of societies. As noted in the introduction to this volume, children and race have become a prime optic through which to understand struggles over identity in the global north. With a specific interest in whiteness, I explore European whiteness through figurations of the child and the question of 'what makes an innocent child'? As case of study, I will turn to mediated representations of children framed as being in a position of an out-of-place-ness that disturbs the alignment of race and space (Ahmed, 2006: 121), and thus, serves to constitute them as objects of public awareness and emotional investment. I will pay specific attention to British and Danish media reporting on the case of Maria, a white girl who was found in a Romani neighborhood in Greece in 2013. The emotional orientation of her in the media reporting on the case unfolded as an affective intervention (Smedegaard Nielsen and Myong, 2019: 498) from the public aimed at moving her from her locality of living, and thus, repair her situation of being out-of-place. Analytically, I will approach the case by attending to Sara Ahmed's (2006) queer phenomenology, that suggests to examine 'how bodies are gendered, sexualized, and raced by how they extend into space …[…]… how bodies become orientated by how they take up time and space' (Ahmed, 2006: 5). One space of particular interest of this chapter is what can be thought of as the Northern European mediated public space, and within this I will investigate how mediated representation allows bodies to take up time and space, and thus how they are racialized by becoming orientated in certain ways. I will pay specific attention to the alignment of race and space (Ahmed, 2006: 121), and investigate if and how racialization aligns itself with the spatial orientation of bodies as being 'in place' or 'out of place'. In that sense, what may be contested is the question of some bodies as inhabiting some spaces more appropriately than others. This question is indeed relevant for the question of mobility, in the sense that the recognizability of the body as belonging at certain places heavily affects its possibilities of moving between different places. The analysis suggests that through representations of compassionable children, European whiteness is constituted as a matter of reproduction in its proper families and places. As these are suggested to belong to primarily Northern and Western Europe, this part of Europe becomes orientation point for where whiteness extends itself (Ahmed, 2006: 109 f) in European public space.

## Child innocence and public compassion

In September 2015 the Kurdish-Syrian toddler Alan Kurdi tragically drowned and washed ashore on a beach in Turkey after a failed attempt to cross the Mediterranean to Europe together with his family, having fled the war in Syria. An image, depicting him lying head down at the seashore, went viral in its rapid spread on social media such as Twitter and Facebook, and it also hit the agendas of the journalistic news media in most of the world. Indeed, his little dead body, for at least some time, took up space in the mediated public space (D'Orazio, 2015: 20 f). Although the lasting effects may be disputed, the media attention on the case did cause a response of raised public awareness of the situation of the refugees from the war in Syria, and their efforts to obtain protection in Europe and beyond (Armbruster, 2018: 2).

Alan Kurdi was immediately recognizable as an innocent child falling victim to atrocities far beyond his control or intent. As his case illustrates, imagery of children has a potential to raise awareness of atrocities and inequalities, as children often perform well as ideal victims, and appeal for unconditioned compassion and empathy (Seu, 2015: 656–657). Nevertheless, although it may seem obvious that children can have no guilt or responsibility for the atrocities they may face, and in that sense are innocent, it is still the case that some children seem to be met as more innocent than others, and thus in greater need of our compassion, empathy and help than others. Across the world children are exposed to abuse, violence, death, and other kinds of atrocities all the time, and some of the atrocities become objects of public witnessing through media and other kinds of representation. Yet, not all of these children are put forward as objects of public emotional investments of compassion and mourning, that is, as grievable lives (Butler, 2004: 19 f). For example, migrant children travelling without their parents are 'often caught between protectionist discourses and ones of delinquency' (Rosen and Crafter, 2018: 68), and thus, the migrant child is figured in a discrepancy between innocence and dangerousness. Moreover, the Western/European public may feel overexposed to imageries of suffering children appealing for compassionate investment for the benefit of some humanitarian cause. The public may react with a compassion fatigue or even aversion, when morally compelled to feel empathy and compassion by their mediated witnessing of suffering others (Berlant, 2004: 4; Seu, 2015: 656). In this sense, it does not seem to be enough to be a child, in order to obtain public compassion and empathy. In the chapter, I will consider how the political economy of the emotions of compassion and empathy orientates children as innocent, and how some children may come forward as more innocent, as more worthy of care and protection, than others.

## The thing about the parents

Linda Gordon (2008) examines the historical development of the putting-children-first policy, and the related best-interest-of-the-child principle, along the development of so-called 'Western modernity'. She argues that often children's needs have been operationalized as being in opposition to their parents (or: mothers), which effectively often has led to interventions that have worsened the conditions of children, rather than improved them (Gordon, 2008: 341–342). Notwithstanding, that of course sometimes parents are not doing good for their children, the flip side of this approach has been, that often the best interest of the child has been effectuated as a rescue from the future offered them in the settings of their families, legitimated through the motive of providing the children a better future. This goal of providing a better future, as Gordon puts it (with reference to a case of poverty): 'arises from the notion of childhood innocence, the idea that children should not have to bear the burden of their parents' poverty; that children deserve opportunity precisely because of their youth' (Gordon, 2008: 335–336). Where the ideal of ensuring children the best conditions and opportunities in life seems indisputable, it may evolve as a politically contestable issue to determine which conditions and opportunities are best, as well as which actors are most adequate of securing them. Public imaginaries and representations of children can play into such processes of determining how and by whom a child's future is best secured. In my investigation of this issue, I am particularly interested in the effects of the affective economies (Ahmed, 2004: 44 f) within which mediated stories about children in need are unfolded.

In the case of Alan Kurdi, it was obviously too late to secure his future, when the image of his dead body was brought to the global agenda of refugee politics. However, the responsibility of the neglect that led to the tragic end of his life was disputed, with some arguing that his father, as the only survivor of the family, was to blame for taking his family on the risky boat trip across the Mediterranean, whereas others placed the responsibility at the level of politics (Adler-Nissen et al., 2019). As such, also this case positioned the question of the innocent child's right to protection and a 'better future' in the indeterminacy between the parents, or the state as institution, as its proper caretakers. It seems as if these two parts must be invested in a struggle of out-weighting, insofar as the state is figured as a body to take over, when the parents are deemed incapable of securing the good life of their child. But, where the idea(l) of childhood innocence has brought about the ideal that 'children should not have to bear the burden of their parents' poverty', as Gordon (2008: 335) points out, it seems as if the state does not impose any other kind of burden on the children to bear, if rescued from a situation of 'bad parenthood'. This chapter aims at exploring if and how it may be fruitful to think about the racialized structuring of society as imposing a burden on children, that has significant effects on the way a child is publicly figured as innocent and object of compassion, empathy, and perhaps 'rescue'.

## The thing about whiteness

Penelope Papailias (2019: 1062) suggests that one of the reasons why the case of Alan Kurdi gained attention and caused public mourning may have been because of his resemblance of whiteness. Despite his Kurdish-Syrian origin, he could pass as a white European child from the image of him lying dead on the beach. Furthermore, he looked as if he was just sleeping (Papailias, 2019: 1062). In this sense, for a white European public he may have resembled one of 'our own children'.

Robin Bernstein (2011: 4–19) places the historical origins of the idea of child innocence in the late eighteenth and early nineteenth centuries. Here, it originated from ideas of children as uncorrupted nature and even holy angels, paving the way for an understanding of children as embodiments of innocence itself, however being developed in a close attachment to white children, particularly girls. Additionally, Bernstein (2011: 6) shows, an important part of the figure of 'the innocent child' was its obliviousness, which included ignorance and transcendence of categories and inequalities based on for example class, gender and race. In this sense, although the figure of the innocent child may be imagined as transcending racial categories, it effectively, from historic reasons, comes to align itself with whiteness. Thus, it allows a white child to embody innocence in a more immediate manner than a racialized child. Nevertheless, imaginaries of children as pure and blank may also invite for an investment of meaning onto the child figure. As far as the child figure is invested with mutability, as not yet fully formed (Castañeda, 2002: 108), it may be posited as transformative and able to transgress categories of identity and inequality.

Thus, the child figure is invested with both a sense of mutability and transformation, and with the idea of bearing a heritage, maybe even a burden, from its kin. Being invested with such oppositional orientations in the world, a child can easily, when represented as in need of rescue, come to constitute an orientation point where its kin, the public and the child itself become orientated along axes of meaning attached to categorized differentiations, as for example race and age. With my specific interest in European whiteness and racialization, I will in the following pay attention to a case that works to contest European whiteness and its margins.

## Maria, the angel – moving in and out of whiteness

The white child Maria was 'discovered' in October 2013 in a Romani neighborhood in Greece, during a police raid. The small girl was about 4–5 years-old, and the police took her with them, as they from her light skin, blue-green eyes, and blond hair judged that she could not be the biological child of the Romani parents, with whom she was living. While her parents were arrested and charged with child abduction, Maria was brought to the orphanage of a humanitarian children's organization, and a search for her 'real' parents was initiated. Thus, Maria's visible racial difference from the family became a marker of her believed forced and violent transgression of the racialized boundaries structuring society. The story highlights how the entanglement of racialized societal boundaries and ideas of proper kinship of racial likeness within families can work to make race come forth as something that marks relations between children and their caring environments as matters of public concern.

The search for Maria's parents was catapulted through the media of Northern and Western Europe with speculations that Maria could have been abducted from parents from these areas. Her portrait was distributed widely, depicting a very blond and fair skinned child, in parts of the media she was even referred to as the 'blonde angel' (Spencer, Evans and Reilly, 2013). The police made DNA-test of the child and her alleged parents and found that they did not match, which fueled the suspicions of her being abducted. Additionally, the speculations led to even further speculations about if other missing white children could have been abducted by Romas (Murphy, 2013). Thus, the reporting drew heavily on the myth of 'Gypsy' child stealing (Matthews, 2010: 138 f), which was also critically addressed in an opinion piece published in the Danish newspaper Information as response to the case (Eichen, 2013). The parents themselves, as well as other family members, testified that they had not abducted the child, but had her given to them as a baby by her biological Bulgarian mother who was unable to take care of her herself (see e.g. Spencer, Evans and Reilly, 2013; BBC News, 2013a; Jessen, 2013).

The media reporting leaves no doubt that it was because of Maria's whiteness that she was 'discovered' and removed from her home in the Romani neighborhood. An article from The Telegraph explains: 'The prosecutor conducting the raid "saw a little blond head poking out from under the bedclothes," said Costas Giannopoulos, director of the charity A Child's Smile, which is now looking after her. "It struck her as odd, and that's how it all started"' (Alexander, 2013). Thus, Maria's whiteness put her forward as of interest to the state apparatus and the public, and it made her able to take up public space through the police's search for her believed white parents, and the media's reporting on her case. The visual side of the reporting played a significant role, as her portrait was widely spread with the purpose of getting people to recognize her in the search for her biological parents. However, it was not her whiteness in itself that attracted attention, but rather her whiteness situated as being out of place. A white child was not meant to be in a Romani neighborhood, it was 'odd' as put by the charity director in the above quotation. Indeed, the notion of the child as being out-of-place was heavily invested by the reporting, stating, among other, that the police removed her from 'her involuntary captivity' [sit ufrivillige fangenskab] (Jessen, 2013: n.p.), and that she was found 'dirty and shocked' (Alexander, 2013: n.p.). It was also suggested that she had been 'trafficked' (Spencer, Evan and Reilly, 2013), and a description of her Romani neighborhood tells: 'Scruffy-looking children play among the rubbish – none of them with Maria's distinctive blonde hair and blue eyes' (Alexander, 2013: n.p.). In this sense, her whiteness served as evidence that she was in her wrong place, even suggesting her being violently brought there, and consequently Maria was constituted as an innocent child who should be rescued. Indeed, the contrast set up in the quote to the other children in the community underlines this interpretation. The other 'scruffy-looking' children were apparently not framed as innocent, and worth rescuing from a destiny similar to what Maria was rescued from. As it appears, they did not embody a whiteness of 'blonde hair and blue eyes' to shine through the dirt and rubbish. Thus, it was the whiteness that Maria's body revealed that caught public attention and consequently let itself extend in space.

Alongside the spatial extension of whiteness embodied by Maria and diffused by the police and media searching her parents, other bodies became restricted in space (Ahmed, 2004: 69; Ahmed, 2006: 109 f). People from the Romani community, where Maria was living, were reported to express their love, grief, and longing for her, when she was removed. However, their emotional orientation towards Maria did not extend spatially as it was not put forward as being the central issue of concern in the media reporting, which centered the public mourning of an imagined white loss. The case was not a case of the loss of a child for the Romani parents and their community. Instead, it was a case of the believed loss of a child of white parents, which allowed for whiteness, and not Romani raciality, to extend and take up space. Or, the Romani raciality could be said only to extend in the sense of being taking into the extension of whiteness as that which 'is not' (Ahmed, 2006: 115). Additionally, the extension of whiteness happened alongside a diffusion of the story about Maria itself, moving from Greece at the margins of Europe to Northern Europe, with its encompassing of the hegemonic and 'whitest' whiteness (Dyer, 1997: 13). In this movement, the Romani underwent a reproductive racialization into its 'proper position' of that which is not. It was neither the marginal European whiteness nor the hegemonic Nordic whiteness. Instead, both kinds of whiteness orientated themselves towards the concerns of the Nordic whiteness, as a believed loss of white Northern European parents as what the case was about. In this sense, the marginal Greek whiteness orientated itself in an idealizing and desiring manner towards the hegemony of the Nordic whiteness, through an agreed racialization of the Romani as constituting that which the desirable Nordic whiteness, embodied by Maria, should be rescued from.

The media made a sudden shift in their framing of the case when it was revealed that Maria's parents were not white Europeans, but a Romani couple living in Bulgaria, seemingly in even worse poverty than her adoptive parents in Greece (Kristensen, 2013a, 2013b; BBC, 2013b). Illustratively, in the Danish public service media DR's reporting, the images shown of Maria's biological family and their community bear testimony of great poverty. They show a very skinny woman as Maria's mother, and her siblings, some of them without proper clothing, and sitting in a room looking dirty and poor (Kristensen, 2013b). The reporting explains that Maria was a Romani child, but appeared as white due to a genetic Albino variation in the family, which was also evident from the pictures showing that some of her siblings also were blonde. The finding of Maria's biological family was not framed as a celebration of their reunion, as the reporting had anticipated by its hitherto framing of the case as a matter of an abducted white European child and the search for her lost parents. Instead, the Bulgarian Romani couple was reported on as being 'suspected' of being Maria's biological parents, as well as it was reported that they were suspected of having sold Maria to the Greek Romani couple (Kristensen, 2013a). Thus, when it was settled that Maria's parents were not white, she became somehow deprived of parents at all, in the sense of being seemingly rescued from both her biological and her adoptive parents. Both her biological and her adoptive parents were set under suspicion of having violated her rights, in terms of having traded her. As such, there was a clear and direct alignment between Romani parenthood and the out-weighting of the parents as the proper caretakers of Maria, which worked to uphold the responsibility of the Greek state to rescue her from 'the burden' of her kin.

Although it was Maria's believed whiteness that configured her as being out-of-place in the Romani neighborhood, the revelation that she was not 'real' white did not roll back the expansion of whiteness that had worked to place Maria within white space as represented by Northern European media, by the search for her believed white parents. Additionally, as she was not returned to neither of her Romani parents, she continued to be barred from the Romani raciality. Instead, the revelation that Maria was not 'real' white worked to orientate her differently within mediated white space, now as being primarily an object of white compassion and rescue from the burden of her parents' poverty (Gordon, 2008: 335–336), including the racialized marginalization of the Romani population (Fekete, 2014). Hence, although the case turned out not to be about the rescue of an abducted white child, a public sentiment of having rescued a child in need could be upheld by not returning her. It may even be that the revelation that Maria was not 'real' white afforded the white public a sense of non-racist moral soundness, insofar that it may have served to proof the white public's and its state institutions' will to save also a non-white child. In this sense, it seems that the innocence of children may depend on a public feel-good, stemming from the belief of being able to save the child from its predestined burdens, and promise it a better future. Indeed, the upholding of such sentiments may feel much more pleasant, than the opposite response would have requested in Maria's case. This would have required the concession of the Greek state to have wrongly removed a child from its primary caregivers, and of the European media and public to have approved and engaged itself in this.

## Concluding remarks

Analytical attention to cases of children represented as objects of public emotional investment can work to bring to the foreground those mechanisms that are at work in the racialized structuring of society and in contestations of identities. As children may be regarded as reproducers of race and kin, the question of which children are positioned as in need of rescue from 'the burden' of their descent, and why, can tell something about how races are seen as properly reproduced. Concerning the case of Maria, it seems that her body became a battleground for contestation of whiteness. From the media attention on her small white body, it became evident, firstly, that whiteness belongs primarily to Northern and Western Europe. Secondly, it became apparent that whiteness involves the question of children as reproducers of race and kin in the proper families and localities, and thirdly, that whiteness continuously extends itself throughout Europe by the taking in of other racialized subjectivities, as e.g. the Romani, as that which is not. Furthermore, the case revealed that these processes worked through a mediated public emotional investment of the feel-good of compassionate rescue of an innocent child, construing the compassionate white European public, and its state institutions, as humanitarian and as working in the best interest of the child. Furthermore, it may have strengthened the sense of a united European whiteness, that the marginal whiteness of Greece at Europe's margins orientated itself in an idealizing and desiring manner towards the Northern European 'center' of Nordic whiteness.

In the case of Maria, it seems as if her white body as well as her once-belonging to whiteness invested her with a greater sense of innocence than other Romani children, and thus, the need for rescuing her. As opposed to those children who were left to the life and destiny that Maria was supposedly rescued from when the police found her. An innocence, which stuck insofar as she was not returned to that life after the revelation of her Romani kin. However, the case does question if it should always be considered an advantage for a child to be constituted as innocent, as it here caused the removal of Maria from her adoptive parents who seemed to have functioned as Maria's primary caregivers. Thus, she may have been removed from a safe life with her family.

The case of Maria bears certain similarities to the tragic case of Alan Kurdi, which may tell something about the way visible whiteness, in terms of bodily features, interrelates with imaginaries of race as biologically reproduced through kinship. Both children were visibly recognized as white, which may have afforded them the news value that in the first place made them objects of public attention and intervention. However, for both children the context revealed that they could not lay claim to the imaginary of whiteness as an attribute of Northern-/Western European heritage, as they were ascribed Romani and Kurdish ethnicity respectively. In this sense, both children accentuate that race and whiteness must be understood as a complex phenomenon, involving different constitutive imaginaries. It involves both visible, bodily features from which race is recognized, and for example makes one pass as white or not, it involves imaginaries of racial categories as residing in genes, and thus, as matters of biological reproduction, and it involves imaginaries about which ethnicities, including their geographical places of living, that can lay claim to 'real' whiteness.[1] It may be suggested that a child subject's race may not be settled at all, but instead be thought of as being in a state of constant contestation between these different axes of racial meaning. Within this field of contestation the child subject seems positioned in an indeterminacy between its racial heritage in terms of kinship, and its possibility of transgression and movement into other racial categorizations. How the child subject is orientated towards kinship or transgression, and how it through these orientations is ascribed racial meaning, may be less dependent on the child subject itself, but rather how it plays into broader racialized structures of society, such as in the case here, to afford the white public a morally good sentiment of saving an innocent child.

## Bibliography

Adler-Nissen, R., Andersen, K. E. and Hansen, L. (2019). 'Images, Emotions, and International Politics: The Death of Alan Kurdi', Review of International Studies, doi:10.1017/S0260210519000317

Ahmed, S. (2004). The Cultural Politics of Emotion. Edinburgh: Edinburgh University Press.

Ahmed, S. (2006). Queer Phenomenology. Orientations, Objects, Others. Durham and London: Duke University Press.

Armbruster, H. (2018). '"It Was the Photograph of the Little Boy": Reflections on the Syrian Vulnerable Persons Resettlement Programme in the UK', Ethnic and Racial Studies, DOI: 10.1080/01419870.2018.1554226

Berlant, L. (2004). 'Introduction: Compassion (and Withholding)'. In L. Berlant (ed.), Compassion: The Culture and Politics of an Emotion, pp. 1–14. London: Routledge.

Bernstein, R. (2011). Racial Innocence: Performing American Childhood from Slavery to Civil Rights. New York: New York University Press.

Butler, J. (2004). Precarious Life. The Powers of Mourning and Violence. London and New York: Verso.

Castañeda, C. (2002). Figurations. Child, Bodies, Worlds. Durham and London: Duke University Press.

1 Additionally, and as I have discussed in earlier work (Smedegaard Nielsen, 2015), race is also in many cases constituted alongside imaginaries of culture. A question I, in consideration of this chapter's scope and focus, have left aside here.

D'Orazio, F. (2015). 'Journey of an Image: From a Beach in Bodrum to Twenty Million Screens Across the World'. In F. Vis and O. Goriunova (eds.), The Iconic Image on Social Media: A Rapid Research Response to the Death of Aylan Kurdi*, pp. 11–18, Visual Social Media Lab, https://pure.royalholloway.ac.uk/portal/files/41164696/iconic_image_on_social_media.pdf.

Dyer, R. (1997). White, London: Routledge.

Fekete, L. (2014). 'Europe against the Roma', Race and Class, 55 (3), 60–70.

Gordon, L. (2008). 'The Perils of Innocence, or What's Wrong with Putting Children First', Journal of the History of Childhood and Youth, 1 (3), 331–350.

Matthews, J. (2010). 'Back Where They Belong: Gypsies, Kidnapping and Assimilation in Victorian Children's Literature', Romani Studies 5, 20 (2), 137–159.

Papailias, P. (2019). '(Un)seeing Dead Refugee Bodies: Mourning Memes, Spectropolitics, and the Haunting of Europe', Media, Culture & Society, 41(8), 1048–1068.

Rosen, R. and Crafter, S. (2018). 'Media Representations of Separated Child Migrants: From Dubs to Doubt', Migration and Society, 1 (1), 66–81.

Seu, I. B. (2015). 'Appealing Children: UK Audiences' Responses to the Use of Children in Humanitarian Communications', The International Communication Gazette, 77 (7), 654–667.

Smedegaard Nielsen, A. 2015. 'If it had Been a Muslim: Affectivity and Race in Danish Journalists' Reflections on Making News on Terror'. In R. Andreassen and K. Vitus (eds.), Affectivity and Race: Studies from Nordic Contexts, pp. 43–58, Farnham: Ashgate.

Smedegaard Nielsen, A. and Myong, L. (2019). 'White Danish Love as Affective Intervention: Studying Media Representations of Family Reunification Involving Children', Nordic Journal of Migration Research, 9(4), 497–514, DOI: 10.1515/njmr-2019-0038.

Vis, F. and Goriunova, O. (Eds.). (2015). The Iconic Image on Social Media: A Rapid Research Response to the Death of Aylan Kurdi*. Visual Social Media Lab, https://pure.royalholloway.ac.uk/portal/files/41164696/iconic_image_on_social_media.pdf.

## Media archive

Alexander, H. (2013). 'Inside Farsala: the Roma camp in Greece where blonde four-year-old was found', telegraph.co.uk, 19, October, https://telegraph.co.uk/news/worldnews/europe/greece/10390790/Inside-Farsala-the-Roma-camp-in-Greece-where-blonde-four-year-old-was-found.html, accessed 31 October 2019.

BBC News. (2013a). 'Maria: Greek Roma couple charged with abduction', bbc.com, 21 October, https://www.bbc.com/news/world-europe-24605954, accessed 31 October 2019.

BBC News. (2013b). 'Mystery girl Maria's parents found in Bulgaria by DNA', bbc.com, 25 October, https://www.bbc.com/news/world-europe-24673804, accessed 6 November 2019.

Eichen, B. C. (2013). 'Selvfølgelig stjæler romaer hvide folks børn', Information, 7 November, https://www.information.dk/debat/2013/11/selvfoelgelig-stjaeler-romaer-hvide-folks-boern, accessed 14 November 2019.

Jessen, C. (2013). 'Maria: Hendes lille hoved stak ud under sengetæppet', ekstrabladet.dk, 19 October, https://ekstrabladet.dk/112/article4573626.ece, accessed 31 October 2019.

Kristensen, S. W. (2013a). 'Bulgarsk politi mistænker romapar for at være "Marias" biologiske forældre', dr.dk, 24 October, https://www.dr.dk/nyheder/udland/bulgarsk-politi-mistaenker-romapar-vaere-marias-biologiske-foraeldre, accessed 6 November 2019.

Kristensen, S. W. (2013b). 'Se billederne af den familie, der kan være Marias biologiske', dr.dk, 24 October, https://www.dr.dk/nyheder/udland/se-billederne-af-den-familie-der-kan-vaere-marias-biologiske, accessed 6 November 2019.

Murphy, S. (2013). 'Was missing Ben Needham at the same gypsy camp as "Maria"? Police probe claims that abducted British boy was seen at site where blonde girl, four, was found', dailymail.co.uk, 20 October, https://www.dailymail.co.uk/news/article-2468431/Police-probe-claims-Ben-Needham-spotted-gypsy-camp-Maria.html, accessed 27 November 2019.

Spencer, B., Evans, R. & Rilley, J. (2013). 'First pictures of gypsy couple "who snatched little Maria" as they appear in court accused of abduction and face up to 20 years in prison', dailymail.co.uk, 21 October, https://www.dailymail.co.uk/news/article-2470062/Blonde-Angel-Maria-Gypsy-couple-court-abduction-charges.html, accessed 31 October 2019.

Steffen Jensen

# Chronotopes of Displacement in a Cape Town Squatter Camp

Mitch, a young Malawian man, is sitting on top of the 3-meter wall outside his compound in Overcome Heights, a squatter camp in the Southern Cape Peninsula near Muizenberg. It is a late evening in April 2018 and trouble has been brewing for days. Mitch is watching in horror as a group of young boys from the neighbourhood are throwing stones and rocks at a Somali-owned spazashop while they are singing freedom songs from the anti-apartheid struggle. This was not the only attack on Somali shopkeepers that night – or other nights. A little down the road, the youngsters had tried to get in through the roof. The Somali shopkeeper had mortally hurt one of the intruders with a knife. Mitch was distraught by the incidents. For him, the ferocious violence against the Somali shopkeepers was reminiscent of past as well as a foreboding of future xenophobic attacks against foreign nationals in South Africa.

This brief vignette draws our attention to two related concerns in writings about South Africa, namely migration from the rest of Africa and the violence against migrants that has become all too commonplace in the country. Since the 2008 xenophobic attacks displaced hundreds of thousands foreign nationals and wounded or killed hundreds, much has been written about anti-migrants violence (Eliseev et al., 2008; Worby, Hassim and Kupe, 2008; Robins, 2009). In many ways, the attacks in 2008 constituted what Patha Chatterjee (2005) calls a moment of pure politics where new political modalities come into existence often through shocking forms of violence. Hence, the attacks on for instance the Somali shopkeepers that Mitch witnessed were performances that follow particular, choreographed scripts. The other strain of writings on migration, often linked to the former, explores how South African migrants survive and cope with the hostile environment (see for instance Landau and Pampalone, 2018; Landau, 2014; Kihato, 2013; Zulu and Solomon, 2015; Worby, 2013). The combination of these two research foci – understanding South Africa as a violent migration hub and understanding migrants' strategies – is central in much migration study in South Africa and elsewhere. Migration and refugee studies have increasingly become about trans-border, international mobility and the governance of such mobility.[1] While this is clearly relevant as an object of study, there are potential risks associated with such foregrounding when one wants to understand displacement. We cannot reduce Mitch' ordeals to a simple relationship between migrants struggling to form a future and a hostile host-population and state. At the exact time as Mitch was hanging on to the wall, some few hundred meters away, others demonstrated for housing. A Molotov cocktail was thrown at a house in middle-class Marina da Gama. The demonstrations spilled over into the near-by shopping centre where shops were being looted. At the back of the settlement, a land occupation progressed near the landfill. A few days before, the multipurpose hall at the back of the settlement was torched. Towards the northern edge of the settlement, the gang war that had engulfed the settlement continued, left Elise and Nandi scrambling for safety. While none of these incidents is easily absorbed into a migration narrative, they are intimately related to both historical and contemporary processes of displacement. In order to see this, we simply need to zoom in on the area in which the attacks on the Somali shopkeeper took place and take serious the entangled logics between displacement, political histories and violence. We cannot understand the land invasions, the service delivery protests or the gang war without understanding overlapping and sedimented forms of displacement and the struggle to stake a claim on the hallow Capetonian space. By paying attention to these interlocking and sedimented processes of displacement and urban claims, we are also able to understand the extent to which different instantiations of historical and colonial processes are sedimented in these structures of displacement. Hence, in the chapter I ask, 'What forms of displacement and urban claims co-exist in Overcome Heights and what does that reveal about the colonial instantiations in present-day Cape Town?'

Theoretically, it is useful to invoke Loren Landau's adaptation of Mikhail Bakhtin's concept of chronotopes to understand the simultaneous temporality and spatiality of displacement (Landau, 2019). True to Bakhtin's literary theorization (Bemong et al., 2010), Landau stresses how chronotopes signify particular temporal-spatial configurations of people's narration of the relationship between time and space. Landau explores three different chronotopes among a multitude

1 Refugee studies must be concerned with cross-border flight as legally a refugee is defined by the act of crossing borders, however it is clear that the moment we begin to position refugees in broader social and historical contexts that we need to broaden our study beyond the moment of flight. See for instance Michel Agier's insightful analysis of refugee camps turning into urban slum in time (Agier, 2019).

of chronotopes, existing parallel to each other in Johannesburg.[2] By focusing on chronotopes, we are able to understand the contemporaneity and entanglement of different trajectories as we find then in people's narration of their everyday life, past and present. Importantly, and Landau would never dispute this, displacement relates to political economy that is both spatial and temporal (Hammar, 2013). While most people, including Mitch, Elise and Nandi, three protagonists of this article, would recognize the precarious and unstable nature of their lives, they would not necessarily understand this as displacement. Displacement is primarily an analytical concept. To understand the contemporary and multiple histories of displacement analytically we need to begin by tracking people's often forced movement before ending up in Overcome Heights. These stories relate to family and kin relations, informalization and precaritization of labour, urban politics around land and property, violence and rural-urban migration that in different ways animate the various chronotopes that co-exist in Overcome Heights. These stories all highlight processes of crisis and displacement relating to the contemporary political economy of Cape Town. However, and as the second theoretical layer, I want to ask to what extent and how the processes of displacement relate to colonial structuring of urban life. In this analysis, I draw on Ann Laura Stoler (2016) and Christina Sharpe (2012) analyses of the continuous structures of colonialism and slavery. I propose to explore how and to which extent, if at all, we can trace overlapping and sedimented colonial structures in the chronotopes of displacement in contemporary Overcome Heights.

Empirically, the article is based on four periods of fieldwork in Overcome Heights from 2009 to 2019, fieldwork in greater Cape Town between 1995 and 2002 as well as fieldwork in rural South Africa between 2003 and 2007. I organize the argument in two parts. Firstly, following this introduction, I briefly describe the emergence of Overcome Heights as a post-apartheid urban space, followed by an exploration of the processes or chronotopes of displacement that saw them end up in Overcome Heights. Secondly, I ask tentatively and with some hesitation if it is useful analytically to trace colonial structures in the chronotopes of displacement in contemporary Overcome Heights.

2 Landau refers to these three as dislocated futures, deferred distanciation, and marooned malaise (2019: 1).

## Chronotopes of displacement in Overcome Heights

Overcome Heights began to grow rapidly around 2005. Until then it had been a scarcely populated sandy area to the south of the townships of Seawinds and Lavender Hill, east of the predominantly middle-class gated community Marina da Gama and north of Vrygrond. While it is possible to determine ownership and residence in the archives and identify the emergence of the first significant wave of settlers in the area around 2000, the history of Overcome Heights is deeply contested. Different claims about who has most legitimate rights to occupy the land proliferate, and any history told about Overcome Heights is invariably also a politically situated history. Wary of the risks, we follow a group of research participants to Overcome Heights, beginning with Ouma.[3]

Ouma got off the train from De Arr in the mid-1960s as a young girl, running away from the impoverished Western Cape hinterlands. In 1971, while working as a domestic worker for and living with families of rail workers, she was told about Vrygrond where she could get her own place and build her own home. Vrygrond means 'free land' in Afrikaans and was referred to as such by the people who had come to live there as squatters after being evicted from their homes as part of the forced removals in relation to the racialized politics of apartheid. For Ouma it was indeed a free land as no one claimed rent or fees from her. For complicated reasons, Vrygrond had remained largely untouched by the transformations of large squatter camps to become the equally huge housing projects – what would become the townships on the Cape Flats. Vrygrond had been settled in the early 1940s along with dozens of other informal settlements on the periphery of the growing city. Ouma stayed there until she moved to Overcome Heights around 2010 with her granddaughter whose drug addicted mother had moved to nearby Lavender Hill, one of the most notorious townships in Cape Town.

Walter also moved to Vrygrond from Lavender Hill in the early 1970s. In his own narrative, he became a community organizer from the mid-1970s, invading land around the Cape Town municipal area. Over the years, the area of Vrygrond was settled in several waves, and the authorities repeatedly sought to move residents to other, more peripheral areas and townships. The resistance entwined with the anti-apartheid struggle and often led to armed battles between authorities and residents in the area. At the end of apartheid, the City began the construction of a new housing project under the Reconstruction and Development Programme (RDP) and in 1999–2000 around 1600 housing units were built in

3 This account is based on a four-month diary study with 15 participants in Overcome Heights. See Schneidermann et al. (2020) for information about methods.

Vrygrond. Those of Vrygrond's residents who did not qualify for RDP housing were displaced to the sandy area north of the settlement. Following a court-case in the mid-2000s, the City of Cape Town had to accept that they could not get rid of the squatters that had begun occupying this area which became Overcome Heights. Walter and a small group of community organizers became central in organizing the settlement of Overcome Heights. The period between 2004 and 2007 represented the major settlement of people in Overcome Heights and the majority of the research participants moved to Overcome Heights in this period. Each of these arrivals traces journeys across and into Cape Town. Like Ouma, decades earlier, most of the people who moved to Overcome Heights learned about the opportunity to 'take the land' and erect a housing structure in Overcome from close friends or family members.

When we did our first round of research in 2009, Vrygrond had grown exponentially from the early 2000s when only around four thousand people were registered in the area. This figure had grown to almost forty-thousand people (Jensen, Naidoo and Polatin, 2011). As we were sampling for the 2009 survey, we had to create a new team to accommodate the growth of Overcome Heights that had not made it onto any official maps and registers at the time. Since 2009, the area has primarily densified. This means that all space between houses has been claimed and that most, not all, yards have been built-up to accommodate incoming residents, especially foreign nationals. This is where Mitch now stays along with thousands of other migrants. In some of these yards, the original inhabitants have built up to ten rooms or shacks that they rent out for considerable amounts.

The trajectories described above largely describe the existence of three distinct groups – coloureds, Africans and foreign nationals. These groups relate to apartheid and post-apartheid categories. The apartheid regime divided the population into four essentialized, racial groups, White, Africans, coloureds and Indians. These categories, centrepiece of apartheid ideology, came to structure people's lives and opportunities. Despite attempts to deracialize South African politics, the categories still hold meaning. Especially the term 'coloured' has been embroiled in constant and decade-long debates. While I agree with the criticisms launched against apartheid usages and categories, I also note that despite this criticism, people in Overcome Heights consistently refer to themselves or their neighbours as coloureds in seemingly effortless ways. At the same time, the coloured group is far from unitary and it makes little sense to collapse middle-class and township residents.[4] The concept of foreign nationals has

4 For some of the debates see Jensen (2008), Erasmus (2017) and Adhikari (2005).

gained importance in post-apartheid South Africa. The category only applies to migrants from the rest of Africa and hence, they could be seen as Africans. However, in the racialized world of South Africa that category applies to Bantu-speaking Africans. In the case of most Africans in Cape Town, they belong to the isi-Xhosa speaking group. Hence, in the warped, racialized world of South Africans, foreign nationals almost assume the character of another racialized group distinct from South African Africans.

While each of these three groups have distinct experiences of displacement and strategies for handling crisis in everyday life, there are also overlapping and interlocking mechanisms. Let us briefly revisit each of these displacement processes that constitute specific temporal-spatial configurations or chronotopes. The coloured residents of Overcome Heights constitute one chronotopes. They overwhelmingly see themselves as backyarders. 'Backyarders' is a concept used by people themselves to describe a history of marginalization or internal social hierarchies within the townships. Backyarders never owned houses or had prior rights to occupancy. They most often lived at the mercy of the 'front-yarders', those whose names were on the legal documents of apartheid and post-apartheid states. As families grew, increasing numbers of residents were forced into precarious housing arrangements in backyard shacks or in sleeping arrangement inside houses. These housing arrangements were often conflictual – over noise, behaviour, rent, food, toilets and so on. Backyarders almost invariably lost these conflicts, often resulting in perpetual humiliations and frequent internal displacements. All coloured interlocutors had moved several times before ending up in Overcome Heights where they, for the first time, literally occupied the front yard. While life in Overcome Heights in no way signalled the end to struggle the move inaugurated a new phase in their relation and claims to hallow Cape Town land.

While there seemed to be a majority of coloured backyarders among the first wave into Overcome Heights, Africans (mostly isiXhosa speakers) followed suit in large numbers, constituting a different chronotope. As most plots had already been occupied, many, including our interlocutors, ended up in the Road Reserve, the part of Overcome Heights that had been set aside for road construction. This part was also not included in the legal proceedings that made Overcome Heights a legal reality. Consequently, the Road Reserve is significantly worse serviced than the 'official' part of Overcome Heights. Most of the African residents came a few years after the initial coloured settlers. In our sample, three out of four came from Site 5, a vast African squatter camp near Fishhoek on the False Bay coast. Site 5 was part of an on-going, century old circular migration between the Eastern Cape and Cape Town where people would move to Cape

Town as youngsters and return to the Eastern Cape to retire or be buried. The Road Reserve seems much denser than the 'front' of Overcome Heights. There are no roads going through wide enough to allow cars (let alone fire engines) to pass and almost all land within an ever-moving boundary has been occupied. The over-crowding, the lack of sanitation, water and garbage collection together with the fact that almost all residents in the Road Reserve are isiXhosa speaking Africans resonate with and reproduce potentially racialized grievance. This grievance is also fuelled by the fact that the African National Congress to which the majority of residents in the Road Reserve affiliated has very little influence in Cape Town and in Overcome Heights.[5]

While the Road Reserve appears more crowded than the front, the front is dense in a different way. Many of the residents who came after 2005 have subsequently built rooms or accommodation on the plot. It is in accommodation like this that all Malawian interlocutors stayed. Reason, for example lived in a room sharing a yard with nine other, mostly Malawian younger men. Mitch stayed with five other families in a yard or compound. Hence, while the streets are relatively wide, the compounds may be very crowded. Renting out has become a very important economic activity, bankrolling hundreds of families. As Mitch says, 'We are their income'. The great influx of especially Malawians to Cape Town had begun in the early 2000s. Malawians had gone to South Africa for decades but had in the past mostly ended up in and around the mining industry in the Northern part of the country around Johannesburg. Due to the increasing capitalization of mines and nationalistic policies in the post-apartheid era, migration from Malawi was informalized as well as diversifying to the rest of the country (Jensen and Buur, 2007). The life of informalized migrants is tough and violent in the townships and squatter camps and all foreign nationals engaged in torturous reflections of whether to stay or to go home. Hence, the spatial-temporal configuration was much different from both coloureds and Africans.

In many ways, it makes sense to discuss the chronotopes of displacement individually. However, there are also entanglements. Some forms of entanglements are less benevolent as when foreign nationals are caught up in gang fights and service delivery boycotts and quasi-riots – or when African youth are drawn into gang structures that used to be reserved for coloureds. However, most entanglement emanate from the very intimate lives of people in Overcome Heights. It is

5 Cape Town and the Western Cape have been dominated politically by the Democratic Alliance that draws its support mainly from White, Indian and coloured voters. Coloured voters represent more than half the electorate in the province.

simply impossible not to know anything about the other groups or in one way or the other cross paths. Most of these entanglements are amical, everyday relations borne out of shared lives. At other times, like in 2008 during the xenophobic violence where coloureds and isiXhosa speaking Africans engaged in horrendous but also heroic acts of civil courage to protect their Malawian and Zimbabwean neighbours. In this way, Overcome Heights has become a radical illustration of post-apartheid South Africa at the bottom of society in the world's most unequal country in the most unequal city of that country.

## In the wake … colonial chronotopes

Above, I have explored contemporary chronotopes as we found them in Overcome Heights in the second decade of the twenty-first century. However, I would like to ask if it would perhaps make sense to think of these chronotopes of displacement as having a much longer history and that these contemporary forms of displacement happen as part of and in the wake of colonial displacement. This is what African-American scholar Christina Sharpe (2016) suggests in her book entitled 'In the wake …' For Sharpe we cannot understand black lives in America without understanding the persistent reproduction of chattel slavery. Sharpe writes,

> To be in the wake is to occupy and to be occupied by the continuous and changing present of "slavery's as yet unresolved unfolding. To be "in" the wake, to occupy that grammar, the infinitive, might provide another way of theorizing, in/for/from what Frank Wilderson refers to as "stay[ing] in the hold of the ship" (Sharpe, 2016: 13–14).

For Sharpe, 'in the wake' elicits a number of associations regarding the afterlife of crisis and disaster, from funeral wakes to the currents created in the wake of a tsunami for instance, where debris and unpredictability define the possibilities of life. If we follow Sharpe's argument, it means that we need to ask different questions about displacement. At the danger of reducing the complex history of Overcome Heights and racial, gendered and class struggle in South Africa, I would like to suggest as a thought experiment to explore what happened in Overcome Heights as different instantiations of displacement with historical roots in colonialism. Colonialism produced displacement to an extent where it is difficult not to see displacement as a defining characteristic of colonialism. Take Elise and her coloured neighbours. As I write about elsewhere in detail (Jensen, 2008), the racialized stereotypes that have defined and structured coloured life for centuries emanate from a history of slavery and genocide that rocked the life worlds of the Khoisan at the eve of the nineteenth century (Crais and Scully,

2010). Historiography of coloured displacement – including my own – have often begun at the end of slavery and genocide and prioritized the emergence of the modern city, the transition to the South African union and of course the forced removals during apartheid and the production of the townships (Jeppe and Soudien, 1990; Bickford-Smith, 1995; Western, 1996; Adhikari, 2005; Jensen, 2008; Erasmus, 2017). While this literature has excellently established the parameters for coloured subjugation, displacement and struggle in Cape Town, the literature has arguably overplayed the exceptionalism of Cape Town and underplayed the extent to which the stereotypes resemble stereotypes of other indigenous and enslaved people during for instance the genocidal, colonial incursion in the Americas. These stereotypes have repeatedly been central in legitimizing displacement processes seemingly motivated by different rationalities.

The circular migration of Nandi relates to a yet another instantiation of colonialism. It harks back to the destruction of the African peasantry in the mid-nineteenth century and the cataclysmic events that gave rise to the messianic movements during the ten frontier wars in Southern Africa between white colonialists and the Xhosa people. As Clifton Crais (2002), Colin Bundy (1979) and Jeff Peires (2003) suggest, the frontier wars throughout the nineteenth century resulted in the profound proletarianization in which working in the Cape Colony became an integral part of survival for isi-Xhosa speaking Africans. When gold was struck around Johannesburg, that same circular migration became central to the rise of racial capitalism, that is, the emergence of forms of accumulation relying on racial politics, as described by for instance Moodie and Ndatshe (1994) and Mamdani (2018). While much focus has been on the migration between rural parts of the Eastern Cape and the mining industry, the links between the Eastern Cape and Cape Town are as important (Bank, 2001). Despite the fact that the migratory route is sedimented, it assumes the form of circular migration where people will migrate to Cape Town but frequently return their dead to be buried in the rural homes (Bähre, 2007). While circular migration has almost taken on the form of culture, it can be seen as internalized displacement founded on the continued marginalization of the homelands (Jensen and Zenker, 2015). In this way, Nandi's ordeals were part of a much longer and continuing history of dispossession, displacement and constant marginalization of isi-Xhosa speaking Africans in Cape Town as well as in South Africa.

Finally, Mitch' route into Cape Town also related to particular forms of racialized capitalism inherent in agro-industry and mining for the past hundred years. Following the land-dispossessions of the African peasantry, the rise of agro-industry and the mineral revolution in the later part of the nineteenth century, a massive migration system emerged over the next century to satisfy agriculture and the mining industry's almost insatiable need for labour. This system extended into Tanzania with formalized labour recruitment offices and deals between individual countries (post-independence) and mining and agro-industrial companies. In this way, apartheid South Africa's economy was for all purposes Southern African. Mining and agricultural companies actively encouraged the employment of different ethnic groups, de facto entrenching conflict between them (Moodie and Ndatche, 1994). For the industry it mattered less whether people came from inside or outside the internationally recognized borders of the country, especially if that meant controlling the labour force better. However, with the fall of apartheid and the increased capitalization of the mining and agricultural industry, hundreds of thousands of non-South African migrant workers were made redundant. They did not stop coming but their status was increasingly informalized, no longer with fixed labour contracts and a migration infrastructure (Jensen and Buur, 2007). Mitch and his family provide an illustration of this process. Whereas generations in his family had gone to South Africa to work under formal conditions, he had to find more informalized routes – including applying for asylum or overstaying his visa. In this way, we can clearly see the extent to which Mitch' migration has been part of an equally long history of mutually re-enforcing processes of dispossession, displacement and capitalist accumulation around mineral and agricultural political economies that encompassed the entire southern African subcontinent.

With these brief accounts of very long historical developments in mind, we may ask if Elise, Nandi and Mitch are indeed still 'in the hold of the ship', as Christina Sharpe (2016) puts it. Critiques may ask (and have done so) whether such long, mono-causal explanations do not reduce the complexity of history in ways that obscure more than they explain. Clearly, the problem with this kind of postcolonial reading is that it tends to reduce history and agency to mere reflections of a colonial past. What happens to all the different small events that we reduce to a retrospective function of one political structure? What happen to Elise', Nandi's and Mitch's resourceful and innovative responses to everyday crisis? Are they also simply pawns of a one-dimensional history? While I think these questions are pertinent, I want to take Sharpe's question serious. In one influential intervention, Ann Laura Stoler suggests that many events and processes are in fact 'intimately tied to imperial effects and shaped by the distribution of demands, priorities, containments, and coercions of imperial formations' (2016: 1). Inspired by this, we might begin to reconstruct what she calls the imperial debris to see the recurrent effects and connections to the present (Stoler, 2013). These effects are, she suggests, not easy to see because 'They wrap around contemporary problems; adhere to the logics of governance, are plaited through racialized distinctions and hold tight to [...] less tangible emotional economies of humiliations, indignities and resentments' (Stoler, 2016: 1–2). Reading our data and the ordeals of Elise, Nandi and Mitch through the insights of Sharpe and Stoler allow us, I think, to ask a different set of questions about and transcend the presentism of the displacement that we saw in Overcome Heights. All three were arguably still struggling with finding their bearings in the wake of the cataclysmic crisis of colonialism, albeit different instantiations of it. This understanding of chronotopes of displacement allows us to see both the extent to which displacement are interlocked as well as how different forms of colonialism make their mark in one place, creating different parameters for struggle and claim-making. These chronotopes have long histories that each influences also what they will be today. In this way, the contemporary displacement we describe in Overcome Heights relate to – but is not reducible – different instantiations of (post)-coloniality in Cape Town.

## Bibliography

Adhikari, M. (2005). *Not White Enough, Not Black Bnough: Racial Identity in the South African Coloured Community*. Cincinnati: Ohio University Press.

Bank, L. (2001). Living Together, Moving Apart: Homemade Agendas, Identity Politics and Urban-Rural Linkages in the Eastern Cape, South Africa. *Journal of Contemporary African Studies*, 19 (1), 129–147.

Bähre, E. (2007). *Money and Violence: Financial Self-Help Groups in a South African Township*. Leiden: Brill.

Bemong, N., Borghart, P., De Dobbeleer, M., De Temmerman, K., Demoen, K., & Keunen, B. (2010). *Bakhtin's Theory of the Literary Chronotope: Reflections, Applications, Perspectives* (pp. 3–16). Gent, Belgium: Academia Press.

Bickford-Smith, V. (2003). *Ethnic Pride and Racial Prejudice in Victorian Cape Town*. Cambridge: Cambridge University Press.

Bundy, C. (1979). *The Rise and Fall of the South African Peasantry* (Vol. 28). Berkeley: University of California Press.

Chatterjee, P. (2005). Sovereign Violence and the Domain of the Political. In Hansen, T. and F. Stepputat (Eds.), *Sovereign Bodies: Citizens, Migrants, and States in the Postcolonial World*. Princeton: Princeton University Press: 82–100.

Crais, C. (2002). *The Politics of Evil: Magic, State Power and the Political Imagination in South Africa*. Cambridge: Cambridge University Press.

Crais, C., & Scully, P. (2010). *Sara Baartman and the Hottentot Venus: A Ghost Story and a Biography*. Princeton: Princeton University Press.

Eliseev, A., Maruping, R., Glaser, D., Nieftagodien, N., Gelb, S., Pillay, D., & Zack, T. (2008). *Go Home or Die Here: Violence, Xenophobia and the Reinvention of Difference in South Africa*. New York: New York University Press.

Erasmus, Z. (2017). *Race Otherwise: Forging a New Humanism for South Africa*. New York: New York University Press.

Hammar, A. (Ed.). (2014). *Displacement Economies in Africa: Paradoxes of Crisis and Creativity*. London: Zed Books Ltd.

Jensen, S. (2008). *Gangs, Politics & Dignity in Cape Town*. Oxford: James Currey.

Jensen, S., & Buur, L. (2007). The Nationalist Imperative: South Africanisation, Regional Integration and Mobile Livelihoods. In Buur, L., S. Jensen and F. Stepputat (eds.), *The Security-Development Nexus: Expressions of Sovereignty and Securitization in Southern Africa*. Nordiska Afrikainstitutet; Pretoria: HSRC Press: 63–84.

Jensen, S., & Zenker, O. (2015). Homelands as Frontiers: Apartheid's Loose Ends–An Introduction. *Journal of Southern African Studies*, 41 (5), 937–952.

Jeppie, S., & Soudien, C. (Eds.). (1990). *The Struggle for District Six: Past and Present*. Cape Town: Buchu Books.

Kihato, C. (2013). *Migrant Women of Johannesburg: Everyday Life in an In-Between City*. New York: Springer.

Mamdani, M. (2018). *Citizen and Subject: Contemporary Africa and the Legacy of Late Colonialism*. Princeton: Princeton University Press.

Moodie, T. D., & Ndatshe, V. (1994). *Going for Gold: Men, Mines, and Migration*. Berkeley: University of California Press.

Peires, J. (2003). *The Dead Will Arise: Nongqawuse and the Great Cattle-Killing of 1856–7*. Johannesburg: Jonathan Ball.

Robins, S. (2009). Humanitarian Aid Beyond "Bare Survival": Social Movement Responses to Xenophobic Violence in South Africa. *American Ethnologist, 36* (4), 637–650.

Sharpe, C. (2016). *In the Wake: On Blackness and Being*. Durham: Duke University Press.

Stoler, A. L. (Ed.). (2013). *Imperial Debris: On Ruins and Ruination*. Durham: Duke University Press.

Stoler, A. L. (2016). *Duress: Imperial Durabilities in Our Times*. Durham: Duke University Press.

Worby, E., Hassim, S., & Kupe, T. (2008). *Go Home or Die Here: Violence, Xenophobia and the Reinvention of Difference in South Africa*. Johannesburg: Wits University Press.

Zulu, M., & Wilhelm-Solomon, M. (2015). Tormented by Umnyama: An Urban Cosmology of Migration and Misfortune in Inner-City Johannesburg. In Palmary, I., B. Hamber, & L. Núñez (Eds.), *Healing and Change in the City of Gold: Case Studies of Coping and Support in Johannesburg*. New York: Springer.

Brigitte Dragsted

# Dreams: Mobile Bodies and Troubled Temporal Unfolding in Nairobi

## Introduction

Paul had worked as a shoe hawker in downtown Nairobi for twelve years when I met him during fieldwork. On several occasions, I followed him around the city's Central Business District over the course of an evening as he chased the flows of customers and dodged the movements of Nairobi City County Inspectorate vehicles. When we met, he would often invite me to admire his stock of formal men's shoes from the nearby Gikomba market for second-hand clothes and shoes, which he would have spent the day polishing and repairing. Paul always prided himself in having a knack for selecting good quality items that appealed to 'high-end' customers.

We are waiting around in a back alley one early evening when Paul tells me about several other pairs of shoes that he selected at Gikomba market earlier in the day but has not brought with him:

'You can't carry many pairs [of shoes] if you are selling like this. If you have thirty pairs here and you hear that kanjo [City County Inspectorate officers] are just around the corner – already you can start shaking!'

Paul holds out his hand horizontally in front of him and illustrates by making the hand tremble.

'Because if they come here and they take everything, you will just be back to zero. You have to find some money and go to Gikomba, buy 10 pairs and come back here. Start all over.'

And once again, like on several previous occasions, Paul shares his dream of quitting hawking and opening his own shop: 'I don't like selling here on the street. If I had a chance to go somewhere in a shop and sell, that would be much better. But the problem is capital, like I've told you.'

Paul has indeed told me. Many times. By now, Paul's dream of opening a shop enters our conversations with a predictable pattern to it: Hawking is not all bad since it allows Paul to sustain his family, but now, this business of always running from kanjo – eeeeeeh! What kind of life is that? How will he go on running when he gets older and his body is no longer strong? No, what Paul would really like is to open his own shop where he can keep a large number of shoes and customers can come to him. He will be comfortable, sitting in his shop and attending to customers. And he can market the shop using social media, just as he does with his current returning customers. But now, the problem is getting the capital to start up. Securing a lease in the city center alone costs two million shillings under the table, a payment known as 'goodwill'. Added to that would be the cost of stock, easily another million. Paul just doesn't see how he can bring up that kind of capital.

Versions of this dream recur throughout my conversations with Paul. The staggering amounts of two million shillings in 'goodwill' to secure a lease and one million to buy stock are fixed components. They hover over Paul, making the realization of his dream both tangible and unreachable at the same time.

Paul is not the only hawker in central Nairobi who dreams of quitting hawking and opening his own shop. In fact, this dream seems to be so widespread among hawkers as to make it the rule rather than the exception. When asked about their hopes and dreams for the future, hawkers will typically tell you that they hope soon to find themselves in a place where they can be 'settled'; where they do not have to run from City County Inspectorate officers all the time.

The unsettlement experienced by hawkers who constantly run from law enforcement officers in central Nairobi is not only a bodily kind of unsettlement, but also a temporal one. Very few hawkers in central Nairobi actually want to be hawkers. Most are migrants to the city who have come in hope of better opportunities, but who end up stuck in the informal areas that serve as its access points. In their life trajectories, hawkers feel like they are not where they ought to be. There is an urge to move on from their current situation in life, which finds expression in the widespread dream of opening their own shop.

In the following, I discuss how we might understand this layered experience of bodily and existential unsettlement among hawkers. In particular, I am interested in how the hawkers' unsettlement is intimately intertwined with another kind of unsettlement, felt among Nairobi's middle-class residents, about the trajectory of their city. Concerned about not living up to expectations for 'development,' interpreted in this case as an aesthetic vision of urban modernity, better-off Nairobians see the presence of hawkers who become too permanent in the city's streets as a danger of retracting urban development; of temporal regression. The dream of middle-class Nairobians for a modern metropole, and the perceived threat that hawkers constitute to this dream, fuel the violent police crackdowns on hawkers that further deny them the possibility of settling on the streets in which they work.

To discuss this intertwinement of what we might call elite and marginal dreaming, I turn to Neferti Tadiar. 'Of what consequence are Philippine dreams?'

Tadiar asks (2004: 1). Her answer involves a view on international political economy as driven, first and foremost, by work of imagination such as fantasies and dreams. In this view, previously colonized countries such as the Philippines who occupy a subordinate position in international relations will be governed by elites who strive for inclusion in global hierarchies. The aesthetic ideals for modernity to which elites aspire come to be felt concretely on the bodies of poor urban residents who are subjected to 'cleaning drives' that include evictions and violent crackdowns (ibid.: 92–93). I take inspiration from Tadiar's mode of asking about the dreams of countries whose colonial history continue to affect their place in international political economy, and about the violent effects that such dreams can have. However, contrary to Tadiar, I find that in the case of hawkers in Nairobi, elite dreams are not distinct from the dreams of those marginalized persons on whom they bear down in the form of violent crackdowns. I propose that the dream of a shop and the dream of a clean and modern Nairobi are instantiations of the same Kenyan dream for a prosperity that seems imperative but always out of reach.

My argument progresses as follows: I first describe how hawkers in central Nairobi come to dream of a shop, compelled by a combined experience of unsettlement as a bodily state and as an unsatisfactory position in their life trajectories. Next, I introduce what I argue is a particular instantiation of the Nairobian dream for development, namely a twitter storm against the then newly elect governor Mike Sonko in 2017 around what was perceived to be a too-permanent presence of hawkers in the city's streets. I conclude by considering how dreams come to have violent effects, and how distributed experiences of temporal unsettlement become embodied in mobile hawking.

## Mobile bodies

The white City County Inspectorate van has been parked around the corner the whole morning, preventing the hawkers who usually spread their wares on this particular stretch of pavement in central Nairobi from working. Wangari feels the pressure of not having sold a single pair of the socks that are currently tied up in her bundle and hidden away in a nearby backyard. It is almost mid-day.

> 'Come, Brigitte, I want to go and open [start selling]. I can't sit here and not work the whole day'

'But the van is still there?'
'Yes. I need to ficha.'

Wangari is already walking towards where her bundle of socks is hidden. I have trouble keeping up with her on the busy street.

'What is the word you used?'

'Ficha. Playing hide-and-seek with them. I put my things for a few minutes. When kanjo comes, I remove.' She turns to me for a moment and illustrates by swaying from side to side with her upper body like a fighter ready to dodge a blow.

I follow Wangari to a place a bit further up the road, not visible from where the Inspectorate van is parked, but still much closer to the van than what would generally make a hawker feel comfortable. Wangari has stopped minding me altogether. With her back to a wall, trying to look in all other directions at the same time, she puts down her bundle on the pavement and unties the knot, not taking the time to organize the socks neatly as she usually would. A customer walks up to her and asks about prices, and she answers without looking at him, her eyes darting from side to side. After about five minutes, she suddenly jumps towards her pile of socks, collects the corners of the fabric and runs off.

'Kuficha'[1] means 'to hide' in Swahili. In the sense in which Wangari used it, though, the word connotes not just staying hidden but also being alert, looking out, and running to a place where she can hide. It implies mobility. Not just hiding, but 'playing hide-and-seek', as Wangari explained.

While Wangari in the incident above used the word ficha to describe her state of hyper-alertness in a particularly tightly policed area, hawkers also speak of their work in general as marked by a constant readiness to run.

'Kuficha, that is what we do as hawkers,' Mwende tells me on another day. 'You have seen us there in the street. We open, we sell for a little while, and then we pack up and run.'

'We are always on our feet,' says Julia, who is sitting next to us.

Kuficha, as it appeared in my conversations with hawkers, describes a position of precarity as well as a bodily competence. On the one hand, hawkers pride themselves in their skills of being attuned to their environment and able to wrap up their goods and run away within seconds. On the other hand, having to be 'always on your feet' denotes a precarious, vulnerable position on the city's streets.

## Marked bodies

One of the floor-level shops opposite where Wangari, Julia and Mwende work has two loudspeakers attached on each corner of the shopfront. On most days,

1 Swahili verbs carry the prefix 'ku-' to denote the infinitive form.

the overburdened speakers bellow out either gospel music or English-language children's songs, to advertise that these two albums can be bought inside. Today is a good day, however: The speakers screech out local dance tunes, and the hawkers listen with a spring in their step.

'Do you hear this song, Brigitte?' says Wangari.

The loudspeakers now play a song with a dancehall beat and lyrics in Sheng that I can't make out.

'What is it about?'

'You hear how they say "stima" [electricity]? Eh! So this song, it's about – you know – when stima is gone in the ghetto, and then it comes back. And people are so happy and excited they shout: "Stima!"' Wangari laughs.

Julia jumps up and dances to the song. Mwende hums along and rocks her shoulders to the music while sitting on the sidewalk.

'You see Mwende dancing down there?' Wangari says, raising her voice. 'She is a ghetto girl. She stays in Huruma. She is one of those people in the song who will get so excited and shout: "Stima!"'

Wangari laughs. Julia and Mwende laugh. Mwende shouts back that Wangari herself has grown up in Huruma and is no different. Wangari makes a few purposeful dance moves.

Most of the hawkers who come to the city center each day to sell their wares stay in Nairobi's 'Eastlands' in areas such as Huruma that carry entrenched stigma. The high frequency of power outages in such areas, referred to by Wangari, is by no means the only problem faced by residents. Known for being overcrowded and ripe with criminal activity, the bad reputation of these residential areas follows their residents as they move into more affluent areas of the city. Van Stapele's (2016) argument about 'spatial othering' of young men living Mathare, another Eastlands community, could easily be applied to residents of Huruma as well: Once in the city center, they expect to be treated with reservation and suspicion merely by mention of the area in which they stay.

Inspectorate officers and other Nairobians often use reference to the Eastlands areas in which hawkers live to convey other, implied, meanings about their assumed motivations for hawking. Here is an Inspectorate officer called Kuria, explaining how he sees hawkers as people desperate to make money and therefore prone to violence:

> They [hawkers] stay in Mathare.[2] Have you been to Mathare? Do you have slums like that in Denmark? They have children there and there is no food in the house, and they

2 Despite Kuria's conviction that hawkers stay in Mathare, I found that most of the

> know that: "If I come to town, I can make something." [...] If you try to arrest someone who has not eaten for a day – that person will fight you!

Like many other poor urban neighborhoods in Nairobi, Huruma and Mathare grew out of the explosive urbanization of the 1960s and 1970s, when colonial pass laws were abolished and landless residents from rural areas migrated to the city in large numbers in search of opportunities. The municipal government was unable to keep up with the influx of people (Anderson, 2001), and areas such as the Mathare Valley were inhabited by squatters who settled on unoccupied private land (Médard, 2010). Commentators at the time spoke of the divide between the slow, controlled growth of the 'modern' half of the city and the rapid growth of the unplanned, informal 'self-help' city (Hake, 1977). Even as the 'self-help' city filled up with shanties, however, many families continued to live between dual households: One in the city, and one in the rural areas (Hake, 1977: 77; Robertson, 1997: 146). Among the hawkers with whom I worked, a minority were born in Nairobi, and even those who were maintain ties to their families in rural areas.

The 'self-help' city from the 1970s, in this sense, is less an autonomous entity than a site in the ongoing migration of Kenya's poor towards better opportunities. As Kuria's comment shows, however, areas like Huruma and Mathare, while accessible as entry points to the city, leave a mark on hawkers once these move further into the city center. Seen as potentially violent, hawkers are understood to call for violent modes of policing.

## Dreams of permanence and destination

Persistently present throughout 59 interviews with hawkers that were conducted from August to October 2017 as part of my doctoral research, the dream of quitting hawking and owning a shop reoccurs in different shapes.

In some instances, the dream is presented as a natural transition from one career stage to another. Wachira has been a hawker for six years. His cousin introduced him to the work when he had just arrived in Nairobi from his home in Nyandarua County in 2011. Seeing that a lot of young people are becoming hawkers, Wachira feels that he must move on to opening his own business so that the newcomers can 'advance their lives' like he has:

---

hawkers I engaged with live in adjacent areas which nonetheless carry stigma comparable to that of Mathare.

> Since there are still people joining us [becoming hawkers] and it is not to say that I would like to stay here for the rest of my life, I would like to work for the next two to three years so that I can open a big business and give another person an opportunity to work on the street to advance their life.

In other cases, the dream of opening your own shop seems to express a more troubled wish to leave hawking. A doubt, rather than the certainty implied in Wachira's narrative above. Makena is called 'mathee', mother, by the other hawkers. Her children are grown up and she already has her first grandchild at home. Makena continues hawking because she needs the income it brings, but she resents having to run from Inspectorate officers:

> Honestly, when I compare my age with most of the youngsters here [...] I pray that God would help me [...] get a place where I would settle. I will be so happy if I get done with the frequent chases [by Inspectorate officers]. It is circumstances that would make someone be in such a place [hawking]. It is not fun. There is no fun in it.

The dream of opening a shop, as it pervades hawkers' outlook on their own life trajectories, speaks to the physical and emotional pressures of being 'always on your feet': The strain of having to run with heavy goods, the need for constant alertness that never allows them to relax, and the discomfort of being seen by others as criminals both because of the places they live and because of the work they do. Out of this condition, the dream of a shop emerges as a dream of permanence for the mobile body, while at the same time promising a 'respectable' destination for the body marked by stigma.

## National dreams

Hope for a better future is not a universal human experience, if you ask anthropologists. On the contrary, anthropological literature on hope suggests that they ways in which a person hopes are always socially, culturally and historically conditioned (Crapanzano, 2003). Hope may even be conceived of as a social resource that societies have the capacity to 'distribute' among their citizens, such that middle-class persons have the privilege of hoping in specific, long-term ways while those in less privileged positions hope in a utopian, short-term fashion (Hage, 2003). Several studies engage with hope among marginalized persons, suggesting that hope takes on particular qualities in the contexts of economic precarity (Vigh, 2006; Frederiksen, 2011; Pedersen, 2012), and clandestine migration (Lucht, 2011; Turner, 2014; Kleist & Thorsen, 2017). That modes of hoping are shaped by economic and social marginality would seem an adequate description of the dreams of hawkers in central Nairobi. We have seen how the dream of opening one's own shop emerges from the embodied experience of being policed as well as from the social experience of stigma.

However, beyond the importance that marginality has for hawkers' experiences of unsettlement, another important element seems to be a more shared Kenyan experience of troubled temporal unfolding. When hawkers in central Nairobi almost without exception dream of leaving hawking and opening their own shop, they participate in a drive towards improvement and a rejection of the status quo that is described in literature on Kenya as an investment in notions of 'development'. As Haugerud (1997) shows, politics in Kenya have long been centered around a moral bargain between the population and its ruling elites: In return for political support, Kenyans can expect not just stability in their subsistence levels but steadily rising standards of material wealth. From colonial officials promising 'lamps, oil and matches' to rural populations in the 1920s to postcolonial politicians promising infrastructure projects, 'development' has been conceived of as material improvements rewarding political loyalty (Haugerud, 1997: 10–11; 101–102).

Smith (2008) describes how when the post-independence patronage state became cash-strapped in the 1990s under Structural Adjustment Programmes and could no longer uphold its own end of the bargain, discourses around 'development' among ordinary Kenyans became unhinged from the state. Today, 'development' denotes a variety of individual and collective work to transform the present, starting with each person's growing up, as in the statement: 'You have developed well!' (Smith, 2008: 6). Whether referring to individuals, or to formal local or national politics, 'development' implies moving forward; rejecting the status quo. It often involves a relation to another place and time in comparison to which Kenya is seen to be 'behind' (Smith, 2008: 7–11). Crucial moments in history such as the austerity of the 1990s, under which half of the traffic lights in Nairobi were permanently broken, became for Kenyans a strong experience of decline; of a collective feeling that the country was retracting its development, and so was moving backwards (Smith, 2008: 11–15). As part of its colonial history, and combined with religious imaginary, Smith argues, 'development' has at different times had the quality of something withheld, something spectral (Smith, 2008: 38).

As an imperative for progress and a simultaneous experience of troubled temporal unfolding, then, 'development' informs Kenyan temporal imaginaries. This goes not only for hawkers' outlook on their own life trajectories but also for better-off Nairobians concerned about the progress of Nairobi as a metropole, as I show in the following section.

## A Twitter storm and a clean-up

When Mbuvi Gideon Kioko, popularly known as 'Mike Sonko,' was elected governor of Nairobi County in August 2017, a few months followed when the policing of hawkers in central Nairobi was markedly relaxed. Having exerted himself to win the votes of hawkers by citing plans of regulated access to city streets as well as the construction of markets in central locations, Sonko began his career as governor with official radio silence on the matter of hawkers, combined with vast de facto tolerance. As hawkers flocked to town from all directions in which there are deprived neighborhoods, pedestrians were increasingly forced to compete with vehicles on the roads because the sidewalks had become blocked by hawkers' wares. Local news media cried of 'hawker headache' (Omulo, 2017), 'hawkers menace' (Mutavi, 2017a), 'hawkers invasion' (Musambi, 2017), and 'madness in city streets' (Mutavi, 2017b).

This alarm about the increased presence of hawkers was echoed on the social media platform Twitter which in Kenya, like in many other parts of the world, is associated with society's more privileged members; a debate forum driven by the voices of journalists, politicians and celebrities (Muindi, 2018; Al-Saqaf & Christensen, 2019). One such tweet (Ma3Route, 2017) is by a Twitter account on which users share information about the city's traffic conditions. Above a picture of a pavement in the central Nairobi lined with vegetable hawkers, the text sarcastically integrates Nairobi's promotional motto of being a 'green city in the sun' with the common Swahili pseudonym for street traders and open-air artisans 'jua kali', meaning 'under the hot sun':

**@Ma3Route:** How we've made our Nairobi capital city CBD "CITY UNDER UNDER THE SUN [sun emoticon]

[…]

**@WaridiNyambura:** My QUESTION to Sonko is Nairobi an international capital city or a village marketplace?

[…]

**@jimmymbandi:** Unfortunate in Kenya we assume we are very developed but we cannot manage a city.

Here, the contrast between 'modern' Nairobi and 'self-help' Nairobi of the 1970s operates as a moral distinction according to which a 'village marketplace' has no place in the 'international capital city'. Hawkers who become too permanent in the streets of Nairobi, then, threaten the city with temporal regression; with an about-turn of the city's developmental trajectory.

On November 8th, a few days after Twitter exploded with angry conversations about hawkers turning Nairobi into a village marketplace, the governor took to explaining himself via his official Twitter account. Accompanied by four pictures of streets in the city center with Inspectorate vehicles visibly present and no hawkers, Sonko promised to solve the problem of hawkers' obstructing the sidewalks (Sonko, 2017). Comments to his tweet repeat the danger of the 'capital city' being turned into a 'market'. Some also accuse the governor of 'popularity games' in relation to the hawkers, and encourage him to 'crack the whip':

**@MikeSonko:** For the time being, my administration is working on means and ways that will ensure a progressive and humane relocation of hawkers to designated streets and lanes where they can freely do their businesses without obstructing other people as well as other business owners.
[…]
**@kembobill:** […] The millions who walk these streets daily don't approve of their streets being turned into a hop skip n jump jungle. Crack the whip.
[…]
**@mitimbili:** They will return if you don't act firm. The law is on your side, use it. End popularity games.
[…]
**@omondidacon:** Have it done very fast !!!! This is our capital city not capital Market!!!!!!! Get it done!!!
[…]
**@habib_juma:** Nairobi's image must be protected..It represents us out here

The crackdown on hawking by authorities, which the commentators above call for, came a few months later when, according to news media, Sonko finally 'rolled up his sleeves' and had hawkers 'flushed out' of the city center by a combined force of City County Inspectorate officers and police (Orinde, 2018). Afterwards, according to the hawkers I kept in touch with after completing my fieldwork, the state of hawking returned to normal: Hawkers were neither completely evicted from the city nor accommodated. They went back to ficha in the streets.

## Conclusion: Shared dreams and distributed violence

Nairobi's hawkers who dream of the permanence and respectability of a shop can be understood to embody the violent effects of a national dreaming for 'development;' of an imperative for improvement accompanied by the sense that this improvement might not easily come about. This dreaming manifests both in hawkers' own outlook on their life trajectories, and in that of wealthier residents concerned about the troubled temporal unfolding of a city that they understand to belong to them; to those embodying the 'modern' Nairobi.

At this point we can revisit Tadiar's (2004) question, which I quoted in the beginning, about the dreams of a previously colonized country and the consequences of these dreams. Tadiar conceives of dreams for modernity and development as elite dreams, different from the dreams of the masses who bear the violence that these dreams unleash on their bodies. I would like to propose that the unsettlement experienced in emotional, somatic and existential registers by hawkers who ficha in central Nairobi calls for a different approach. Their dreams are not different from or opposed to the dreams of an elite. On the contrary, hawkers and middle-class Nairobians dream the same dreams. However, the violent effects of the Kenyan dreams of development are unevenly distributed, and sharing the dreaming only exacerbates its violence for hawkers. Not only are they unsettled in a spatial sense by the policing that chases them around the city. They are also unsettled in a temporal sense by the elusiveness of their dreams for respectability and a proper destination.

## Bibliography


Al-Saqaf, Walid, and Christian Christensen. 2019. 'Tweeting in Precarious Times: Comparing Twitter Use During the 2013 General Election in Kenya and the 2012 Presidential Election in Egypt'. In Media, Communication and the Struggle for Democratic Change: Case Studies on Contested Transitions, Katrin Voltmer, Christian Christensen, Irene Neverla, Nicole Stremlau, Barbara Thomass, Nebojsa Vladisavljević, and Herman Wasserman (eds.), 133–157. Cham: Springer International Publishing AG.

Anderson, David M. 2001. 'Corruption at City Hall: African Housing and Urban Development in Colonial Nairobi'. AZANIA: Journal of the British Institute in Eastern Africa 36 (1): 138–154.

Crapanzano, Vincent. 2003. 'Reflections on Hope as a Category of Social and Psychological Analysis'. Cultural Anthropology 18 (1): 3–32. https://doi.org/10.1525/can.2003.18.1.3.

Frederiksen, Martin Demant. 2011. 'Marginaliseret tid: Materialitet, fremtid og håb i Georgien'. Tidsskriftet Antropologi 63: 7–23.

Hage, Ghassan. 2003. Against Paranoid Nationalism: Searching for Hope in a Shrinking Society. Annandale, NSW: Pluto Press.

Hake, Andrew. 1977. African Metropolis: Nairobi's Self-Help City. Bd. 1. Chatto and Windus for Sussex University Press; Toronto: Clarke, Irwin.

Haugerud, Angelique. 1997. The Culture of Politics in Modern Kenya. Bd. 84. West Nyack: Cambridge University Press.

Kleist, Nauja, and Dorte Thorsen. 2017. Hope and Uncertainty in Contemporary African Migration. Routledge Studies in Anthropology. London: Routledge. https://doi.org/10.4324/9781315659916.

Lucht, Hans. 2011. Darkness before Daybreak: African Migrants Living on the Margins in Southern Italy Today. fulcrum.org. Berkeley: University of California Press.

Ma3Route. 2017. 'How we've made our Nairobi capital city CBD "CITY UNDER UNDER THE SUN"'. Twitter, 2 November 2017. https://twitter.com/Ma3Route/status/925957382919700480?ref_src=twsrc%5Etfw%7Ctwcamp%5Etweetembed%7Ctwterm%5E925957382919700480&ref_url=https%3A%2F%2Fnairobinews.nation.co.ke%2Fnews%2Fnairobi-turns-hawkers-paradise-sonko.

Médard, Claire. 2010. 'City Planning in Nairobi: The Stakes, the People, the Sidetracking'. In Nairobi Today: The Paradox of a Fragmented City, Deyssi Rodriguez-Torres and Hélène Charton-Bigot (eds.), 25–60. Dar es Salaam: Mkuki na Nyota Publishers.

Muindi, Benjamin. 2018. 'Negotiating the Balance between Speed and Credibility in Deploying Twitter as Journalistic Tool at the Daily Nation Newspaper in Kenya'. African Journalism Studies 39 (1): 111–128. https://doi.org/10.1080/23743670.2018.1445654.

Musambi, Evelyne. 2017. 'Sonko@100: Hawkers invasion real nightmare for Nairobians'. Daily Nation, 29 November 2017. https://nairobinews.nation.co.ke/news/sonko-invasion-nightmare-nairobians.

Mutavi, Lillian. 2017a. 'Sonko Confronted by Hawkers Menace during CBD Tour'. Daily Nation, 20 September 2017. https://nairobinews.nation.co.ke/news/sonko-confronted-by-hawkers-menace-during-cbd-tour-photos.

———. 2017b. 'Nairobians Frustrated by Madness in City Streets'. Daily Nation, 11 December 2017. https://nairobinews.nation.co.ke/news/nairobians-frustrated-madness-city-streets.

Omulo, Collins. 2017. 'The Huge Hawker Headache in City Centre'. Daily Nation, 7 August 2017. https://nairobinews.nation.co.ke/news/huge-hawker-headache-city-centre.

Orinde, Hillary. 2018. 'Sonko Rolls Up His Sleeves and Hawkers Are Flushed Out of the Nairobi Streets (Photos)'. The Standard, 26 February 2018. https://www.standardmedia.co.ke/article/2001271215/sonko-rolls-up-his-sleeves-and-hawkers-are-flushed-out-of-the-nairobi-streets-photos.

Pedersen, Morten Axel. 2012. 'A Day in the Cadillac: The Work of Hope in Urban Mongolia'. Social Analysis 56 (2): 136–151. https://doi.org/10.3167/sa.2012.560210.

Robertson, Claire. 1997. Trouble Showed the Way, Women, Men, and Trade in the Nairobi Area, 1890–1990. Indiana University Press.

Smith, James Howard. 2008. Bewitching Development: Witchcraft and the Reinvention of Development in Neoliberal Kenya. University of Chicago Press.

Sonko, Mike. 2017. 'For the Time Being, My Administration Is Working on Means and Ways That Will Ensure a Progressive and Humane Relocation of Hawkers to Designated Streets and Lanes Where They Can Freely Do Their Businesses without Obstructing Other People as Well as Other Business Owners'. Twitter, 8 November 2017. https://twitter.com/MikeSonko/status/928118567740026881?ref_src=twsrc%5Etfw%7Ctwcamp%5Etweetembed%7Ctwterm%5E928118567740026881&ref_url=https%3A%2F%2Fnairobinews.nation.co.ke%2Fnews%2Fhere-is-how-sonko-plans-to-relocate-hawkers-from-cbd.

Tadiar, Neferti Xina M. 2004. Fantasy Production, Sexual Economies and Other Philippine Consequences for the New World Order. The new Hong Kong Cinema. Hong Kong University Press.

Turner, Simon. 2014. '"We Wait for Miracles": Ideas of Hope and Future among Clandestine Burundian Refugees in Nairobi'. In Ethnographies of Uncertainty in Africa, 173–192. Anthropology, Change and Development. London: Palgrave Macmillan. https://doi.org/10.1057/9781137350831.

Van Stapele, Naomi. 2016. '"We Are Not Kenyans": Extra-Judicial Killings, Manhood and Citizenship in Mathare, a Nairobi Ghetto'. Conflict, Security & Development 16 (4): 301–325.

Vigh, Henrik. 2006. 'Social Death and Violent Life Chances: Youth Mobilization and Social Navigation in Bissau City'. In Navigating Youth, Generating Adulthood: Social Becoming in an African Context, Catrine Christiansen, Mats Utas, and Henrik Vigh (eds.),

Malayna Raftopoulos

# Extractivism, Territorialization, and Displacement in Latin America

## Introduction

The pursuit of extractivist projects by governments throughout Latin America has led to the reconfiguration and fragmentation of territories in distinct forms such as the creation of regulatory boundaries and the emergence of extractive enclaves linked to global markets. Extractivism creates 'a territorial dynamic whose tendency is the intensive occupation of territory and land-grabbing through forms linked to monoculture or single-commodity production' (Svampa, 2019: 11). This has led to the creation of extractivist modes of territorialization through complex state-society relations, different forms of violence, regulative pluralism and intense politics, giving rise to political, social and ecological disputes over resources and contrasting visions of territoriality (Côte and Korf, 2018). Although environmental and development induced displacement is not a recent phenomenon, the proliferation of extractivist activities since the beginning of the twenty-first century has not only led to reterritorialization, challenging existing state and social structures, but has altered the processes of displacement. The dynamics of this extractivist socio-territorial model, based on accumulation by dispossession and valuation strategies, has caused the displacement of populations and other forms of production – both in relation to local and regional economies – and has also redefined land disputes in the region pitting poor and marginalized populations against major economic players (ibid.). Territorialization, which can be considered an organizational process (Deleuze and Guattari, 2005), involves 'a reorganization of functions and a grouping of forces, the likes of which create differentiation and distance' (Paquette and Lacassagne, 2013: 244). Furthermore, the emergence of new modes of resources extraction creates new territories within the dynamic of frontiers and territorialization, dissolving, suspending or dismantling existing social orders and regimes of resource control, including property systems, political jurisdictions, rights, and social contracts. Territorialization then reorders and reorganizes systems of resource control such as rights, authorities, jurisdictions, and their spatial representations within the space. It also establishes authority, which is not necessarily associated with the state, though the introduction of concrete operations that govern access, police boundaries and define space (Rasmussen and Lund, 2018). The reconfiguration of frontier spaces, or reterritorialization, involves four key dimensions: 'establishing a territorial administration, instituting a legal system and with it the creation of rights subjects and laws of property, establishing of boundaries and mapping of space, and, crucially, ensuring the capacity to enforce any and all of this by means of force, if necessary' (ibid.: 393).

Reterritorialization and the consolidation of extractivist territorialities has generated local territorial disputes as well as the deepening of criminalization and distinct forms of violence (Raftopoulos, 2017). In discussing the failure of what he calls 'the imperialism of high-modernist, planned social order', Scott argues that the schemes devised by the modern state to gain greater control over its territory and populations, while targeting the improvement of the human condition, have gone 'tragically awry' (1998: 4–5). According to Scott, for development projects to end in full-fledged disaster, four factors are necessary: The administrative ordering of nature and society, the adoption of a high-modern ideology by the state, the existence of authoritarian state willing and able to its power to implement high-modernist designs and a weakened civil society unable to resist these plans (ibid.). Also, considered to be a spill-over effect of extractivism (Gudynas, 2015), the growing trend of criminalization is oriented towards the subjugation and inclusion of populations into the extractive development model through diverse strategies aimed at dispelling any challenge to the reproduction of the accumulation model and property regimes, neutralizing political claims to land and natural resources and constructing an attack of the rights agenda.

As this chapter explores, the imposition of extractivist activities through the logic of territorialization has led to a number of spill-over effects (Gudynas, 2015), including the displacement – both environmental and development induced – of communities as well as the growing trend of governments in hybrid regimes dealing with social protests criminally rather than socially or politically. Through a discussion of the link between the extractivist imperative and territorialization, this chapter firstly examines the ways in which extractivism has been regularized through the reconfiguration of territory, leading to the displacement of both resources and populations. Secondly, the chapter considers the relationship between natural resource conflicts, human rights and criminalization. It analyses how the extractive model has been politically defended though state-led strategies designed to consolidate, defend and guarantee the functionality of the neoliberal extractivist discourse as well as the socio-territorial consequences that arise from processes of territory reconfiguration.

## Extractivist territorialities and displacement in Latin America

Territorialization based on the dispossession of its commons and the commodification of nature has become a central feature of globalization and neoliberalism (Raftopoulos and Morley, 2020) and has determined 'land privatization, deterritorialization of rural communities, the elimination of rights to natural goods, the transformation of the labour force, and the suppression of alternatives ways of production and use' (Rincón and Fernandes, 2018: 2086). As a consequence of the production of 'surplus population' (Li, 2010), which occurs when only place and resources are deemed useful but not those who reside within that territory, labour absorption becomes detached from the process of rural dispossession and social actors that inhabit those territories are excluded. The creation of a surplus population 'underscores how the frontier dynamics work not only by zeroing out existing orders and erasing the traces of past livelihoods, but also, sometimes, by excluding the dispossessed from the new order of things' (Rasmussen and Lund, 2018: 392). Critical to the expansion of extractivism in Latin America has been territorial reorganization though the deployment of a binary notion of territoriality by transnational corporations and governments based on a viable/unviable division. This zoning of territories has in turn created two dominant imaginaries of national geographic space whereby regional economies are measured according to the rate of return: Firstly, the idea of an efficient territory and secondly, the image of empty territory or sacrificable territory. Furthermore, accompanying the expansion of extractivist activities is the constructed imagery of 'empty spaces' or 'socially empty territories', characterized as isolated and impoverished spaces with a low population density but rich in natural resources. These 'new modalities that the logic of capital accumulation has adopted' which exclude the possibility of other notions territory, have become highly contested, generating a 'tension of territorialities' (Svampa, 2008: 7 and 11). This language of valorization of territories, characterized by their primary landscapes and their large extensions, has becomes so ingrained in Latin American political and cultural imaginary it has allowed governments to justify the sale of large territories and to argue that extractivist activities are the only productive alternative for those regions classified as empty territory (Svampa, 2008: 9).

Through the notion of 'regulation by territorialization', territorial projects and strategies employed by states to produce bounded and controlled space through which to govern both people and resources have shifted access, control and management of natural resources into the hands of the powerful corporations, altering human-environmental relationships and also leading to the loss of physical territory (Bassett and Gautier, 2014: 2). Displacement within the context of extractivist activities is a complex phenomenon in that is closely related to both environmentally-induced and development-induced displacement and resettlement. Change in land use as a result of the expansion of the extractive frontier and the increase in extractive projects have forced peasant and indigenous communities to leave their homes due to either direct physical displacement or indirect livelihood displacement (Betts, 2009). However, the short and long-term local impacts of extractivist projects on the environment, in particular, pollution and extinction of water sources and soil as well as the loss of biodiversity and agrobiodiversity due to deforestation, also leads to environmentally-induced displacement. This is particularly noticeable in cases of extractivist related environmental accidents such as the Brumadinho dam disaster in 2019, which killed around 300 people when a tailing dam from one of Vale's iron ore mines in the state of Minas Gerais collapsed and unleashed a torrent of sludge onto the town of Brumadinho.

Development induced displacement has become widely associated with extractivist activities. Families are increasingly being displaced through a process of expulsion – which often involves violence, armed confrontations and death – and the use of various strategies. This has been most evident with the rapid expansion of agro-business and palm oil plantations in the region. In Guatemala's northern lowlands, the expansion of plantations has led to the displacement of forty-two communities in Sayaxché, the largest palm producing municipality in the department of Petén. These communities include, El progreso (twenty-three families), El Cubil (thirty-two families), El Canaleño (forty-six families), La Torre (seventy-six families), Santa Rosa (eighty-six families), Santa María (forty-three families), and Centro Uno (164 families). Large areas of land have either been purchased from poor farmers by intermediaries who then sell the land at an inflated price to palm oil companies or purchased directly by companies. There have also been reports that subsistence farmers are being coerced though threats and violence by both state and private security forces, deceived or pressured by the own community into selling their land, while others 'voluntarily' sold their land due to indebtedness or for the 'large' upfront payments. In other instances, small farming communities surrounding the soy plantations have been displaced because of contamination or destruction of their subsistence crops by the agro-toxins used in large-scale agriculture. Many of the displaced residents of Sayaxché were also victims of previous displacements, having been forced to flee the regions of Alta Verapaz, Baja Verapaz, and Quiché during the civil war and the scorched earth campaigns against indigenous communities (Verité, 2016a). A study conducted by the World Rainforest Movement on the ways in which palm plantations contribute to displacement, deforestation, and human rights abuses in Ecuador showed that the displacement of local communities had been facilitated by companies obtaining government concessions in the Ecuadorian Amazon with financing acquired from the Inter-American Development Bank; the Ecuadorian government's refusal to respect indigenous peoples' rights as laid out in both the International Labour Convention 169 (ILO 169) and United Nations Declaration on the Rights Indigenous People (UNDRIP); and also the difficulties indigenous communities have faced in obtaining formal land titles (Verité, 2016b).

However, displacement has not been restricted to agri-business but is also widely associated with other extractivist activities such as mining. Examining the department of Caldas in Colombia, Rincón and Fernandes (2018) explain how the region has become an important epicentre for the convergence of different dynamics of the extractive model because of the expansion of agriculture, mining and large-scale infrastructure and dam projects. The district of Marmato, where mining has been at the centre of the economy since the colonial period, has become embroiled in conflicts with the local miners who are being displaced by industrial mining. Despite constitutional decrees in 1957 establishing that the hill where Marmato is located was to be divided into a high region reserved for small-scale miners and a lower region allocated to medium and large-scale mining, following the discovery of massive gold reserves the Colombian government has facilitated the expansion of multinational corporations' exploratory operations in the area. Already affected by the relocation of the municipal town to the valley area following a campaign by the Canadian company Medoro Resources in 2006, 'the situation has created a continuous process of material dispossession of territory and the loss of the traditional social relationships which had roots within the peasant legacy and traditional strategies for mineral extraction' (Rincón and Fernandes, 2018: 2095). Threatened that their properties would be expropriated by the state, a proportion of miners agreed to sell their properties and relocate to other towns where work was available in other industries. Furthermore, following the sale of the company Mineros Nacionales who had been operating in the area to Medoro Resources, eighty-five local mines were closed immediately, leaving 2500 miners unemployed. Later in 2011, when Medoro Resources was replaced by Gran Colombia Gold, more local mines were closed as land titles previously owned by local mine managers who employed sustainable miners were acquired by the company. Even though 18 % of Mormato's population was classified as indigenous, the Colombian government was unwilling to establish consent processes. Miners who remained in the area were also affected by the 2010 reform of the Mining Code aimed to reduce illegal mining, which made it difficult for artisanal miners to operate in the area.

The use of fear of expropriation, economic need, political pressure and intimidation transformed economic displacement in Mormato into forced displacement (US office on Colombia, 2013: 17–23). As these cases demonstrate, despite the territorial turn, which saw governments throughout the region legally recognize indigenous peoples' and Afro-descendants' collective rights to land and resources (Bryan, 2012), the dynamics of dispossession associated with the modes of territorialization that characterize extractivism and the ever-growing demand for raw materials have extended the socio-spatial order and had profound social-ecological consequences.

## State responses to territorial contestation: Criminalizing 'the enemy'

Since colonial times, the tenure of territories and natural resources in Latin America has been unequal. Marked by the dispossession of indigenous lands and concentration of resources into the hands of a few, natural resource development has been characterized by high rates of insecurity and conflict. However, in the last decade or so, the number of socio-environmental conflicts linked to extractive activities have grown exponentially in Latin America in the face of deterritorial processes (Raftopoulos and Powęska, 2017), highlighting growing concerns over the socio-environmental implications of extractivism (Gudynas, 2015), ontological differences (Blaser, 2014), and the dispossession of resources, in particular, territorial sovereignty (Escobar, 2008; Svampa, 2019). Such conflicts should be seen as contrasting visions and values, where the dominating conceptions are imposed upon local visions of environment and development and when 'the meaning and the use of a certain territory by a specific group occurs to the detriment of the meanings and uses that other social groups may employ for assuring their social and environmental reproduction' (Zhouri, 2014: 7). Local communities and social movements are contesting the binary notion of territory deployed by transnational corporations and the state by offering alternative understandings of territory as a space of resistance in which socio-natures are rearticulated and socio-environmental relations reconfigured beyond existing political and economic paradigms (Svampa, 2008).

While conceptions of territory are increasingly at the centre of peasant and indigenous movements demands, which question the current monocultural and destructive development model and demanding the demercantilization of 'common goods' (Svampa, 2008: 11), the defence of territory is also increasingly being used to build territorial alliances among different groups, especially in relation to recovering control over the most fundamental aspects of communal sovereignty – decision-making processes related territory – of which natural resources are essential part (Damonte Valencia, 2011; Avci and Fernández-Salvador, 2016). Governments in the region have continuously shown their willingness to override their commitments human and environmental rights to promote their extractivist development agenda. Even countries such as Ecuador and Bolivia which have attempted to move away from modernist paradigms and adopt original epistemological and ontological narratives though the concept of Buen Vivir [live well] have failed to substantially change the current structure of accumulation and move away from a productivity appropriation of nature and extractivist policies.

Criminalization has become a critical means of maintaining the extractive development model, fashioned through the neoliberal policies implemented since the 1990s, and containing popular protests that threaten or question this model and the notion of regulation by territorialization. Protecting the large revenues associated with extraction often requires high levels of violence and repression in the extractive enclaves as multinational companies and governments seek to guarantee the supply of natural resources though the opening up of remote frontiers and networks of connectivity. While criminalization has for a long time been used as a strategy to limit the spaces available to civil society, since the resource boom in the 2000s, the criminalization of resistance has intensified in Latin America under both progressive and conservative governments. There has been an increasing intolerance towards anyone opposed to extractive projects or any element that disturbs the extractivist model (Olarte, 2014) and criminalization has become embedded in wider discussions over the functioning of democracies (Terwindt, 2014). Criminalization, though its attempts to restrict democracy by making it 'comparable with routinized violence' is a direct attack on democratic practices (Doran, 2017) and has led to the emergence of violent pluralism and new democratic state formations that are entwined with violent practices (Desmond Arias and Goldstein, 2010).

Consequently, criticism of the criminal prosecution of protesters has moved beyond the human rights perspective, which has traditionally separated "the denunciation of human rights violations from moral judgments regarding politics', towards an alternative approach under the term 'criminalization of protests'" (Terwindt, 2014: 165). As Terwindt explains, "this perspective takes into account the power relations between different groups and sectors in society and moves the lens from individual people to the activity or the political position that is defended. It further critically analyses the discursive battle about what is defined as 'peaceful' and what as 'illegal' or 'violent'" (ibid.). The term 'criminalization', understood in criminological terms as 'the process by which behaviours and individuals are transformed into crime and criminals' (Peace Brigades International, 2012: 2), has increasingly been adopted to describe the suppression of protests and protesters. However, as Silva Santisteban points out, 'the criminalization of protests is not the verification of an act of criminality, on the contrary, is the assumption that a leader who participates in a social protest will commit a crime. It is a strategy of governments to dismantle social movements' (2017: 94).

Criminalization should therefore be understood as an evolving phenomenon that is designed to consolidate, defend and guarantee the functionality of the neoliberal extractivist imperative though the employment of a variety of political, juridical and social strategies to counteract and displace processes of resistance and control, remove or exclude any barriers that threaten or disturb the hegemonic model. Furthermore, its seeks to exclude 'the possibility of feeling, thinking, knowing and living in a manner different from what is imposed by the neoliberal and extractivist status quo' (Hoetmer, 2017: 19). Criminalization is not an isolated phenomenon and while it has been produced within a weak judicial system, it has been able to flourish though the creation of mining governments and extractive states (Durand, 2015). In order to promote the hegemonic extractivist discourse, the state becomes benevolent and permissive, allowing corporations to expand their roles and powers to the extent that it resembles a government; organizing territory, investing and executing infrastructural development. Modern extractive enclaves, while reinforcing an asymmetry of power at all levels, generate new forms of political power by assuming social roles and clientelistic practices, conceiving, developing and implementing a varied range of private or privatized social policies as well as developing systems of social and political control (Durand, 2015: 9).

Under the guise of national interest and maintaining national security, criminalization has become the principal means of containing and displacing protests, preserving the prevailing regime, socially and judicially justifying the deepening of repressive politics, and the legalization and institutionalization of violence as well as fundamentally weakening human rights. A number of tendencies have become associated with the criminalization which have far reaching social, political and legal implications. Firstly, criminalization strategies have been orchestrated and normalized at various levels of the state apparatus, including public sector officials and representatives of autonomous public institutions. This includes state security forces and institutions who intervene and control operations to suppress social-environmental conflicts and maintain 'order', law makers who are responsible for the creation or adaptation of laws as well as prosecutors and judges who apply and interpret laws and legal norms. However, these strategies have also been employed by non-state actors, in particular multi-national corporations. State-led criminalization strategies have cast social-environmental conflicts as a law and order problem, designed to depoliticize the conflict and downplay the sense of collective struggle and community support. Secondly, multi-national corporations, who are usually the complainant, have played a significant role in both advancing and perpetrating criminalization measures. In particular, their portrayal of protests as a security threat and the contracting of state security forces and private security firms has led to militarization of policing protests and increased violence. Thirdly, the criminalization of protests has resulted in the serious decline of criminal justice and legal systems in the region, which have been systematically manipulated to suit the narrative of criminalization and the state's discourse of viewing conflicts from a criminal perspective, as well as the redefinition of rights in order to dismantle popular struggles. Despite, the state's responsibility to protect people within its borders, the framework of maintaining national interests and national security acts as a powerful political tool and impacts on human rights and civil liberties. Rights are no longer seen from the eyes of the holders but rather from the needs of preserving the prevailing state, radically altering state-society relations. Moreover, the language of criminalization, while portraying protesters as being criminals for the legal purposes, marks them out as being different than common criminals by labelling and constructing an image of them as enemies of the state. Not only does this label dehumanize and delegitimize protesters, but it also legitimizes state repression and the violation of human rights, creating a culture of impunity. Fourthly, criminalization happens before a protest occurs or a project begins as well as afterwards and reinforces historic patterns of repression and marginalization. Lastly, it is a series of targeted punitive acts rather than a single act of persecution and is a multifaceted process that involves juridical, political, and psychological aspects. Threats, torture, surveillance, and violence place enormous pressure on protesters and their families and has a profound impact on the individual(s) psychological and emotional well-being.

The political adaption of legal and judicial mechanisms aims to destigmatize violence and the extraction project through establishing a criminal norm which is perceived to be legitimate because it sustains the given social order. The process of criminalization often begins with establishing criminal policy through the creation or modification of laws and criminal regulation by classifying an action as a criminal offense or increasing penalties on acts already defined as crimes. Ecuadorian authorities have limited the right to freedom of assembly by requiring protest organizers to gain permission from the municipality and police superintendent to hold a protest and criminalizing through imprisonment or fines demonstration leaders without the relevant paperwork. In Bolivia, government officials have the power to dissolve any non-governmental organizations without using any judicial process (Raftopoulos, 2017). While in Peru, authorities have increased penalties for committing a public order offences, which made it easier for the military to intervene in social-environmental conflicts, and supported impunity for official abuses. For example, the 2006 Law 28820 broadened the definition of attacks and disturbances against public services to include the normal functioning of the provision of hydrocarbons, carrying a penalty of four to six years which was later raised to six to eight years in 2010 (law 29583). Later in 2016, gas and hydrocarbon products were included as public services not to be impeded (Legislative Decree 1245). In 2006, the penalty for assault on common security were increased to six to ten years (Law 29583) and its definition modified in 2010 to include gas and electricity infrastructure. Infrastructure for hydrocarbon production was later added in 2016 (Legislative Decree 1245). Moreover, the militarization of policing protests was also aided by the adoption of Legislative decree 1095 in 2010 which authorized the deployment of military forces during times of civil unrest, the use of lethal weapons in case of social conflicts, and permitted armed forces to intervene or act in support of the National Police following the declaration of a state of emergency. The decree also established that any 'illicit conduct' committed by military personnel during the course of their duties would be subject to the jurisdiction of military courts, fostering a culture of impunity. Furthermore, Law 29986 (2012) permitted the removal of corpses without the presence of the Prosecutor by members of the Armed Forces or the National Police in areas under a state of emergency, and Law 30151 (2014), facilitating the impunity of Armed Forces and Police Forces who caused injury or death through the use of guns or other weapons while on duty.

Baseless judicial prosecutions, which involves the enactment and reinforcement of legal laws and regulations by organs of control and the selection of which illegal acts should be the subject of criminal prosecution and who should be criminalized, serves to weaken opposition by engaging protesters and organizations in lengthy legal procedures. High-level smear campaigns and the stigmatization of protesters have also played a key role in laying the groundwork for the process of criminalization by delegitimizing, undermining and tarnishing individuals, organizations and the actual protest itself. Labels such as anti-mine terrorists, development enemies and destabilizers of the economy have produced a climate of polarization and hostility, and created an association between protests, chaos and civil disorder in the public imagination. Governments throughout Latin America have employed a zero-tolerance policy towards anyone opposing the extractive imperative and have led a campaign to vilify and stigmatize indigenous groups and social movements opposed to extractive imperative. By labelling voices of dissent as environmental extremists or terrorists, authorities have attempted to build a framework of acceptance for curtailing human rights, and legitimatizing aggression and persecution against them.

## Conclusion

As a consequence of the continual expansion of the extractive frontier and corporate control of land, extractivism has become a key driver of displacement throughout Latin America due to its direct and indirect impact on the socioeconomic reality and health of affected communities as well as the environmental consequences. The imposition of extractivist activities through the logic of territorialization has led to the occupation, reconfiguration and fragmentation of territories. The dynamics of displacement within the context of extractivism have expanded beyond the displacement of populations but also encompasses the displacement of resources and territory as well as social mobilizations. The struggle over territory and sovereignty, as well as the absence of participatory democracy, in particular the lack of public and political debate and the power asymmetry that surrounds this current development model, has given rise to cycle of protests that look to transcend traditional ideological and class divisions and unite around the negative impacts of extractivism, alternative notions of development and also the defence of the commons and biodiversity. The socio-environmental movements that have emerged in recent years in response to the effects of reterritorialization, including the displacement of both people and resource, find themselves in an exceptionally difficult situation; 'on the one hand, they must directly confront the global action of the large transnational corporations, coming from the developed North, who in this new stage of accumulation of capital have become the clearly hegemonic actors of the extractive-export model. On the other hand, at the local level, they must confront the policies and general orientations of the governments – both at the provincial and national levels' (Svampa, 2008: 17). The imposition of extractivist activities and reconfiguration of space has led to the deepening of criminalization and distinct forms of violence against voices of dissent as states throughout the region adopt authoritarian tendencies to push through extractivist projects and take steps to contain and displace social mobilization by introducing measures to limit economic, social, political and civil rights. At the core of the conflicts and deeply ingrained into the narrative of indigenous and peasant movements is the notion of territory both as a space of resistance to contest processes of territorialization and defend the common goods, but also a space in which socio-natures are rearticulated and alternative models of development, including an alternative to development are formulated. As Escobar (2008) has argued, it is these subaltern knowledges emerging through social movements and indigenous organizations and shaped by the experience of coloniality that have the potential to become spaces for the articulations of alternative projects and facilitate the pluriversality of socionatural formations. However, such ontology does not fit the modernist developmentalist and capitalist logic though which the extractive imperative is framed.

The creation of extractivist modes of territorialization has also profoundly impacted the way in which processes of displacement are carried out. While displacement within the context of extractivism has been closely related to land grabbing and the application of violence, the expansion of extractivist activities and reprimatization of Latin American economies has altered underlying processes of displacement which have been compounded by the central state's efforts to enforce the extractive imperative. Processes of displacement within extractive enclaves, which are intrinsically connected to global capital interests and the struggle over the control of natural resources, have been deepened by the employment of various mechanisms by the state. Politically, the displacement of populations has been orchestrated by the weakening of democratic practices. This has occurred through the curbing of politics of plurality whereby participatory mechanisms such as consultations are limited for local communities and instead decisions are taken by the central state as well as the diminishing of judicial systems with the state making use of legal mechanisms and rolling back of regulative frameworks to suspend, disrupt or redefine the application of human and environmental rights and control those citizens opposed to extractive activities. Socially, the condition of displacement has not only led to fundamental territorial changes and the separation of citizens from their homes but has also disrupted the relationship between humans and nature, displacing indigenous knowledge, traditions and cultural identity which is inextricably linked to their land and destabilizing social structures. As a consequence of the enhanced processes of displacement, displaced communities receive little acknowledgement, protection or assistance from the state despite its responsibility to protect and promote human rights in their territories.

## Bibliography

Avci, D. & Fernandez-Slavador, C. (2016). Territorial Dynamics and Local Resistance: Two Mining Conflicts in Ecuador Compared, Extractive Industries and Society, 3 (4), 912-921.

Bassett, T. J. & Gautier, D. (2014). Regulation by Territorialization: The Political Ecology of Conservation & Development Rerritories: Introduction, EchoGéo [Online], 29, 1–7.

Betts, A. (2009). Forced Migration and Global Politics. UK: John Wiley and Sons.

Blaser, M. (2014). Ontology and Indigeneity: On the Political Ontology of Heterogeneous Assemblages, Cultural Geographies, 21 (1), 49–58.

Bryan, J. (2012). 'Rethinking Territory: Social Justice and Neoliberalism in Latin America's Territorial Turn', Geography Compass, 6 (4), 215–226.

Côte, M. & Korf, B. (2018). Making Concessions: Extractive Enclaves, Entangled Capitalism and Regulative Pluralism at the Gold Mining Frontier in Burkina Faso, World Development, 101: 466–476.

Damonte Valencia, G. (2011). Mineria y Politica: La Recreacion de Luchas Campesinas en Dos Comunidades Andinas. In Bebbington, A. (ed.), Minería, Movimientos Sociales y Respuestas Campesinas: Una Ecología Política de Transformaciones Territoriales, pp. 147–192. Lima: IEP.

Deleuze, G. and Guattari, F. (2005). A Thousand Plateaus: Capitalism and Schizophrenia, translated by Brian Massumi. US: The University of Minnesota Press.

Desmond Arias, E. & Goldstein, D. M. (2010). Violent Pluralism: Understanding the New Democracies in Latin America. In: E. Desmond Arias and D. M. Goldstein (eds.), Violent Democracies in Latin America, pp. 1–34. Durham, NC: Duke University Press.

Doran, M. C. (2017). The Hidden Face of Violence in Latin America: Assessing the Criminalisation of Protest in Comparative Perspective, Latin American Perspectives, 44 (5), 183–206.

Durand, F. (2015). Poder Político y Gobierno Minero. Lima: Cuadernos de CooperAccion.

Escobar, A. (2008). Territories of Difference: Place, Movements, Life, Redes. Durham, NC: Duke University Press.

Gudynas, E. (2015). Extractivismo: Ecología, Economía y Política de un Modo de Entender el Desarrollo y la Naturaleza. Bolivia, Cochabamba, Centro de Documentación e Información.

Hoetmer, R. (2017). "Esta Democracia ya No Es Democracia ..." Siete Hipótesis Exploratorias sobre Biopolítica Extractivista, La Criminalización de la

Disidencia, y Alternativas, http://economiassolidarias.unmsm.edu.pe/sites/default/files/Hoetmer_Biopol%C3%ADtica%20Per%C3%BA.pdf, accessed 18 January 2021.

Li, T. (2010). To Make Live or Let Die? Rural Dispossession and the Protection of Surplus Populations, Antipode, 41 (1), 66–93.

Olarte, M.C. (2014). Depoliticization and Criminalization of Social Protest Through Economic Decisionism: The Colombian Case, Oñati Socio-Legal Series [online], 4 (1), 139–160.

Paquette, J. & Lacassagne, A. (2013). Subterranean subalterns: Territorialisation, Deterritorialisation, and the Aesthetics of Mining, Culture and Organization, 19 (3), 242-260.

Peace Brigades International (2012). Criminalisation of Human Rights Defenders, <https://www.peacebrigades.org/fileadmin/user_files/groups/uk/files/Publications/Crim_Report.pdf>, accessed 18 January 2021.

Raftopoulos, M. (2017). Contemporary Debates on Social-Environmental Conflicts, Extractivism and Human Rights in Latin America, The International Journal of Human Rights, 21 (4), 387–404.

Raftopoulos, M. and Morely, J. (2020). Ecocide in the Amazon: The Contested Politics of Environmental Rights in Brazil, The International Journal of Human Rights, 24 (10), 1616–1641.

Raftopoulos, M. & Powęska, R. (eds.) (2017). Natural Resource Development and Human Rights in Latin America; State and Non-State Actors in the Promotion and Opposition to Extractivism. London: Human Rights Consortium and Institute for Latin American Studies.

Rasmussen, M. B. & Lund, C. (2018). Reconfiguring Frontier Spaces: The Territorialization of Resource Control, World Development, 101, 388–399.

Rincón, L. F. and Fernandes, B. M. (2018). Territorial Dispossession: Dynamics of Capitalist Expansion in Rural Territories in South America, Third World Quarterly, 39 (11), 2085–2102.

Scott, J. C. (1998). Seeing Like a State: How Certain Schemes to Improve the Human Condition Have Failed. New Haven, CT: Yale University Press.

Silva Santisteban, R. (2017). Mujeres y Conflictos Ecoterritoriales: Impactos, Estrategias, Resistencias, <https://www.demus.org.pe/wp-content/uploads/2018/02/Mujeresyconflictos_Convenio.-2017.pdf>, accessed 18 January 2021.

Svampa, M. (2008). La Disputa por el Desarrollo: Territorio, Movimientos de Carácter Socio-Ambiental y Discursos Dominantes, <http://www.maristellasvampa.net/archivos/ensayo43.pdf>, accessed 18 January 2021.

Svampa, M. (2019). Development in Latin America: Towards a New Future. UK: Fernwood Publishing.

Terwindt, C. (2014). Criminalization of Social Protest: Future Research, Oñati Socio-Legal Series, 4 (1), 161–169.

US office on Colombia. (2013). Large-scale Mining in Colombia: Human Rights Violations Past, Present and Future. Retrieved from <https://reliefweb.int/sites/reliefweb.int/files/resources/large-scale-mining-full-report.pdf>, accessed 18 January 2021.

Verité. (2016a). Labor and Human Rights Risk Analysis of the Guatemalan Palm Oil Sector. Retrived from <https://www.verite.org/wp-content/uploads/2016/11/RiskAnalysisGuatemalanPalmOilSector_0.pdf>, accessed 18 January 2021.

Verité. (2016b). Labor and Human Rights Risk Analysis of the Ecuador's Palm Oil Sector. Retrieved from <https://www.verite.org/wp-content/uploads/2016/11/Risk-Analysis-of-Ecuador-Palm-Oil-Sector-Final.pdf>, accesses 18 January 2021.

Zhouri, A. (2014). Mapping Environmental Inequalities in Brazil: Mining, Environmental Conflicts and Impasses of Mediation. Berlin: DesigALdades.net.

Morten Lynge Madsen

# Do Human Rights Matter When You Are Stuck in an Urban Informal Settlement?

Henry has a difficult decision to make. A few days earlier, the police confiscated his boda. Henry, aged 20, dropped out of school several years' ago. He makes a living as a boda boda driver but without his motorbike – his boda – he has no source of income. Now, his boda has reappeared, but there is a catch. The boda is parked outside the residential area where Rashid stays. Rashid is not just anybody. Rashid is a known police officer, who has been involved in numerous incidents that have resulted in the death of young men from Mathare and other informal settlements in East Nairobi. Henry is from Mathare and it is not the first time he and Rashid crosses paths. He is terrified of Rashid and fears that the boda-incident is a trap. He fears that he will be shot dead the moment he goes to pick it up. On the other hand, the boda is his only source of income and a primary means of mobility. Without it he is literally stuck.

In Mathare, the fear and uncertainty that the episode sparks in Henry and the constant reality of having to deal with a highly unpredictable state in the form of the police is normal. Furthermore, the incident speaks to the precarity of life as a young man in Mathare, where seemingly random events, large and small, constantly lurk to nullify hard-won gains. These events push Henry and his peers back to start, thereby bringing about a sense of stuckness or immobility, which has nothing to do with stillness but rather implies constant movement, leading nowhere (Jefferson, Turner and Jensen, 2019).

My ambition with this chapter is to investigate this sense of stuckness, as it is experienced and described by numerous young men at the urban margins of Nairobi. I am particularly interested in the ways in which stuckness is amplified, even generated, in encounters with authority and the relevance of rights – first and foremost the right to life – in these encounters. As a development practitioner, Human Rights Based Approaches have become the modus operandi of development interventions. Yet, as a researcher, investigating the relevance and effectiveness of Human Rights Based Approaches in urban settings characterized by high levels of violence, Human Rights appear to be of little relevance.

This leads me to a simple but central question that I will explore in this chapter: Why do Human Rights – in particular the right to life – appear to offer so little meaningful protection in an informal settlement like Mathare?

The argument brought forth here is not that we should abandon Human Rights or Human Rights Based Approaches, far from it. Rather, I am interested in exploring the day-to-day encounters between authorities and citizens in order to better understand the challenges and shortcomings in claiming rights at the urban margins. Through two case studies, I will highlight how these encounters take place in the form of violent exchanges between police officers, young men and their families and I will argue that connections and relations currently mean more for young men's ability to survive than does a constitutionally inscribed right to life. In a final discussion, using Loic Wacquant's term territorial stigmatization (Wacquant, 2008), I will relate the denial of rights that is evident in the violent exchanges between police and young men to a sense of stuckness. In Stephen Lubkemann's terms, rights violations lead to involuntary immobility, or a form of 'displacement in place' (Lubkemann, 2008).

## Methodology

The research informing this chapter is a part of a Danida (Danish International Development Assistance) funded urban development programme implemented by Plan International Denmark and eight civil society partners in 13 informal settlements in Ethiopia, Kenya, Uganda and Zimbabwe, entitled the 'Safe and Inclusive Cities Programme'. The chapter draws on two sources of data. Firstly, a baseline study carried out in 2018, aimed at assessing the prevalence of violence, victim and perpetrator profiling and young people's civic engagement. The study included 4889 Survey interviews with young people (age 15–25) in 13 urban locations, 46 Focus Group Discussion with the same target groups, and 81 Key Informant Interviews with young people and local and city level authorities.

Secondly, taking a mixed methods approach (Creswell, 2014), investigating key quantitative findings further in order to obtain an in-depth understanding of the interrelations between police violence, human rights, and young people's interaction with authority, a qualitative research process in the form of a diary study was initiated. The diary study was a collaborate research initiative of three young researchers from Mathare and the author of this chapter. During the course of seven months, 12 young men kept a diary and completed biweekly semi structured interviews with the three local researchers. The 12 participants were selected based on their affiliation with local grassroots' youth groups and with a focus on ensuring a geographical spread. The study took place between November 2019 and June 2020.

## Human Rights and Human Rights Based Approaches to development

The Safe and Inclusive Cities programme embraces a Human Rights Based Approach to development, focusing on reducing Urban Violence through strengthening young women and men's rights to participate in decision-making and claim their rights to security and social services from local authorities. This approach was inspired by OECD's annual State of Fragility Report from 2016 and a growing body of research and reports that call for more attention to integrating urban violence reduction within local civil society led development interventions (World Bank, 2011; IDRC, International Development Research Centre, Muggah 2012; Jensen and Bjarnesen, 2014; Muggah, 2014; OECD, 2016).

The Human Rights Based Approach to development cooperation has become increasingly influential over the past 15–20 years, with the 'UN Common Understanding on the Human rights Based Approach (HRBA) to Development Cooperation' (UN, 2003) as a common reference point. Ultimately, with a Human Rights Based Approach to development, the goal of develop programmes is the fulfillment of human rights.

However, whereas the HRBA is founded in the Human Rights Conventions and international human rights treaties, Civil Society Organizations applying Human Rights Based Approaches rarely address Human Rights Conventions, specific articles or Instruments directly in their programming. Rather, within a Human Rights Based Approach, the key modus operandi is to identify rights-holders and their entitlements, on the one hand, and duty-bearers and their obligations, on the other, and work towards strengthening both the capacity of rights-holder to make claims and duty-bearers to meet their obligations.[1]

Applying a Human Rights Based approach to development that centers on strengthening citizens' claims to rights vis-a-via local authorities takes as its starting point that rights are a static property that people have.

However, Christian Lund's analysis of state formation allows for a more dynamic conceptualization of rights and authority (Lund, 2016). Lund argues that public authority is not static but constantly in the making. Authority and citizenship are mutually constitutive and constantly negotiated and contested through claims to rights (Lund, 2016: 1201). Making claims to a right, for instance to a service – public welfare, education, security – acknowledges authority of

1 See Vandenhole and Gready (2014) for further discussions on the differences between Human Rights Organizations and Human Rights Based approaches to Development, as these are implemented by development actors.

the institution, to which the claim is made. Simultaneously, granting the right or providing the service to the claimant acknowledges the claimant's rights. In other words, citizenship, rights and authority are mutually constitutive through an ongoing process of recognition.

However, what if the mutually constitutive process of recognition follows an entirely different logic? What if the encounters between authority – in this case the police – and citizens – in this case young men from the urban margins – take the form of violent exchanges (Jensen et al., 2017), where violence, or the threat of violence, is exchanged for money – or in some cases other resources or services? A 'violent exchange' in this conceptualization, is 'an exchange between an authority and a citizen based on or featuring elements of violence […]' (Jensen et al., 2017: 20). This perspective on the interaction between authority and citizen changes the focus from recognition to relation, as the negative exchange, like all exchanges between people, build and maintain relations (Jensen et al., 2017: 20). Moreover, it becomes evident that the young men from Mathare do not encounter authority as such. They interact with and build relations with people; with individual police officers, who build and maintain the relationship based on their mandate to use violence. How does that affect young men's ability to claim rights? In the following, I will unfold this question through the case of two young men from Nairobi's informal settlement, Mathare.

## The case of Mathare: Urban violence, recognition and the state

The choice of Mathare as the setting for the present case study was no coincidence. Across the 13 settlements, Mathare stands out. In the quantitative data, the area registers higher levels and perceptions of violence than any of the other settlements. However, the most striking difference is that the victims are predominately male and that a much higher proportion of the registered violence has been carried out by the police than in any of the other settlements. For those who know Mathare, this is hardly a surprise. In recent years, the extreme extent of police brutality and Extra-judicial Executions – predominately of young men – that takes place in Mathare has received growing attention by local Human Rights Organizations (MSJC, Mathare Social Justice Centre 2017). In this extreme capacity, the findings from Mathare are not representative of the other informal settlements in the study, nor of informal settlements in general. Rather, following Javier Auyero's analyses of violence at the urban margins in Argentina (Auyero and Berti, 2015), exploring police violence and human rights in this particular setting enables us to clearly see and address some of the key challenges in young men's endeavors to make a life for themselves at the urban margin. Further, we can link these challenges to the particular presence of the state in an urban setting that is extreme but not unique.

Here, I will focus on two of the participants, Henry and Jackson. Henry is 20 years old. Jackson is 23. They were both born in Mathare.

## Henry

We first met Henry in November 2019. This is almost a year before his boda went missing. Henry had two older brothers, but in mid-November, he lost one of his brothers. Just before midnight, his eldest brother called to check up on where he was. There were rumors of police shootings in the neighborhood and gunshots were audible from inside the house. Henry was safe at home. His brother told him to stay inside and went to check up on their other brother, who did not have a phone.

Neither of Henry's two brothers came home that night. While searching for the missing brother, Henry's eldest brother was arrested and charged with murder. He is still in prison, a year later, while he awaits trial.

Henry's other brother was shot dead by the police. The circumstances around the tragic incident are not clear. There has been no investigation and no one has been charged.

Less than a month later, an early afternoon in December 2019, Henry, walking from his home with two friends, was stopped by a police officer. 'He searched me, but I had nothing. He then started insulting me and intimidating me. He ordered me to kneel and I couldn't defend myself because he was holding a bamboo stick'. While Henry was on the ground, the police officer called for backup. 'More police arrived in a "Probox" [a heavy-duty patrol vehicle]. I had seen them before. At that moment, my mother arrived. She asked what was going on, but no one bothered to answer her. I was forced into the boot of the car. My mother resisted and told them that she was getting into the boot, too, if they did not tell her, what they were arresting me for. One of the police officers just said that they would kill me, like they had my brother'. After a short while they demand 20,000 Kenyan Shillings (close to 200 USD) to release Henry, but his mother refuses. She does not possess 20,000 Shillings. Henry recollects the events in this way: 'They pulled her away [from the police vehicle] and took me to Amana Petrol Station, to a known "killer cop" called Rashid. He ordered them to take me back, because my mother is stubborn, and go collect the money instead'. The incident constitutes what Steffen Jensen et al. refer to as a 'violent exchange' (Jensen et al., 2017), where police threats of violence and arbitrary imprisonment are sought exchanged for a bribe. In Nairobi's informal settlements, these exchanges usually follow gendered patterns; where police officers harass and threaten young men with a view to solicit bribes from their mothers (Gudmundsen, Hansen and Jensen, 2017: 103).

Henry was eventually released. It is unclear if his mother paid a bribe to secure his release and if so, what she paid. Later, Henry concludes the description by stating: 'I then shifted [moved] to my mother's place and I usually don't go to work. I don't want to be killed'.

## Jackson

Jackson was invited to be a part of the research project as an 'outlier' – an exception – because he had only been arrested once. The other participants of the study were randomly selected, but one of the local researchers pleaded to include Jackson in the study. The researcher had come across a 23-year old young man from Mathare, who had only been arrested once and quite easily made his way out again. This, she considered too exceptional to ignore.

On a December day in 2019, Jackson boarded a Matatu taxi to go from Mathare, an informal settlement on the Eastside of Nairobi, where he stays, to town. About ten minutes into the journey, a police officer enters the Matatu. In Jackson's own words: 'The Matatu stopped. A big man entered. I later found out that he was a police officer. He came right to me, grabbed the young man next to me and forced him out of the Matatu. A few seconds later, he came back and asked me if I had boarded the Matatu at the same stage [stop] as the other guy. I said yes. He grabbed me, too, and forced me out of the Matatu. There was another police officer outside. They were both in civilian clothing. We were put in the car and handcuffed. They started driving us back towards Mathare. We were driven around Mathare while they interrogated us. I decided to send my parents a (text) message telling them I had been arrested, since I did not trust the officers. They eventually released us, when they found out that we were not suspects or planning to rob people at the stage. They warned us not to be found idling at that stage again. I then boarded another Matatu and went to town – as planned'.

Later on, Jackson reflected on the incident. 'There are so many cases of police arresting 'suspects' the same way I was arrested and then murder them in cold blood. I have heard of so many cases where the police kills just for a mistaken identify. I was told I was lucky. If it wasn't for the quick intervention from my dad, I would have been dead by now'.

It is not clear exactly who Jackson's father contacted in order to intervene in his son's arrest. All we know is that Jackson sends his father a text message from the back of the police vehicle. About an hour later, he is released. It is generally known that Jackson's father has strong connections with local police officers and the chief due to his involvement in the illicit Chang'aa brewing trade. However, exactly how he utilized these connections remain unknown, at least to the researchers, as Jackson chooses not to disclose any more information about the incident. (During the course of the research, Jackson's father intervened on at least one more incident, securing his son a temporary position on a Government funded Covid-19 recovery programme, which the other young men of the study perceived as extremely difficult to gain access to).

While the selection of Jackson obviously calls for a discussion on methodological rigor, comparing Jackson's experiences to Henry's – and to all the other young men of the study – is illustrative. The comparison underscores a simple but central point of the study – and highlights the overarching challenge of the Human Rights Based Approach to reducing urban violence through strengthening rights-holders' capacity to make claims and duty-bearers' capacity to meet their obligation. The way in which rights-holders (the young men) and duty-bearers (the police and other local authorities, including chiefs, councils of elders) interact around a claim to basic services (security and access to justice) in Mathare does not follow the conventional procedure, nor Kenyan law for that matter.

Henry's trouble with the police (which are still unfolding as the boda incidence is still – at the time of writing – unresolved) are extreme but not unique. Expect for Jackson, all participants in the diary study had multiple encounters with the police over the seven months' of research. The encounters range from harassment and soliciting bribes to beatings, incarcerations for days without trial, threats of violence, physical violence and death threats. Several of the participants have been involved in incidents where the police has shot at, wounded and in two cases killed their peers.

During the research, the participants also record several incidents of crime and interpersonal violence that are not related to the police. Hardly any of these are reported and none has yet been resolved through the formal legal system. Enquiring into the reasons for not reporting crime and not complaining about police harassment and abuse of power, answers universally revolve around resignation and fear.

As Henry puts it, when asked why he has not reported the numerous incidents that he has been subjected to: 'I can't. If it's a police, no action will be taken upon him. Most probably, if the police gets to know you, he will obviously avenge … Or even kill you and get done with the issue. The Chief and the village elders work closely with the police. The same may happen. Or they will pay people to beat you up … I can't report anything. Unless God sends down another institution [laughs]'.

What can we tell from the two cases above? Two simple points. Firstly, that human rights – in this case the right to life – are not the decisive factor in young men's ability to survive in Mathare. Connections and relations are. Secondly, that living in Mathare as a young man under these conditions, where the ability to survive hinges on connections and relations –most often their parents' connections – and where their freedom of mobility is extremely restricted – constitutes a sense of being stuck.

Let us address the first point, first and return to the latter in the final discussion. In Henry and Jackson's cases above, their ability to survive is a matter of intricate connections and relations between individual police officers (not the police as an institution), elders, parents, chiefs. Moreover, these relations span and connect an illegal trade (the brewing of Chang'aa) and law enforcement and are not either illegal or legal. In fact, the position and relations that Jackson's parents have built through an illicit trade is the deciding aspect in securing Jackson's release, and possibly survival, from a formal institution, the police.

Javier Auyero's ethnographic research on urban violence in Buenos Aires (Auyero et al., 2014; Auyero and Berti, 2015) offers a useful perspective on the state's presence, law enforcement and citizenship at the urban margins. Auyero describes the presence of the state on the urban margins in Buenos Aires as constituted through intermittent, selective and contradictory law enforcement. The state's presence at the urban margins, Auyero argues, perpetuates rather than prevents violence. The state is not absent. Rather, the state has an intermittent, selective and frantic presence. Some petty criminals are chased and incarcerated, while others are not, and some forms of crime are hardly ever investigated (Auyero et al., 2014: 106). Furthermore, the police is both the repressive arm of the state against criminals and a perpetrator of crime, both directly and through being entangled with and connected to illegal networks. This deters people from seeking assistance from the police – the state – to resolve crime and ensure justice and safety, which in effect leaves the urban poor with no formal protection or mechanism of seeking justice. The connections between state actors and perpetrators of violence constitute an 'engagement' that erodes the rule of law and institutes 'a separate, localized, order' (Desmond Arias in Auyero et al., 2014: 108).

Auyero, citing Guillermo O'Donnell, describes this as a form of 'low-intensity citizenship', where democracy works in terms of the right to vote but where the liberal component of democracy is systematically violated, i.e. one can vote but cannot expect proper treatment from the police or the courts (Auyero et al.,

2014: 108). James Holston reaches a similar conclusion in his work on urban citizenship Brazil, using the term differentiated citizenship to describe the plight of Brazilians at the urban margins, effectively having inferior rights than Brazilians in middle class and better of areas (Holston, 2011: 341).

Aurero's accounts of violence on the urban margins of Buenos Aires are strikingly similar to those in Mathare, Nairobi. Law enforcement is intermittent and frantic and formal Kenyan citizenship offers little in terms of claiming rights. Consider, again, the case of Jackson. His release had nothing to with rights or citizenship. He was released because of his parents. Jackson is the son of a well-known Chang'aa brewer in Mathare (Chang'aa brewing is an illicit but highly profitable trade in Mathare). A single text message was enough to restore Jackson's freedom, and – attesting to the arbitrariness of law enforcement in Mathare – the freedom of the other young man (a total stranger to Jackson) that the police dragged out of the Matatu at the same time.

## Stuckness as a denial of rights

Why does the formal right to a life offer so little protection in these cases – even despite formal Kenyan Citizenship? Returning to Christian Lund's argument that rights and authority are mutually constitutive through reciprocal processes of recognition can help us. 'Rights entailed through recognition as a political subject may be limited or extensive. In fact, the recognition may entail no rights at all, as the capacity to recognize rights is also the capacity to deny and expurge them' (Lund, 2016 1206).

In their own way, every single one of the young men from Mathare referred to this process of being stripped of their rights by authorities (formal and informal) by being labelled as thugs, gang members, criminals, that did not deserve rights – not even the right to life.

In her work on extra-judicial killings in Mathare, Naomi van Stapele has written extensively on this subject offering a comprehensive historic, political and socio-economic account of the processes whereby young men from Mathare become stripped of their rights to protection and justice by being cast as dangerous gangsters and as such 'non-citizens' (van Stapele, 2016: 314). Her analysis resonates with Nancy Scheper-Hughes' work on Street Children in Brazil and marginal young people in Urban South Africa, where Scheper-Hughes describes these as processes of structural violence that reduce 'the socially vulnerable into "expendable non-persons", thus allowing the license – even the duty – to kill them' (Scheper-Hughes, 2004: 13).

In van Stapele's analysis, the location, the ghetto, plays an important part in this process. Being from the ghetto, and particularly from Mathare, is a central part of being labelled a thug and therefore less of a real citizen, even a non-citizen. The location contributes to a particular recognition that, paraphrasing Lund, entails no rights at all.

The stigma and disadvantage associated with growing up in a ghetto, an informal settlement or a slum area, constitutes what Loic Wacquant has termed 'territorial stigmatization' (Wacquant, 2008). Territorial stigmatization describes the process and experience of being stigmatized on grounds of the specific locality or territory that one comes from, be it the ghetto, the slum, or a social housing project. Several of the participants of the study describe this experience of being stigmatized on the grounds of being from Mathare. However, age and gender are invariably mentioned as additional stigmatizing factors, effectively rendering young men from Mathare to be perceived as a form of outlaws.

The point here is that the location itself contributes to a particular form of recognition that undermines young men's ability to claim rights – rights to security, to freedom of movement, to justice and in some cases to life. This, obviously, makes them extremely vulnerable to exploitation and crime and it makes it exceedingly difficult to plan and achieve ambitions. Several of the accounts of the participants in the diary study refer to constant struggles of making money and planning ways forward in life, only to be robbed, conned, or extorted by the police thereby losing it all and having to start over. These are accounts of constant movement, seeking and seizing opportunity, moving goods and wares across town and narrowly escaping the police (mixed in with extended periods of boredom and stagnation). These accounts attest to their ability to survive and to navigate the particular marginal urban setting, in which they live. However, the same accounts describe their constant setbacks and losses and their difficulties in guarding themselves against risks, exactly because of their inability to effectively claim rights to protection and recourse to justice, partly brought about by the location in which they live. Relating this situation to Henry Lefebvre's seminal call for 'the right to the city' (Lefebvre, 1967), which has subsequently turned into a social movement calling for every urban dweller's right to participate in the continuous process of making the city while simultaneously making a life for oneself in the city (International Alliance of Inhabitants, 2005), it is clear from the experience of Henry and so many other young men from Mathare and other 'ghettos' that more than 50 years since Lefebvre first voiced these thoughts, the right to the city is far from realized. Their particular origin within the city in effect denies them access to the rest of city, to use the city, and to participate in making the city. This effectively leads to a sense of being stuck.

Andrew Jefferson, Simon Turner and Steffen Jensen introduce the concept of stuckness as a novel way to explore the lived experience of people that are coping with, escaping from and 'making life' in sites of confinement (Jefferson, Turner, and Jensen, 2019: 2). Sites of confinement includes the prison, the camp, the 'ghetto' and the informal settlement – like Mathare – and are characterized by flows and enclosures of people that are dislocated or confined. Stuckness in these sites does imply physical immobility, but refers to '[...] the way confinement is experienced, sensed and lived. The experience of stuckness is not simply an expression of physical confinement and spatial closure but expresses the way people make sense of confining dynamics and practices' (Jefferson, Turner, and Jensen, 2019: 2).

Furthermore, stuckness is as much temporal as it is spatial. The intersection of temporality and spatiality is critical in understanding the stuckness that Henry experiences, in his struggle to survive and create a meaningful live for himself in a site of confinement.

The temporal aspect of being stuck is reminiscent of waiting, even chronic waiting, often with no clear sense of when the wait might be over, or what exactly one is waiting for (Jeffrey, 2008: 955). Henry's experiences of stuckness clearly attests to this sense of indefinite and intangible waiting as well as the intersection of temporality and spatiality in the process of waiting. Firstly, when Henry loses his brother(s) and subsequently fears for his own life, he moves to his mother's place (a perceived place of relative safety compared to the public space where he works) to wait. Secondly, while he weighs his options regarding retrieving his Boda from notorious 'killer cop' Rashid, balancing the risk of being shot with the actuality of not having any source of income to rely on, he again retreats to relative safety away for the public space and waits. For how long he will have to wait, and for what exactly, is not clear. However, it is clear that Henry's temporal as well as spatial stuckness, exemplified here in his recurrent states of waiting, is brought about by a fear – and a very real risk – of death, of being killed by the police.

Henry's sense of stuckness is a direct consequence of his effective lack of a right to life, or more precisely, that the right to life in effect does not apply to Henry.

At the same time, stuckness becomes a rights violation in itself. Henry's freedom of movement is not secured, far from it. Moving around the public space in Mathare and beyond is a constant risk to Henry and his peers, several of whom have, as described above, been subjected to numerous incidents of police brutality, extortion and violence. As most of these young men rely on the public space for their source of income – including through street trading, casual labor and engagement in the transport sector – the restrictions in their freedom of mobility also hampers their opportunities to make a living and carve out a viable future for themselves, in Mathare or elsewhere.

In other words, stuckness constitutes a rights violation in a double sense. Henry is neither able to pursue social mobility and a future existence outside of Mathare – escaping, as it were, the site of confinement – nor does he have the freedom of mobility to pursue a viable life within Mathare, thereby contributing to transforming, even destigmatizing, Mathare.

Henry has lived his entire life in Mathare. He is neither a migrant, nor a refugee, nor a conventional IPD ('Internally Displaced Person'), for that matter. His experience of stuckness is similar to what Stephen Lubkemann terms 'displacement in place' (Lubkemann, 2008: 455) to describe the predicament of young Mozambicans who were forcefully immobilized during the Mozambican civil war (1977–1992). Lubkemann argues that involuntary immobility undermined highly common life strategies founded in various forms of migration and mobility, leading to a sense of 'displacement in place' and calls for 'analytically de-coupling displacement from migration per se' (ibid.). Instead of analyzing displacement a priori in relation to 'movement', Lubkemann calls for taking the social strategies for coping with various forms of crisis and their social, economic and political effects that generate displacement as our analytical starting point (Lubkemann, 2008: 469, see Hammer, 2014 for a similar argument on 'Displacement Economies'). Returning to the case of Henry in Mathare, he is 'displaced in place' – literally confined within his mother's house in the exact area where he grew up. His displacement was not brought about by migration or war but by a potentially lethal human rights crisis that has its most severe consequences in particularly stigmatized urban settings.

In this chapter, I have offered an account of how Human Rights – most importantly the right to life – fall short of offering any meaningful sense of protection for young men on the urban margin of Nairobi. I have attempted to show how the particular presence of the state on the urban margins renders young men's ability to survive more a question of connections and relations – and resources – than a matter of rights or citizenship.

I have then attempted – through the concept territorial stigmatization – to bridge the discussion of urban violence, rights and the state's presence with a parallel discussion of the experience of temporal and spatial stuckness, (im) mobility in sites of confinement and 'displacement in place'. From the lived experience of stuckness, as exemplified through the case of Henry, it is clear that the state's presence, through violence, extortion and police brutality generates and reinforces stuckness. The territory – the informal settlement – contributes to a stigmatization that is used by the police to legitimize inhumane treatment of young Kenyan Citizens, effectively rendering them without a right to life and to free mobility. Henry and his peers may have the ability to survive in this state, but the challenge of escaping the site of confinement, which is the stigma of being a young man from Mathare, rather than the actual locality Mathare, remains insurmountable.

## Bibliography

Auyero, J. and Berti, M. (2015). In Harm's Way. The Dynamics of Urban Violence. Princeton: Princeton University Press.

Auyero, J., de Lara, A., and Berti, M. (2014). 'Violence and the State at the Urban Margins'. Journal of Contemporary Ethnography, vol. 43 (1), pp. 94–116.

Creswell, J. W. (2014). A Concise Introduction to Mixed Methods Research. Los Angeles: Sage Publications.

Gudmundsen, L., Hansen L., and Jensen, S. (2017). 'Gendered Violence in Informal Settlements in Kenya'. In S. Jensen and M. K. Andersen (eds.), Corruption and Torture: Violent Exchange and the Policing of the Urban Poor, pp. 95–118. Aalborg: Aalborg Universitetsforlag.

Hammer, A (2014). 'Introduction'. In A. Hammer (ed.), Displacement Economies in Africa: Paradoxes of Crisis and Creativity, pp. 3–32. London: Zed Books.

Holston, J. (2011). 'Contesting Privilege with Right: The Transformation of Differentiated Citizenship in Brazil'. Citizenship Studies, vol. 15 (3–4), pp. 335–352.

IDRC, International Development Research Centre, Muggah, Robert. (2012). Researching the Urban Dilemma: Urbanization, Poverty and Violence. <https://www.idrc.ca/sites/default/files/sp/Images/Researching-the-Urban-Dilemma-Baseline-study.pdf>.

International Alliance of Inhabitants. (2005). World Charter for the Right to the City. <https://www.right2city.org/wp-content/uploads/2019/09/A1.2_World-Charter-for-the-Right-to-the-City.pdf>.

Jefferson, A. Turner, S. and Jensen, S. (2019), 'Introduction: Stuckness and Sites of Confinement'. Ethnos: Journal of Anthropology, vol. 84 (1), pp. 1–13.

Jeffrey, C. (2008). 'Editorial'. Environment and Planning D: Society and Space, vol. 26, pp. 954–958.

Jensen, S., Andersen, M. K., Larsen, K., and Hansen, L. (2017). 'Introduction: Towards Violent Exchange'. In S. Jensen and M. K. Andersen (eds.), Corruption and Torture: Violent Exchange and the Policing of the Urban Poor, pp. 5–38. Aalborg: Aalborg Universitetsforlag.

Jensen, S. and Bjarnesen, J. (2014). 'Introduction'. In H. Moksnes and M. Melin (eds.), Claiming the City: Civil Society Mobilisation by the Urban Poor, pp. 163–171. Uppsala: Uppsala University.

Lefebvre, H. (1967), 'Le droit à la ville', L'Homme et la société, vol. 6, pp. 29–35.

Lubkemann, S. (2008), 'Involuntary Immobility: On a Theoretical Invisibility in Forced Migration Studies'. Journal of Refugee Studies, vol. 21 (4), pp. 454–475.

Lund, C. (2016). 'Rule and Rupture: State Formation through the Production of Property and Citizenship'. Development and Change, vol. 47, pp. 1199–1228.

MSJC, Mathare Social Justice Centre. (2017). Who Is Next? A Participatory Action Research Report against the Normalization of Extrajudicial Executions in Mathare. <https://drive.google.com/file/d/0B2NZry_SioNhWEFyQWNuVVBJV2M/view>, Accessed 15 February 2021.

Muggah, R. (2014). 'Deconstructing the Fragile City: Exploring Insecurity, Violence and Resilience'. Environment and Urbanization, vol. 26 (2), pp. 345–358.

OECD. (2016). STATES OF FRAGILITY 2016: Understanding Violence. <http://www.oecd-ilibrary.org/docserver/download/4316101e.pdf?expires=1516023904&id=id&accname=guest&checksum=F2527712D18298E74A989CE2C4DE9DE1>.

Scheper-Hughes, N. (2004). 'Dangerous and Endangered Youth: Social Structures and Determinants of Violence'. Annals of the New York Academy of Sciences, vol. 1036 (1), pp. 13–46.

van Stapele, N. (2016). '"We Are Not Kenyans": Extra-Judicial Killings, Manhood and Citizenship in Mathare, a Nairobi Ghetto'. Conflict, Security & Development, vol. 16 (4), pp. 301–325.

United Nations. (2003). 'The Human Rights Based Approach to Development Cooperation. Towards a Common Understanding Among UN Agencies'. <https://unsdg.un.org/sites/default/files/6959The_Human_Rights_Based_Approach_to_Development_Cooperation_Towards_a_Common_Understanding_among_UN.pdf>.

Vandenhole, W. and Gready, P. (2014). 'Failures and Successes of Human Rights-Based Approaches to Development: Towards a Change Perspective'. Nordic Journal of Human Rights, vol. 32 (4), pp. 291–311.

Wacquant, L. (2008). Territorial Stigmatization in the Age of Advanced Marginality. In Symbolic Power in Cultural Contexts. Leiden, The Netherlands: Brill | Sense.

World Bank. (2011). Violence in the City: Understanding and Supporting Community Responses to Urban Violence. Washington: The World Bank. <http://documents.worldbank.org/curated/en/524341468331181450/pdf/638880WP0Viole00BOX361532B00public0.pdf>.

Ahlam Chemlali

# Understanding 'Gendered Border Violence': The Case of Libya

## Introduction

Irregular migration, and migration from and through North Africa in particular, has been declared synonymous with the European Unions purported 'loss of control' of its borders. This has supplied the pretext for what has in fact been not only a continuous intensification of militarized control of the southern border, but also an externalization of the borders into Africa (Akkerman 2018; Fine 2019). This expansion and externalization of borders has transformed the North African countries into militarized border zones and unescapable transit borderlands. Using the legitimizing argument that it is a 'humanitarian move' that 'protects human rights and saves lives' (EC 2018; EP 2021) because it will result in fewer migrants taking the dangerous journey across the Mediterranean, the EU borders have become flexible, mobile, shifting and omnipresent in the region (Balibar 2009; Abderrahim 2019). Yet, in the wake of this externalization, human rights organizations have catalogued a spectrum of violence in the North African borderlands including torture, forced labour, sexual violence, and death conducted by State as well as non-State actors (HRW 2019, 2020, 2021; AI 2020, 2021).

Using a plethora of new instruments, in particular the EU Emergency Trust Fund for Africa (EUTF), the Migration Partnership Framework and The Mobility Partnership Agreement, the EU is funneling millions of Euros into North Africa to stop migration (EC 2018; Zanker 2019; EP 2021). Under the banner of 'combatting illegal migration', the EU has engaged in new partnerships with Libya. With the support and funding of other EU member states and institutions, Italy has pursued cooperation with Libya to externalize EU borders even throughout years of conflict in Libya (Amnesty International 2021). In particular, the Memorandum of Understanding between Italy and Libya, signed in 2017 and renewed without modification in 2020, extended Italian efforts to keep refugees and migrants from reaching its shores by focusing on reconstructing Libyan maritime forces to intercept and return people crossing the central Mediterranean to Libya (Amnesty International 2021). Framed as a 'humanitarian intervention' by the EU that 'builds local capacity, protects human rights and saves lives', a continuum of violence and human rights abuses, has however, been meticulously documented by human rights organizations and the UN (Amnesty International 2021). These forms of violence specific for the border, has continuously exposed, undermined and challenged EU's migration policies, international role, and its avowed humanitarian values.

## Masculinized and feminized forms of violence

The portrayals of border violence and violence in transit are often sensationalized and framed as 'spectacular' such as slave markets, mass rape, human trafficking, sex slavery and sexual violence, types of violence that are specifically gendered. In these instances, European policymakers, media and humanitarian actors frame migrant women as a specific victim group in need of rescue. In this way, concerns over women and women's bodies have come to play a legitimizing role in the European humanitarian border or 'humanitarian intervention through externalization of border control' policies.

While the majority of migrants – in transit and crossing the Mediterranean – are men (IOM 2019a, 2019b; UNHCR 2021), policymakers and humanitarian actors have portrayed the migrant women as the main victims in need of rescue. This construction is however two-sided as migrants are not only understood as 'at risk' but also as 'a risk' to the EU (Aradau 2004), with both categorizations intrinsically linked to each other through gendering and racialization. In this construct the masculinization speaks to the other dominant narrative which 'invoke the fantasy of an invasion from the South' (Andrijasevic & Mai 2010), as chaos to Europe's order (Stachowitsch & Sachseder 2019) or most significantly, the construction of the 'violent and unscrupulous smuggler'. While those who are feminized are portrayed as the true legitimate victims worth saving, which allows the EU to present themselves as saviours of racialized women and children, reproducing the colonial narrative of 'white men saving brown women from brown men' (Spivak 1993). This narrative has particularly circled around and portrayed how irregular migration lead to violence against migrant women, to 'human trafficking', 'sex slavery' and 'sexual violence'. Mirrored in a semantic shift that has taken place during the past years, legitimating border externalization from 'the fight against irregular migration' to 'the fight against human trafficking' (Tyszler 2019; Gross-Wyrtzen 2020). In effect the border externalization as a humanitarian intervention has been legitimated by political desires to rescue migrant women, enabled by gendered and racialized constructions of victimhood in discourses on migration management.

However, exactly how the EU migration politics shapes gendered experiences and the ways in which border violence manifest in North African borderlands remains unexplored. We need to ask how gender and constructions of victimhood play part in context of border control and externalization in new spaces of transit. I argue that it is essential to explore the gendered dimensions to border violence, a specific form of violence inextricably linked to EU's border migration politics. To further our understanding of migrant women as humanitarian subjects between simple dichotomies of 'victims' and 'criminals', I propose to develop the concept of gendered border violence to capture how and the extent to which border management is gendered. Relating this to the larger issues in this volume, this approach helps us understand, in new ways, gendered processes of displacement, mobility and immobility. It suggests that the space and the time between displacement and whatever arrival possible are crucially gendered in the ways in which men and women's lives can be lived.

As Elsa Tyszler (2019) argues, looking at the experience of women gives a deeper insight of the interweaved systems of border control and the entangled systems of border violence in the North African borderlands. This is further underlined by Nawyn (2010: 710) since 'gender is […] a system of power relations that permeates every aspect of the migration experience, one cannot understand the opportunities or barriers to migrate, […] without understanding how migrants are embedded in a gendered system of relations, with one another and with macrostructures.' Importantly, migration control at the border shapes the corporeal experiences of migrants differently, owing to classed, gendered, and racialized understandings of otherness, as power operates through intersectional patterns of domination (Sahraoui 2020).

In this chapter I aim to contribute to a discussion and conceptualization of gendered border violence by focusing on the ways in which violence against migrant women in transit is recognized, reframed, and reinforced and on the role of gendered images and representation in contemporary European migration politics, using the case of Libya. I first briefly outline the Libyan context pre- and post-the fall of Gaddafi and the EU border policies towards Libya. I then describe the system of detention and the transition from transit to confinement and how these changes have particularly reinforced and routinized sexual violence against migrant women. A third section explores how gender constructions in migration management are produced in the borderlands and how this fall under 'sexual humanitarianism' using the case of sex-slave imagery. A closing remark draws out the relevance of my argument for debates on the framing and reconfiguration of gendered violence, and why it is essential to have a gendered understanding of border violence in transit.

## The case of Libya

For decades, oil-rich Libya has been a destination country for migrants, attracting workers from sub-Saharan Africa, the Maghreb, Sahel and several Asian countries, such as Pakistan and Bangladesh, and from the 1990s onwards Gaddafi also used Libya's presidency of the African Union to attract seasonal and casual workers to the Libyan agricultural, construction and oil sectors (Lemberg-Pedersen & Chemlali 2018). After first being designated a postcolonial hero and then international pariah, in his last years before the uprising, Gaddafi was known as an effective partner in Western countries' fight against terrorism and in Europe's desire to avoid asylum seekers and migrants. Just months before his death, he exchanged handshakes and bank transfers with European leaders, from Blair over Sarkozy and Malmstrøm to Prodi (ibid.). While Colonel Gaddafi was in power, the EU and Italy both struck contentious deals with Libya, providing funding in return for a promise to keep unwanted migrants and refugees away from Europe (Hamood 2008; Andersson 2014).

Ever since, the country has been torn apart by armed conflict, as rival governments and militias fight for control, and public services have collapsed (MPI 2020). The chaos that set in after the second Libyan civil war began in 2014 has provided a fertile ground for a dark economy to grow, based on plundering resources and illicit activities such as trafficking in oil, drugs, weapons, and people. The system, which exploited workers, migrants, and refugees, was further decentralized, and more people made money from controlling, smuggling, selling and exploiting migrants. This subsequently turned Libya into the main and most dangerous gateway to Europe for those fleeing repression, conflict and poverty in the region (MSF 2019).

To stem the flow of new arrivals, European states have implemented containment and push-back policies (Morone 2019; Amnesty International 2021). Dismantled search and rescue capacities at sea have been coupled with sponsoring the Libyan coastguard to intercept refugees and migrants in international waters and forcibly return them to Libyan detention centres, in violation of international law (MSF 2020). As a result, human trafficking, abduction, detention and extortion of migrants and refugees continue to flourish in Libya while people's chances of dying in the Mediterranean have only increased (MSF 2019; HRW 2021).

## From transit to confinement

The political fragmentation and violence in Libya have created a prolonged volatile situation of uncertainty and insecurity in society. Violence and fighting have resumed or maybe never really stopped but this time not against a common adversary but as fragmented across the country, South, East and West, over access to resources, infrastructure, territory, and political identity (Ali & Chemlali et al. 2014). According to IOM, there were approximately 2.5 million migrant workers in Libya before the conflict started and despite years of conflict and insecurity, 576,000 migrants of at least 41 nationalities were present in Libya according to IOM estimates from February 2021 (IOM 2021). Today, Libya is notoriously perilous for refugees, asylum seekers, and migrants, who often suffer abuses, including at the country's numerous detention facilities (Global Detention Project 2021). Conditions at these facilities, many of which are under the control of militias, have been criticized by the UN and human rights organizations. There are frequent shortages of water and food; over-crowding is rampant; detainees can experience physical mistreatment and torture; sexual violence, forced labour and slavery are rife; and there is a stark absence of oversight and regulation (ibid. 2021). Nevertheless, Italy and the European Union continue to strike controversial migration control deals with various actors in Libya aimed at reducing flows across the Mediterranean. These arrangements include equipping Libyan forces to return intercepted migrants and refugees at sea, investing in detention centres, and paying militias to control migration ( InfoMigrants 2021; The Libya Observer 2021).

In a recently released report, Amnesty International (2021) documents that in 2020 and 2021 the Libyan authorities held individuals returned from sea to arbitrary and indefinite detention in DCIM centres (Directorate for Combating Illegal Migration, placed under the Ministry of Interior). Here they were systematically subjected to 'torture and other ill-treatment, frequently for the aim of extracting ransoms; sexual or gender-based violence; forced labour and other exploitation; and cruel and inhuman detention conditions that in themselves violate the absolute probation of torture and other ill-treatment' (Amnesty International 2021: 35). Despite the overwhelming available evidence, the conditions of migrant detention have received little attention in the scholarly literature, which has mainly addressed the politics of abandonment and death at sea (Kirby 2020). Sexual violence occurs at border crossings; in transit as 'payment' to smugglers; as a feature of torture for extortion; as an element of forced labour; as rape and in street harassment fuelled by anti-black racism (Refugees

International 2017; Women's Refugee Commission 2019; Kirby 2020; Amnesty International 2021).

## The framing of the sex-slave

It is evident, that migrants in Libya are exposed to brutal and systematic violence, which often takes sexualized or gendered forms. However, Paul Kirby (2020) argues that the disregard of sexual violence and other abuses against detained migrants in EU policy is 'sustained by the framing of the crisis in terms of "human trafficking", where pullback and containment are understood not as exacerbating vulnerability so much as disrupting criminality and therefore ultimately benefiting migrant populations' (1221, emphasis added). This framing is aligned with gendered constructions that fall under sexual humanitarianism, a term coined by sociologist Nicola Mai in 2014 which plays a role in restricting the freedom of movement of groups of migrants who have been strategically reduced and 'othered' to 'pure' victims of oppression and sexual exploitation e.g., sex-trafficking and victims of sexual slavery (Mai 2014). This gender-specific notion of humanitarianism has been instrumentalized in various cases surrounding migrant women, where a particular focus on sexual violence often leads to the fetishization of the bodies of migrant women of colour. This obscures the very strategies that migrant women often deploy for their own protection and that of those who travel with them, as well as the relationships they may forge along the way for survival, company, and care (Sanchez 2019). I argue that sexual humanitarianism has been instrumentalized in Libya, by using the 'slave market and sex-slave case' in late 2017, when a video documenting the slave-auction of sub-Saharan African migrants in Libya started circulating on social media, giving rise to an international wave of outrage. The video was filmed by journalist Nima Elbagir for CNN and featured her investigation of a slave auction outside Tripoli (Elbagir et al. 2017; Gabriell 2019). This triggered a global outcry, even though trafficking in multiple forms throughout Libya had been extensively documented well before the release of the CNN video. Already in 2015, Amnesty International began using the term 'slaves' to qualify the status of sub-Saharan African migrants trapped in hellish conditions in Libya (Gabriell 2019).

Not surprising, the images of slave markets reinforced the gendered constructions, whereas the male migrants were 'slaves', migrant women were 'sex slaves' (see Brut 2020; Baker 2019; France24 2019; Middleberg 2018), as well as invoking racial tropes of 'African slaves' and 'African slave traders' to support government interventions and legal instruments. As such, Libyan slave markets caught the attention of politicians and policy makers in their attempts to justify more restrictive border controls and repatriation. President Emmanuel Macron, not long after the release of the CNN video, was quoted saying to thousands of students at the University of Ouagadougou during his visit to Burkina Faso in 2017: '"Who are the traffickers? They are Africans ... Show me a Belgian, French or German smuggler or whatever else. You will not find one," he said and continued, "There are African slave traders who trade other Africans; that is the reality"' (Telesur 2017, emphasis added). By focusing on 'African' slave traders, the effects of EU policies and border externalization were invisibilized.

The 'slave markets' and 'sex slaves' in Libya created the perfect storm, prompting mass protests in France and beyond and a special session of the UN Security Council called by President Emmanuel Macron (Gabriell 2019). It further enabled certain forms of political action desired by the EU that were inaccessible earlier, including mass repatriations (Wintour & Chrisafis 2017). Thus, gender was made visible and incorporated in the broader sociopolitical agenda of controlling the borders and justifying mass deportations (Oloruntoba et al. 2018) in ways that de facto exonerated European policies for any stake in the matter.

## Conclusion

From my early field work in Tripoli and Benghazi, after the fall of Gaddafi, a study I conducted on victims of torture and related violence, already pointed towards rampant human-rights violations against migrants and locals in Libya (Chemlali 2013; Ali & Chemlali et al. 2014). Since then, the country has experienced increasing violent conflict in the east, west, and south. The experiences of migrants in Libya have changed dramatically in the post-Gaddafi years, as the 2017 Italy agreement transformed the country from one of transit to one of containment. I have sought to illustrate how concerns over women and women's bodies have come to play a legitimizing role in the European 'humanitarian border' or 'humanitarian intervention through externalization of border control' policies. By drawing up the Libyan transit, confinement, and borderland and how the EU externalization not only produce but reinforce and exacerbates the risks and vulnerabilities, it is clear that EU migration politics not only shape gendered experiences and gendered constructions of victimhood, but also reframe and reconfigure the masculinized and feminized migrant categories. Furthermore, drawing on sexual humanitarianism and the empirical case of 'slave markets' and 'sex slavery' I exemplify how these images are reframed by policymakers and governments to justify and legitimize further restrictive migration and border control. At the same time, the fight against irregular migration and human trafficking relies on placing 'gendered bodies right at the center of the crossfire' (Hegde 2014). In the words of Ruben Andersson (2014: 278) migrants become 'tokens of communication' in a claims-making process through which a small, containable 'problem' is hugely inflated, as was illustrated by Libya's Gaddafi, who in 2010 asked for five billion euros a year to 'stop illegal migration' in order to prevent Europe 'turning black'. Similarly, I argue that migrant women become 'tokens of victimhood' and thus central players in the construction of 'the migrant women' as a humanitarian subject which shape and challenge discourses, policies, and interventions in the realm of European border externalization. As such, gendered and racialized constructions entail violent consequences for migrants, particularly for women (Gerard & Pickering 2014). It also shows how the image and construction of the migrant woman continues to capture public and political attention. In stark contrast to the limited legal mobility afforded to the women, the image of the migrant woman travels with ease across borders and mobilizes responses from media, humanitarian and political, actors globally. Based on this, I propose the need for an intersectional conceptualization of gendered border violence. This cannot only be based on reading policies and human rights reports, as I have endeavoured here, but must also include the experiences and strategies from the women themselves in the borderland.

## Bibliography

Abderrahim, T. (2019). A Tale of Two Agreements: EU Migration Cooperation with Morocco and Tunisia. European Institute of the Mediterranean.

Akkerman, M. (2018). Expanding the Fortress: The Policies, the Profiteers and the People Shaped by EU's Border Externalisation Programme. The Transnational Institute (TNI) Amsterdam, May 2018.

Ali, F., Chemlali, A., Andersen, M. K., Skar, M, Roensbo, H., and Modvig, J. (2014). Consequences of Torture and Organized Violence. Libya Needs Assessment Survey. Dignity publication series no.8. https://www.dignity.dk/wp-content/uploads/pubseries_no8.pdf.

Amnesty International (2020). 'Libya: UN Rights Council members must address widespread torture during periodic review, November 2020'. Amnesty International, https://www.amnesty.org/en/latest/news/2020/11/libya-un-rights-council-members-must-address-widespread-torture-during-periodic-review/, accessed 15 February 2021.

Amnesty International (2021). 'Libya: "No one will look for you": Forcibly returned from sea to abusive detention in Libya, July 2021', Amnesty

International, https://www.amnesty.org/download/Documents/MDE194439 2021ENGLISH.pdf, accessed 16 August 2021.

Andersson, R. (2014). Illegality, Inc.: Clandestine Migration and the Business of Bordering Europe. Oakland, CA: University of California Press.

Andrijasevic, R., and Mai, N. (2016). 'Editorial: Trafficking (in) representations: Understanding the recurring appeal of victimhood and slavery in neoliberal times', Anti-Trafficking Review, 7, 1–10.

Aradau, C. (2004). 'The perverse politics of four-letter words: Risk and pity in the securitisation of human trafficking', Millennium, 33 (2), 251–278.

Baker, A. (2019). 'It was as if we weren't human. Inside the modern slave trade trapping African migrants', Time, https://time.com/longform/african-slave-trade/, accessed 15 February 2021.

Balibar, E. (2009). 'Europe as borderland', Environment and Planning D: Society and Space 27, 2, 190–215.

Brut. (2020). 'Libya: Migrants sold as sex slaves', Brut., https://www.brut.media/us/news/libya-migrants-sold-as-sex-slaves-c38e6e2d-982f-4787-84f3-3680d7e62fdc, accessed 15 February 2021.

Chemlali, A. (2013). Victims of Torture and Related Violence in Libya: A Qualitative Assessment with a View to Enhance a Quantitative Needs Assessment in a Post-Conflict Context. University of Copenhagen. Retrieved from http://doc.rct.dk/doc/mon2013.046.pdf, accessed 3 January 2021.

Elbagir, N., Razek, R., Platt, A., and Jones, B. (2017). 'People for sale: Where lives are auctioned for $400', CNN, https://edition.cnn.com/2017/11/14/africa/libya-migrant-auctions/index.html, accessed 15 February 2021.

European Council. (2018). 'Improving migration management in the North of Africa region', European Commision, https://ec.europa.eu/neighbourhood-enlargement/news_corner/news/improving-migration-management-north-africa-region_en, accessed 15 February 2021.

European Parliament. (2021). The European Neighbourhood Policy (ENP), Southern Partners. https://www.europarl.europa.eu/ftu/pdf/en/FTU_5.5.7.pdf, accessed 15 February 2021.

Fine, S. (2019). All at Sea: Europe's Crisis of Solidarity on Migration. Policy Brief. European Council on Foreign Relations.

France24. (2019). 'The story of "Mariam", held captive as a sex slave in Tripoli', France24, https://www.france24.com/en/20190712-story-mariam-ivorian-captive-sex-slave-tripoli-infomigrants, accessed 15 February 2021.

Gabriell, J. (2019). '"Free our brothers!": On the politicization of slavery in Libya within the French context', South Atlantic Quarterly, 118 (3), 686–693.

Gerard, A., and Pickering, S. (2014). 'Gender, securitization and transit: Refugee women and the journey to the EU', Journal of Refugee Studies, 27 (3), 341–352.

Global Detention Project (2021). 'Immigration Detention in Libya, 2021', https://www.globaldetentionproject.org/countries/africa/libya, accessed 15 February 2021.

Gross-Wyrtzen, L. (2020). 'Contained and abandoned in the "humane" border: Black migrants' immobility and survival in Moroccan urban space', Environment and Planning D: Society and Space, 38(5), 887–904.

Hamood, S. (2008). 'EU–Libya cooperation on migration: A raw deal for refugees and migrants?', Journal of Refugee Studies, 21 (1), 32–35.

Hegde, R. S. (2014). 'Gender, Media and Trans/National Spaces'. In Cynthia Carter, Linda Steiner and Lisa McLaughlin (eds.), The Routledge Companion to Media and Gender, 92–102. London: Routledge.

Human Rights Watch. (2019). No Escape from Hell: EU Policies Contribute to Abuse of Migrants in Libya. https://www.hrw.org/sites/default/files/report_pdf/eu0119_web2.pdf, accessed 5 January 2021.

Human Rights Watch. (2020). Italy: Halt Abusive Migration Cooperation with Libya. https://www.hrw.org/news/2020/02/12/italy-halt-abusive-migration-cooperation-libya, accessed 5 January 2021.

Human Rights Watch. (2021). World Report 2021. Events of 2020: Libya, 420–428. https://www.hrw.org/sites/default/files/media_2021/01/2021_hrw_world_report.pdf, accessed 5 January 2021.

InfoMigrants. (2021). Libya: Nearly 1,000 Migrants Intercepted at Sea and Returned to Libya in 3 Days, https://www.infomigrants.net/en/post/28284/libya-nearly-1-000-migrants-intercepted-at-sea-and-returned-to-libya-in-3-days accessed 4 January 2021, accessed 5 January 2021.

IOM. (2019a). World Migration Report 2020, https://publications.iom.int/system/files/pdf/wmr_2020.pdf, accessed 5 January 2021.

IOM. (2019b). Towards Safer Migration in Africa: Migration and Data in Northern and Western Africa. Migration Data on the Central Mediterranean Route: What Do We Know? https://publications.iom.int/books/migration-data-central-mediterranean-route-what-do-we-know, accessed 5 January 2021.

Kirby, P. (2020). 'Sexual violence in the border zone: The EU, the Women, Peace and Security agenda and carceral humanitarianism in Libya', International Affairs, 96 (5), 1209–1226, https://doi.org/10.1093/ia/iiaa097

Lemberg-Pedersen, M., and Chemlali, A. (2018). 'Europa drømmer om en ny Gadaffi i Libyen', Politiken. https://politiken.dk/debat/kroniken/art6355178/Europa-dr%C3%B8mmer-om-en-ny-Gadaffi-i-Libyen.

Mai, N. (2014). 'Between embodied cosmopolitism and sexual humanitarianism: The fractal mobilities and subjectivities of migrants working in the sex industry'. In Baby-Collins, V. and Anteby, L. (eds.), Borders, Mobilities and Migrations, Perspectives from the Mediterranean in the 21st Century, 175–192. Brussels: Peter Lang, 2014.

Middleberg, M. (2018). 'How to stop the slave trade in Libya and beyond', CNN, https://edition.cnn.com/2018/01/05/opinionsmaurice-middleberg-stopping-the-slave-trade/index.html, accessed 15 February 2021.

Migration Policy Institute (2020). Once a Destination for Migrants, Post-Gaddafi Libya Has Gone from Transit Route to Containment. https://www.migrationpolicy.org/article/once-destination-migrants-post-gaddafi-libya-has-gone-transit-route-containment, accessed 15 February 2021.

Morone, A. M. (2019). 'International migration and containment policies: Lessons from Libya', Nation and Security, 4, 44–58, DOI: 10.32576/nb.2019.4.5.

MSF. (2019). Trading in Suffering: Detention, Exploitation and Abuse in Libya, https://www.msf.org/libya%E2%80%99s-cycle-detention-exploitation-and-abuse-against-migrants-and-refugees, accessed 15 February 2021.

MSF. (2020). Stemming the Flow of Arrivals to Europe, https://msf.lu/en/news/all-news/stemming-the-flow-of-arrivals-to-europe, accessed 15 February 2021.

Nawyn, S. (2010). 'Gender and migration: Integrating feminist theory into migration studies', Sociology Compass, 4 (9), 749–765.

Oloruntoba, F. A., Ogwezzy-Ndisika, A. O., Faustino, B. A., and Amakoh, K. O. (2018). 'Transnational gendered narratives on migration: The Nigerian media and female migrants en route to Italy from Libya', Feminist Media Studies, 18 (6), 1130–1132.

Refugees International (2017). "Hell on Earth": Abuses Against Refugees and Migrants Trying to Reach Europe from Libya, 11, https://www.refugeesinternational.org/reports/2017/libya, accessed 15 February 2021.

Sahraoui, N. (2020). 'Gendering the care/control nexus of the humanitarian border: Women's bodies and gendered control of mobility in a EUropean borderland', Environment and Planning D: Society and Space, 38 (5), 905–922.

Sanchez, G. (2019). 'The experiences of women on the migration pathway – And the stories we tell ourselves', Oxford Border Criminologies, https://www.law.ox.ac.uk/research-subject-groups/centre-criminology/centreborder-criminologies/blog/2019/03/experiences-women, accessed 15 February 2021.

Spivak, G. C. (1993). "Can the Subaltern Speak?" In P. Williams and L. Chrisman (eds.), Colonial Discourse and Postcolonial Theory. A Reader, 66–111. Hemel Hempstead: Harvester Wheatsheaf.

Stachowitsch, S., and Sachseder, S. (2019). 'The gendered and racialized politics of risk analysis. The case of Frontex', Critical Studies on Security, 7 (2), 107–123, DOI: 10.1080/21624887.2019.1644050

Telesur (2017). 'Macron blames "African traffickers" for Libya's slave trade', Telesur. https://www.telesurenglish.net/news/Macron-Blames-African-Traffickers-for-Libyas-Slave-Trade-20171129-0005.html, accessed 15 February 2021.

The Libya Observer (2021). 'NCHRL: In excess of 11,000 migrants returned to Libya having been rescued at sea', The Libya Observer, https://www.libyaobserver.ly/inbrief/nchrl-excess-11000-migrants-returned-libya-having-been-rescued-sea, accessed 15 February 2021.

Tyszler, E. (2019). 'From controlling mobilities to control over women's bodies: Gendered effects of EU border externalization in Morocco', CMS 7, 25.

UNHCR (2021). Operational Portal: The Mediterranean Situation. https://data2.unhcr.org/en/situations/mediterranean, accessed 15 February 2021.

Wintour, P., and Chrisafis, A. (2017). 'Voluntary evacuation planned for migrants as Libya battles slavery claims', The Guardian, https://www.theguardian.com/world/2017/nov/29/voluntary-evacuation-planned-for-migrants-in-libya-detention-camps, accessed 15 February 2021.

Women's Refugee Commission (2019). 'More Than One Million Pains': Sexual Violence against Men and Boys on the Central Mediterranean Route to Italy, https://reliefweb.int/sites/reliefweb.int/files/resources/Libya-Italy-Report-03-2019.pdf, accessed 15 February 2021.

Zanker, F. (2019). 'Managing or restricting movement? Diverging approaches of African

Tamirace Fakhoury[1]

# Governing displacement: A Polycentric Perspective

## Introduction

The governance of displacement and mobility has evolved into a key policy-making field, becoming a fashionable term concept over the last decades (Betts 2011; Lippert 1999). Yet what does the governance or the regulation of displacement mean and entail? Who governs who and what? To what end? and by what means? And is governing displacement better understood as the process of regulating refugees' lives through the production of order, the exercise of power, the allocation of resources or the politics of humanitarian care and wellbeing?

Refugee governance is often understood in narrow institutionalist ways as it implies ordering and establishing policy and legal norms and practices in the international refugee regime. In reality, however, scholars have increasingly conceptualized refugee governance through the lens of contrasting approaches (Fiddian-Qasmiyeh et al. 2014; McConnachie 2014). Refugee governance entails the involvement of multiple scales of authority (Milner 2017). Scales of authority are polycentric: They encompass state and non-state actors as well as formal and informal institutions.

Towards the second half of the twentieth century, with the formal establishment of the international refugee regime following the adoption of the 1951 Refugee Convention, scholars have taken an increasing interest in discussing states' governing styles towards refugees, and the strategies they develop either to host, repel or govern refugees from a distance (Betts and Loescher 2010; Chimni 1998; Fitzgerald 2020). They have also focused on how non-state actors such as civil society, faith-based actors or international organizations practice and perform the politics of refugee humanitarianism (Harrell-Bond 2002; Loescher 2014). Adding to this, literature has placed emphasis on the ways informal actors seek to regulate refugee flight even if they have no legal mandate in the field (Chalcraft 2008; Fakhoury 2020; Sanyal 2017). An increasingly dominant stream

---

1 Tamirace Fakhoury is associate professor at the Department of Politics and Society at Aalborg University in Denmark.

of thought has shed light on refugees as governing actors, highlighting themes of bottom-up leadership (LERRN 2021; McConnachie 2014).

Mapping the typology of actors involved in governing displacement may seem like a straightforward affair. Understanding however how and why various actors cooperate and diverge on refugee norms and assessing the implications of their actions for refugee realities remains a complex endeavour. Governance may be fundamentally 'concerned with creating the conditions for ordered rule and collective action' (Stoker 1998: 17). In reality, it leads to colliding logics of action (Campomori and Ambrosini 2020; Gómez-Mera 2016). Reflecting on the production of authority in refugee spaces, scholars have thus increasingly inquired into how complex power differentials derail consensus around refugee protection. Friction over collective policy ends up backfiring on peoples' lives, creating divergences on their rights (Fakhoury 2019a; Fee 2021; Fine and Thiollet 2020; Wolff 2015)

Drawing on the Middle East as a key empirical site for displacement where more than 60 % of the world's 26 million refugees are located (UNHCR 2020), this chapter sets out to explore how the governance of displacement is best understood through a polycentric or multi-level perspective. This perspective necessitates an inquiry into how multiple actors, facets, circuits, and pathways of power regulate refugees' lives. To that end, it looks at the rich scholarship on forced migration in the region, and reviews illustrative streams of thought that have sought to grapple with the polysemous concept of refugee governance.

I proceed as follows. The first section draws on literature strands that look at governance as an act of ordering through crafting policies and norms. These strands explore how states and non-state actors have sought to govern displacement through a variety of policies and governing methods ranging from the so-called durable solutions to securitization and externalization. Second, it delves into literature strands that unpack governance as an act of disordering. In doing so, it refers to some of the work that explores how governing displacement leads on the ground to fragmentation and friction. This spells out numerous consequences for refugees' realities. Intended and unintended consequences encompass temporality and urgency in humanitarian governance as well as protractedness and precarity in displacement. Third, shifting the gaze from policy-making from above to refugees as actors in their own right, the chapter goes on to explore streams of literature that focus on alternative modes of governance or governance from below. Such works divert our attention from policy to refugee-centric fields, inquiring into how refugees challenge, contest and reorder the 'order of things'.

By accounting for the many facets through which governing refugee displacement manifests itself, this chapter builds on various works that have conceptualized refugee policy as an assemblage of ordering and disordering structures (Allen et al. 2017; Campomori and Ambrosini 2020; Milner and Wojnarowicz 2017). In this viewpoint, there is no monocentric or unitary authority regulating the politics of refuge. Rather understanding how authority is devolved, shared, diffused as well as contested among multi-level actors emerges as the privileged area of enquiry (Bache and Flinders, 2004).

## Refugee politics as an ordering process: Multiple governing actors at multiple scales

In the Middle East, refugee governance is generally considered to be weak as nation-states have historically refrained from developing full-fledged asylum systems in line with the 1951 Refugee Convention. Refugee governance may stray far from the principles of the international refugee regime in the region. Yet it is far from weak. Rather, it is codified and articulated through a web of ordering structures spanning the local to the global.

Against this backdrop, analysts have explored how various entities including states, regional as well as international organizations have produced norms and practices that have governed refugees' predicament (Carpi 2019; Fee 2021; Hanafi 2014; Khallaf 2019). Strands of literature have delved into the national ordering structures that authorities have set up to govern refugees. In this instance, analytical frameworks have unpacked how states' historical legacies, political systems and human rights regimes have shaped refugees' experiences (Culcasi 2017; Dorai and Clochard 2006; Lenner 2020). Authors have further explored variation and commonalities in Middle Eastern states' responses to forced migration (Tsourapas 2019a). Here, they have expanded our understanding of how forms of authoritarian state governance concentrated in elites, institutions, and informal practices have muzzled the freedom of refugees and migrants including their right to mobilize politically and to join trade unions (Hilal and Samy 2008). Equally important is the focus on the role of local actors such as municipalities and civil society organizations in providing refugee services, and how such actors interact with the state's central authority on the one hand and with supranational organizations on the other (Boustani 2014; Mourad 2017). Focus is placed on understanding how both formal and informal local actors govern refugee mobility, dispense services, or implement social cohesion regimes between refugee and host communities (Carpi and Şenoğuz 2019; Zakharia and Knox 2014).

Examining regional refugee governance or how the regional state system as well as regional organizations regulate the politics of refuge is yet another significant field of enquiry. Scholars have endeavoured to understand the dynamics that have conditioned the positions of regional blocs and organizations such as the Arab League (LAS) and the Gulf Cooperation Council (GCC) towards refugee flight (Malit and Tsourapas 2021; Thiollet 2011). Indeed, to understand refugee ordering structures in the region, analysts have focused on the specific protocols that states have developed through the mechanism of the Arab League in the wake of refugee-producing conflicts. Examples vary from the Casablanca protocol of 1965 that sought to provide temporary protection to Palestinian refugees to the Declaration on the Protection of Refugees and Displaced Persons in 1992 and the Arab Convention on Regulating the Status of Refugees in the Arab Countries, adopted in 1994 (Janmyr and Stevens 2021; Zaoitti 2006). Recently, in the context of displacement from Syria since 2011, increasing focus has been laid on how the regional bloc of the GCC states has evolved through financial burden-sharing into an important actor in protracted refugee crises (De Bel-Air 2015; Martin 2016).

Notwithstanding these regional instruments, policy trends, and practices, neither inter-Arab cooperative platforms nor regional organizations have considered asylum as one of their key policy foci. Most of the regional refugee law instruments have not had traction as states either signed them with reservations or never acceded (Janmyr and Stevens 2021). In practice, regional organizations namely LAS and the GCC have instead focused on regulating Arab nationals' free mobility and employment schemes, leaving refugee politics to the prerogative of the state (Fakhoury 2019a).

Against this background, scholars have taken increasing interest in understanding why the regional Arab state system has been reluctant to doing collective policy over refugees, and what instead motivates its Realpolitik towards refugees. Rosemarie Sayegh explores how, in the context of conflicts such as the Arab Israeli War, concerted action over the fate of Palestinian refugees is cast aside as states privilege their own geopolitical agendas (Sayigh 2001). Maja Janmyr analyses why Arab states have downplayed the importance of the 1951 Refugee Convention, arguing instead for alternative refugee-related arrangements (Janmyr 2017a). Since most refugee waves come from the region itself, she argues, Arab states have shied away from accusing their fellow states of political persecution, a condition considered as key for attributing refugee status according to the Convention and its 1967 protocol. In this regard, they have privileged instead good neighborliness principles.

This however does not mean that regional refugee governance is absent. Instead, it articulates itself through the particularities of the regional state system and the geopolitical drives that have motivated the politics of refuge.

Another key strand of scholarship that has extensively delved into refugee governance in the region is fundamentally concerned with the role of international actors or externally induced initiatives in this field. Here, analysts and practitioners have explored how supranational organizations such as the European Union (EU) and the UN Refugee agencies[2] have established governing structures in the region to cater to refugee livelihoods and rights (Anholt and Sinatti 2020; Fakhoury 2019a). A strand of literature is particularly interested in how these agencies negotiate refugee rights and seek to influence Middle Eastern states' readiness to adopt the 1951 UN Convention (Janmyr 2017b; Stevens 2016).

Within this climate, scholars have critically looked at the effects of the international refugee order on the region (Fakhoury 2021; Carpi 2019). Some have for inquired into how and why international humanitarian agencies and organizations have developed 'semi-permanent presence' in the region (Brand and Lynch 2017) and what the consequences of their humanitarian practices are (Carpi 2019). Here two themes have arisen as central research areas: How Arab states have shifted responsibility to supranational organizations, and how supranational organizations, by seeking to govern displacement, perform core functions at the heart of migration control. Thus, scholars have explored on the one hand how states such as Jordan, Egypt, Lebanon, and Iraq have delegated key refugee assistance and protection functions to international agencies such as the UNHCR and UNRWA, obscuring accountability over refuge or shifting governance away from the state (Fakhoury 2020; Norman 2020). A vibrant field of study has on the other hand looked at how and why organizations such as the EU have evolved into key actors regulating displacement in the Middle East. An influential school of thought looks at the EU's refugee policy in its 'Neighbourhood' as reflective of the desire to extraterritorialise migration control far from EU borders (Fakhoury 2021; Fitzgerald 2020; Lavenex 2019). By contributing to building regional states' capacity to host refugees in the first countries of asylum, external actors attempt to govern migration from a distance (Fakhoury 2019b).

Researching the governance of displacement as an act of ordering and regulating refugee lives and statuses has recently taken central stage with the case of refugee flight from Syria. Analysts have explored variation and commonalities

2 Namely the UN Refugee Agency (UNHCR) and the United Nations Relief and Works Agency for Palestine Refugees in the Middle East (UNRWA).

in how states and non-state actors have set up governing structures to regulate the lives and mobility of displaced Syrians (Içduygu, and Nimer 2020; Secen 2020) At the heart of their analysis is why states and non-state actors respond to displacement the way they do and what logic of power underlies their governing styles (Baban, Ilcan, and Rygiel 2017).

## Refugee politics as a site of disordering: Colliding logics and disparities of power

At first glance, refugee governance in the Middle East may seem structured around visible and determined loci of power. Still, in practice, refugee regulation frameworks have been highly conflictual, reminding us of broader literature framing governance as a series of colliding regimes (Gómez-Mera 2016; Humrich 2013). Scholars studying refugee journeys have been concerned with the ways multi-levelled scales of authority intersect and clash, leading to a fragmented universe of responses and governmentalities (Fakhoury 2019a, b). Take for instance the case of widespread displacement from Syria whereby analysts have traced how state and non-state responses resemble on the ground an assemblage of incoherent refugee practices (Carpi and Şenoğuz 2019; Fakhoury 2020; Nassar and Stel 2019). These practices are profoundly shaped by geopolitical conflicts, political expediency, and economic interests (Yahya and Muasher 2018).

At the outbreak of refugee-producing conflicts, most states in the region have historically adopted open-border policies only to enforce at a later stage restrictive practices that reinforce protracted displacement and emergency (Brun 2016; Fakhoury 2020). In such a context, scholars have sought to understand how security-centred practices such as setting up camps or enforcing restrictive policies have tightened refugee access to wellbeing (Khallaf 2019; Yahya and Muasher 2018). Camps and informal settlements heightening refugee precarity have thus proliferated in countries such as Lebanon, Jordan, and Turkey. Particular attention is devoted here to capturing refugee spaces as sites of dysfunctional governance (Sanyal 2017). In such spaces, multiple governance actors ranging from the local to the international seek to enforce authority, creating however more chaos over refugee rights (Fakhoury 2020). Additionally, various formal and informal governance actors compete to transform refugee spaces into extensions of state hegemony. Here again, the case of governing displacement from Syria arises as a case in point (Carpi 2019; Nassar and Stel 2019).

Scholarly interest has further inquired into how international refugee policy fails to capture the legacies and complexities of Middle Eastern states and societies (Chatty 2017). International agencies also negotiate on behalf of refugees, solutions that do not necessarily represent their voices and realities. Within this climate, policy dissonance emerges. An example revolves around the funding instruments that organizations such as the EU and the UNHCR have adopted to promote refugee self-reliance in the context of displacement from Syria (Fakhoury 2019b; Turner 2020). Critical scholarship has looked at these supranational instruments as extraterritorial tools that seek to discourage departure to the Global North (Lavenex 2019; Lavenex and Fakhoury 2021). A prominent wave of literature has started to vociferously debate the international political economy of displacement in the Middle East. By offering host economies schemes that link refugee employment with financial aid, supranational organizations develop ordering processes that turn refugees into entrepreneurs rather than actors deserving legal protection (Tsourapas 2019b; Turner 2020). Emphasis is also placed on how international responses to displacement often aggravate divisions among refugee groups (Brun 2016). Humanitarian programming may trigger conflict over resources and privileges as well as tensions between host and refugee communities (Fiddian-Qasmieh 2016; Lehmann and Masterson 2020). With the EU-Jordan compact that focuses on granting 200, 000 job permits to Syrian refugees, other migrant and refugee communities have felt marginalized (Hartnett 2018; Lavenex and Fakhoury 2021). Such frameworks offer both empirical and analytical illustrations as to how the act of governing unravels as an arena of conflicting battlegrounds. These battlegrounds have consequences for refugee lives.

## Refugee politics as a site of bottom-up governance

> Refugees were, are, will be hosts … Hosts also have histories of displacement [3]

As I have shown above, understanding how refugees' lives and pathways are (mis) governed is a dominant field of study. It is however by no means the only overarching approach to understanding how order is produced and reconfigured in refugee spaces. Shying away from policy-centred notions of governance, scholars have increasingly called for understanding how refugee voices interact with established authority and power (Chatty 2017).

Universities have recently hosted an increasing number of research projects looking at refugees as key governors in charge of their narratives and spaces. In 2016, the University College London (UCL) launched in coordination with

3 Elena Fiddian Qasmieh, Refugee Hosts International Conference, 24 October 2019.

universities and stakeholders in Jordan, Lebanon, and Palestine a project integrating participatory and relational methodologies in refugee-related research (Refugee Hosts n.d.). This project places refugees rather than policy at the heart of governance. Researchers have carried out empirical work in refugee camps such as the Palestinian Baddawi Camp in Northern Lebanon to understand 'the complexities of everyday lives in displacement', and the various ways through which people navigate a spectrum of relationships 'between different groups of refugees and hosts, including hosts who are themselves refugees' (Fiddian-Qasmieh 2019). The project emphasizes how hosting communities support refugees and how refugees themselves support displaced individuals. Again, the case of displacement from Syria arises as particularly insightful. Syrians who have been displaced in the wake of the Syrian war have formerly hosted Lebanese citizens fleeing the Israeli-Hezbollah conflict in 2006. Current Syrian refugees in Lebanon have formerly hosted internally displaced Syrians in their hometowns. Palestinians in the Baddawi refugee camp have provided relief services and support to displaced people from Syria in the wake of the 2011 wave of displacement (Fiddian-Qasmieh 2019). Such everyday practices and intersecting practices create a type of 'refugee-refugee humanitarianism' (Fiddian-Qasmieh 2016 & 2019) in which refugees practice humanitarian governance as actors in their own right.

In this view, it is important to account for how refugees create humanitarian practices and structures. By crafting their own safety nets, refugees play the role of donors and aid givers. For instance, during the 2020 Beirut Blasts, Syrian refugees have opened their homes to displaced Lebanese (Da Silva 2020). Marginalized in the framework of the national COVID-19 response, Palestinian refugees in Lebanon have sought to support each other by sharing resources and developing awareness-raising initiatives (Fiddian-Qasmieh and Qasmieh 2020).

As the Refugee Hosts Project reveals, such perspectives deconstruct refugeeness as a permanent condition in that they highlight how refugees are or have been formerly hosts. In doing so, they debunk the narrative of victimhood and vulnerability that often stunts their predicament. Capturing dynamics of 'refugee hosting', 'refugee-refugee relationality' and 'everyday lives in and responses to displacement' (Fiddian Qasmieh 2019) allows us to conceptualize the act and practice of governance as a dynamic and everchanging process: refugees are at the same time hosts, donors, and humanitarian actors.

The Refugee Hosts project aligns itself with a variety of research projects and strands of literature that have looked at the politics of refugee leadership, voices and activism(s).[4] To reconstitute the histories of forced migration, several scholars have cast light on the role of refugees in reshaping geographies of exile and regaining agency under adverse circumstances. Nando Sigona (2014) builds a case for the iconic 2005 protest in Cairo where refugees have challenged the UNHCR politics of livelihoods and resettlement. In the context of widespread displacement from Syria since 2011, scholars have explored how Syrian refugee activists seek to transform the legal and socio-political conditions that govern them (Fourn 2017; Khoury 2017; Western 2020). Journalists have also taken an increasing interest in relating displacement through the lens of storytelling and refugee agency (Ortega 2019). In this view, governance is far from representing an assemblage of policy practices. Rather the everyday politics and representations of refugees creates a sort of 'subaltern geopolitics' (Sharp 2011) which defies hierarchical forms of order and governmentality. In the context of widespread displacement from Syria, displaced Syrians have drawn on art, activism, humanitarian engagement, and storytelling to recast their trajectories (Ortega 2019; Western 2020).

## Final thoughts: In the quest for a multi-level perspective on refugee governance

This chapter has looked at some key analytical pathways that problematize how displacement is governed. In so doing, I have distinguished three scholarly trends that map actors, processes and scales of authority undergirding the governance of displacement. The first scholarly strand is reminiscent of broader social science literature surveying governance as an ensemble of interactions across 'multiple actors' and at 'multiple scales' (Morrison et al. 2017). It tracks the multileveled state and non-state scales of authority that impact refugee regimes and experiences (Culcasi 2017; Fakhoury 2019a). It further focuses on how actors ranging from the local to the global craft rules and norms to regulate refugee displacement. The second strand of literature resonates with the conceptualization of governance as a set of fragmented and colliding architectures (Backer 2016; Gomez-Mera 2016; Krisch 2017). More specifically, it shows how refugee ordering processes, instead of generating synergy, end up creating dissonant geopolitical, cognitive and policy fields (Carpi 2019; Mourad 2017, 2019;

4 See for instance LERRN: The Local Engagement Refugee Research Network at Carleton University, LERRN: The Local Engagement Refugee Research Network – Carleton University.

Sanyal 2017). This literature is particularly interested in exploring refugee spaces as dysfunctional sites of governance reflecting decades of discrimination and policy friction. A third literature strand looks at refugee spaces as a bottom-up site of governance. In such a configuration, refugee narratives and actions create an everyday politics challenging dominant bordering practices and structures of power (Sigona 2014). Shying away from institutional approaches to governance, this literature strand employs actor-centred, participatory, and relational methods of research that intersect with the broader understanding of governing as a site for agency, collaboration, and networks (Latour 2005; Ostrom 2010; Tormos-Aponte and Garcia-Lopez 2018). Academics are interested in the ways refugees unsettle policy as well as asymmetries of power, and in the ways through which they become protagonists, governing their own lives. This literature interrogates our understanding of top-down authority scales, leading us to view governance as decentred and negotiated from below.

The literature strands that I have elaborated upon are neither disconnected from each other nor are they to be understood in counter-position to each other. Rather all of them endeavour to capture interdependencies in the ways policy fields, structures and refugee voices build on each other. To establish an empirical base to these interdependent conceptualizations of refugee governance, I have mapped key streams of thought that analyse the politics of displacement in the Middle East. I have further alluded to some illustrative cases (mostly from the recent wave of mass displacement from Syria) to show how these strands of literature ground their perspectives in real life examples. Indeed, as underscored in the chapter, the case of widespread displacement from Syria emerges as a revelatory site of inquiry for understanding the governance of displacement through a polycentric prism: an act of ordering, an act of disordering and an act of bottom-up governance.

Building on cases from the Middle East in the broader field of refugee studies is in no way an attempt to relegate this region to an area of exceptionalism. Rather the aim is to give an empirical base to the various ways the governance of displacement embodies itself. Further research could draw on such illustrative areas of inquiry to explore how the governance of refugee journeys articulates itself through an assemblage of ordering and disordering structures in various world regions.

Ultimately, by unpacking governance and its derivative articulations, I show how governing processes bear inherently their own contradictions and paradoxes especially when it comes to governing human lives. Here, I seek to amplify the debate on the relevance, limitations, and consequences of 'governing' in shaping our own realities. By looking at responses to displacement and refugee experiences in conjunction to rather than in isolation from overlapping histories, multi-sited arenas of power, and cross-cutting policy fields, we can derive broader insights into how societies, nation-states, and world orders co-constitute as well as collide into each other.

## Bibliography

Allen, W. et al. 2017. "Who Counts in Crises? The New Geopolitics of International Migration and Refugee Governance." Geopolitics, 23(1): 217-243. Doi: https://doi.org/10.1080/14650045.2017.1327740

Anholt R. and G. Sinatti. 2020. "Under the Guise of Resilience: The EU Approach to Migration and Forced Displacement in Jordan and Lebanon." Contemporary Security Policy, 41(2), 311–335.

Baban, F., S. Ilcan, and K. Rygiel. 2017. "Syrian Refugees in Turkey: Pathways to Precarity, Differential Inclusion, and Negotiated Citizenship Rights." Journal of Ethnic and Migration Studies, 43 (1): 41–57.

Bache, I. and Flinders, M. 2004. Multi-Level Governance. Oxford: Oxford University Press.

Backer, L.C. 2016. "Governance Polycentrism or Regulated Self-Regulation: Rule Systems for Human Rights Impacts of Economic Activity Where National, Private, and International Regimes Collide." In Contested Regime Collisions: Norm Fragmentation in World Society. Cambridge: Cambridge University Press, pp. 198-225. Doi: https://doi.org/10.1017/CBO9781316411230.009

Betts, A. 2014. "International Relations and Forced Migration." In Fiddian-Qasmiyeh, E., G. Loescher, K. Long, and N. Sigona (eds.), The Oxford Handbook of Refugee and Forced Migration Studies. Oxford: Oxford University Press. Doi: 10.1093/oxfordhb/9780199652433.013.0004

Betts, A. 2011. "The Global Governance of Migration and the Role of Trans-Regionalism." In Rahel Kunz, Sandra Lavenex, Marion Panizzon (eds.), Multilayered Migration Governance. The Promise of Partnership. London: Routledge.

Betts, A., and G. Loescher (eds.). 2010. Refugees in International Relations. Oxford: Oxford University Press.

Boustani, M. 2014. "Enhancing Municipal Capacities: From Emergency Response to Planning." Civil Society Knowledge Center – Lebanon Support. https://civilsociety-centre.org/pdf-generate/27197.

Brand, L.A. and M. Lynch. 2017. "How the Refugee Crisis Is Transforming the Middle East." The Washington Post. https://www.washingtonpost.com/news/monkey-cage/wp/2017/03/30/how-the-refugee-crisis-is-transforming-the-middle-east/?utm_term=.14c32e8bfa99.

Brun, C. 2016. "There Is No Future in Humanitarianism: Emergency, Temporality and Protracted Displacement." History and Anthropology, 27(4): 393–410. Doi: https://doi.org/10.1080/02757206.2016.1207637

Campomori, F. and M. Ambrosini. 2020. "Multilevel Governance in Trouble: The Implementation of Asylum Seekers' Reception in Italy as a Battleground." Comparative Migration Studies, 8(22). Doi: https://doi.org/10.1186/s40878-020-00178-1

Carpi, E. 2019. "Winking at Humanitarian Neutrality: The Liminal Politics of the State in Lebanon." Anthropologica, 61(1): 83–96. Doi: 10.3138/anth.2018–0006

Carpi, E. and H.P. Senoğuz. 2019. "Refugee Hospitality in Lebanon and Turkey. On Making the 'Other.'" International Migration, 57(2): 126–142. Doi: https://doi.org/10.1111/imig.12471

Chalcraft, J.T. 2008. The Invisible Cage: Syrian Migrant Workers in Lebanon, Stanford Studies in Middle Eastern and Islamic Societies and Cultures. California: Stanford University Press.

Chatty, D. 2017. "The Syrian Humanitarian Disaster: Understanding Perceptions and Aspirations in Jordan, Lebanon and Turkey." Global Policy, 8(1): 25–32. Doi: https://doi.org/10.1111/1758-5899.12390

Chimni, B.S. 1998. "The Geopolitics of Refugee Studies: A View from the South." Journal of Refugee Studies, 11(4): 350–374. Doi: https://doi.org/10.1093/jrs/11.4.350-a

Culcasi, K. 2017. "Displacing Territory: Refugees in the Middle East." International Journal of Middle East Studies, 49(2): 323–326. Doi: 10.1017/S0020743817000095

Da Silva, C. 2020. "Refugees in Lebanon Offer Their Homes, Blood to Beirut Explosion Victims." Newsweek, https://www.newsweek.com/refugees-lebanon-beirut-explosion-1522965

De Bel-Air, F. 2015. "A Note on Syrian Refugees in the Gulf: Attempting to Assess Data and Policies." Migration Policy Centre and Gulf Labour Markets and Migration. [Explanatory Note no. 11/2015] https://cadmus.eui.eu/bitstream/handle/1814/37965/GLMM_ExpNote_2015_11.pdf?sequence=1&isAllowed=y.

Doraï, M.K. and O. Clochard. 2006. "Non-Palestinian Refugees in Lebanon from Asylum Seekers to Illegal Migrants." In De Bel-Air, F., Migration et Politique au Moyen Orient. Beirut: IFPO, 27–143.

Fakhoury, T. (2021). "Refugee Humanitarian Orders and Disorders: The European Union and Syria's Neighbouring Countries." In J. Fiori, B. Taithe, F.E.A. Rigon, and R. Zakaria (eds.), Amidst the Debris: Humanitarianism and the End of Liberal Order. London: Hurst.

Fakhoury, T. 2020. "Refugee Return and Fragmented Governance in the Host State." Special Issue, New Actors and Contested Architectures in International Migration Governance. Third World Quarterly. https://doi.org/10.1080/01436597.2020.1762485

Fakhoury, T. 2019a. "Multi-Level Governance and Migration Politics in the Arab World: The Case of Syria's Displacement." Journal of Ethnic and Migration Studies, 45(8): 1310-1326. Doi: https://doi.org/10.1080/1369183X.2018.1441609

Fakhoury, T. 2019b. "The European Union and Arab Refugee Hosting States: Frictional Encounters." Centre for European Integration Research. [Working Paper no. 01/2019] https://eif.univie.ac.at/downloads/workingpapers/wp2019-01.pdf.

Fee, M. 2021. "Lives Stalled: The Costs of Waiting for Refugee Resettlement." Journal of Ethnic and Migration Studies. Doi: https://doi.org/10.1080/1369183X.2021.1876554

Fiddian Qasmieh, E. and Y.M. Qasmieh. 2020. "Refugees' Pandemic Responses in a Palestinian Camp in Lebanon." Current History, 119 (821): 349–355.

Fiddian-Qasmieh, E. 2019. "Refugee Hosts Team at Mobilizing Global Voices Conference 2019: Perspectives from the Global South." Refugee Hosts. March 25. https://refugeehosts.org/2019/03/25/refugee-hosts-team-at-mobilising-global-voices-conference-2019-perspectives-from-the-global-south/.

Fiddian-Qasmiyeh, E. 2016. "Refugee-Refugee Relationality: Hospitality and 'Being With' Refugees." Refugee Hosts. December 14. https://refugeehosts.org/2016/12/14/refugee-refugee-relationality-hospitality-and-being-with-refugees/.

Fiddian-Qasmiyeh, E., G. Loescher, K. Long, and N. Sigona (eds.). 2014. The Oxford Handbook of Refugee and Forced Migration Studies. Oxford: Oxford University Press. Doi: 10.1093/oxfordhb/9780199652433.001.0001

Fine, S. and H. Thiollet. 2020. "Does Crisis Matter for European Migration Governance? A Framework Paper." MAGYC Working Paper. https://spire.sciencespo.fr/notice/2441/2rarilkpmu8p68752rb0v87uvm.

FitzGerald, D.S. 2020. "Remote Control of Migration: Theorizing Territoriality, Shared Coercion, and Deterrence." Journal of Ethnic and Migration Studies, 46(1): 4-22. Doi: https://doi.org/10.1080/1369183X.2020.1680115

Fourn, L. 2017. "Turning Political Activism into Humanitarian Engagement: Transitional Careers of Young Syrians in Lebanon." [Research Report], Power2Youth. HAL Id: hal-01969969.

Gómez-Mera, L. 2016. "Regime Complexity and Global Governance: The Case of Trafficking in Persons." European Journal of International Relations, 22(3): 1-48. Doi: 10.1177/1354066115600226

Hanafi, S. 2014. "Forced Migration in the Middle East and North Africa." In Fiddian-Qasmiyeh, E., G. Loescher, K. Long, and N. Sigona (eds.), The Oxford Handbook of Refugee and Forced Migration Studies. Oxford: Oxford University Press. Doi: http://doi.org/10.1093/oxfordhb/9780199652433.013.0029

Harrell-Bond, B. 2002. "Can Humanitarian Work with Refugees Be Humane?" Human Rights Quarterly, 24(1): 51–85. Doi: 10.1353/hrq.2002.0011

Hartnett, A. S. (November 2018). "The Effect of Refugee Integration on Migrant Labor in Jordan." Review of Middle East Studies, 52 (2): 263–282. https://doi.org/10.1017/rms.2018.91.

Hilal, L., and S. Samy. 2008. "Asylum and Migration in the Mashrek." Euro-Mediterranean Human Rights Network. https://ec.europa.eu/migrant-integration/index.cfm?action=media.download&uuid=2A9339E1-E12B-E824-A57C5AEF9CF4F31D.

Humrich, C. 2013. "Fragmented International Governance of Arctic Offshore Oil: Governance Challenges and Institutional Improvement." Global Environmental Politics, 13(3): 79-99. Doi: https://doi.org/10.1162/GLEP_a_00184

Içduygu, A. and M. Nimer. 2020. "The Politics of Return: Exploring the Future of Syrian Refugees in Jordan, Lebanon and Turkey." Third World Quarterly, 41(3): 415–433.

Janmyr, M. and D. Stevens. 2021. "Regional Refugee Regimes: Middle East." In C. Costello, M. Foster, and J. McAdam (eds.), The Oxford Handbook of International Refugee Law. Oxford: Oxford University press, 1–22, DOI: 10.1093/law/9780198848639.003.0019

Janmyr, M. 2017a. "No Country of Asylum: 'Legitimizing' Lebanon's Rejection of the 1951 Refugee Convention." International Journal of Refugee Law, 29(3): 438–465. Doi: https://doi.org/10.1093/ijrl/eex026

Janmyr, M. 2017b. "UNHCR and the Syrian Refugee Response: Negotiating Status and Registration in Lebanon." The International Journal of Human Rights, 22(3): 393-419. Doi: https://doi.org/10.1080/13642987.2017.1371140

Khoury, R.B. 2017. "Aiding Activism? Humanitarianism's Impacts on Mobilized Syrian Refugees in Jordan." Middle East Law and Governance, 9(3): 267–281. Doi: https://doi.org/10.1163/18763375-00903001

Krisch, N. 2017. "Liquid Authority in Global Governance." International Theory, 9(2): 237–260. Doi: https://doi.org/10.1017/S1752971916000269

Latour, B. 2005. Reassembling the Social: An Introduction to Actor-Network Theory. Oxford: Oxford University Press.

Lavenex, S. and T. Fakhoury. 2021. "Trade Agreements as a Venue for Migration Governance Potential and Challenges for the European Union," Research Report, Delegationen för migrationsstudier – Delmi, https://www.delmi.se/en/publications/report-2021-11-trade-agreements-as-a-venue-for-migration-governance-potential-and-challenges-for-the-european-union/

Lavenex, S. 2019. "Instruments, Methods, Mechanisms of Externalisation: Trajectory and Implications." Draft Working Paper for the Comparative Network on Refugee Externalization Policies (CONREP).

Lehmann, M.C., and D.T.R. Masterson. 2020. "Does Aid Reduce Anti-Refugee Violence? Evidence from Syrian Refugees in Lebanon." American Political Science Review. Doi: https://doi.org/10.1017/S0003055420000349

Lenner, K. 2020. "'Biting Our Tongues': Policy Legacies and Memories in the Making of the Syrian Refugee Response in Jordan." Refugee Survey Quarterly. doi: https://doi.org/10.1093/rsq/hdaa005

LERRN. 2021. "The Local Engagement Refugee Research Network." Carleton University.

Lippert, R. 1999. "Governing Refugees: The Relevance of Governmentality to Understanding the International Refugee Regime." Alternatives: Global, Local, Political. Doi: https://doi.org/10.1177/030437549902400302

Loescher Gil. 2014. "UNHCR and Forced Migration." The Oxford Handbook of Refugee and Forced Migration.

Khallaf, S. 2019. "Refugee Movements in the Middle East: Old Crises, New Ideas." MENARA Working Papers, no. 29: 1–12. https://www.iai.it/sites/default/files/menara_wp_29.pdf.

Malkki, L. 1996. "Speechless Emissaries: Refugees, Humanitarianism and Dehistoricization." Cultural Anthropology, 11(3): 377–404. Doi: https://doi.org/10.1525/can.1996.11.3.02a00050

Malit, F.T. and G. Tsourapas. 2021. "Migration Diplomacy in the Gulf – Non-State Actors, Cross-Border Mobility, and the United Arab Emirates." Journal of Ethnic and Migration Studies. https://doi.org/10.1080/1369183X.2021.1878875

Martin, S. 2016. "The Global Refugee Crisis." Georgetown Journal of International Affairs, 17(1): 5–11. Doi: https://doi.org/10.1353/gia.2016.0000

McConnachie, K. 2014. Governing Refugees: Justice, Order and Legal Pluralism. London: Routledge.

Milner, J. 2017. "Power and Influence the Global Refugee Regime." Refuge: Canada's Journal on Refugees, 33(1): 3–6. Doi: https://doi.org/10.25071/1920-7336.40443

Milner, J., and K. Wojnarowicz. 2017. "Power in the Global Refugee Regime: Understanding Expressions and Experiences of Power in Global and Local Contexts." Refuge: Canada's Journal on Refugees, 33(1): 7-17. Doi: https://doi.org/10.25071/1920-7336.40444

Morrison, T.H. et al. 2017. "Mitigation and Adaptation in Polycentric Systems: Sources of Power in the Pursuit of Collective Goals." WIREs Climate Change, 8(5): 1. Doi: 10.1002/wcc.479

Mourad, L. 2019. "Open Borders, Local Closures: Decentralization and The Politics of Local Responses to the Syrian Refugee Influx in Lebanon." PhD dissertation.

Mourad, L. 2017. "'Standoffish' Policy Making: Inaction and Change in the Lebanese Response to the Syrian Displacement Crisis." Middle East Law and Governance, 9(3): 249-266. Doi: 10.1163/18763375-00903005

Nassar, J. and N. Stel. (2019). "Lebanon's Response to the Syrian Refugee Crisis: Institutional Ambiguity as a Governance Strategy." Political Geography, 70: 44–54.

Norman, K.P. 2020. Reluctant Reception. Cambridge: Cambridge University Press.

Ortega, A. 2019. "Art and Activism at the Lebanese-Syrian Border." The Conversation, April 29. https://theconversation.com/art-and-activism-at-the-lebanese-syrian-border-116032.

Ostrom, E. 2010. "A Long Polycentric Journey." Annual Review of Political Science, 13: 1-23. Doi: https://doi.org/10.1146/annurev.polisci.090808.123259.

Refugee Hosts. n.d. "Local Community Experiences of Displacement from Syria: Views from Lebanon, Jordan and Turkey." Refugee Hosts. https://refugeehosts.org.

Sanyal, R. 2017. "A No-Camp Policy: Interrogating Informal Settlements in Lebanon." Geoforum, 84: 117–125. Doi: https://doi.org/10.1016/j.geoforum.2017.06.011

Sayigh, R. 2001. "Palestinian Refugees in Lebanon: Implementation, Transfer or Return." Middle East Policy, 8(1): 94–105. Doi: https://doi.org/10.1111/1475-4967.00009

Secen, S. (2020). "Explaining the Politics of Security: Syrian Refugees in Turkey and Lebanon." Journal of Global Security Studies, ogaa039.

Sharp, J. 2011. "Subaltern Geopolitics: Introduction." Geoforum, 42(3): 271-273. Doi: 10.1016/j.geoforum.2011.04.006

Sigona, N. 2014. "The Politics of Refugee Voices: Representations, Narratives, and Memories." In Fiddian-Qasmiyeh, E., G. Loescher, K. Long, and N. Sigona (eds.), The Oxford Handbook of Refugee and Forced Migration Studies. Oxford: Oxford University Press. Doi: 10.1093/oxfordhb/9780199652433.013.0011

Stevens, D. 2016. "Rights, Needs or Assistance? The Role of the UNHCR in Refugee Protection in the Middle East." The International Journal of Human Rights, 20(2): 264-283. Doi: 10.1080/13642987.2015.1079026

Stoker, G. 1998. "Governance as Theory: Five Propositions." International Social Science Journal, 50(155): 17–28. Doi: https://doi.org/10.1111/1468-2451.00106

Thiollet, H. 2011. "Migration as Diplomacy: Labor Migrants, Refugees, and Arab Regional Politics in the Oil-Rich Countries." International Labour and Working-Class History, 79: 103–121. Doi: https://doi.org/10.1017/S0147547910000293

Tormos-Aponte, F., and G.A. García-López. 2018. "Polycentric Struggles: The Experience of the Global Climate Justice Movement." Environmental Policy and Governance, 28(4): 284-294. Doi: https://doi.org/10.1002/eet.1815

Tsourapas, G. 2019a. "The Syrian Refugee Crisis and Foreign Policy Decision-Making in Jordan, Lebanon, and Turkey." Journal of Global Security Studies, 4 (4): 464–481. Doi: https://doi.org/10.1093/jogss/ogz016

Tsourapas, G. 2019b. "Syrian Migration and the Rise of Refugee Rentierism." Crisis Magazine, October 1. https://crisismag.net/2019/10/01/syria-the-european-migrant-crisis-and-the-rise-of-refugee-rentierism/.

Turner, L. 2020. "'#Refugees Can Be Entrepreneurs Too!' Humanitarianism, Race, and the Marketing of Syrian Refugees." Review of International Studies, 46(1): 137-155. Doi: https://doi.org/10.1017/S0260210519000342

UNHCR. 2020. "Figures at a Glance." UNHCR. https://www.unhcr.org/uk/figures-at-a-glance.html.

Western, T. 2020. "Listening with Displacement: Sound, Citizenship, and Disruptive Representations of Migration." Migration and Society: Advances in Research, 3(1): 294-309. Doi: https://doi.org/10.3167/arms.2020.030128

Wolff, S. 2015. "Migration and Refugee Governance in the Mediterranean: Europe and International Organisations at a Crossroads." IAI Working Papers, 15(42). https://www.iai.it/sites/default/files/iaiwp1542.pdf.

Yahya, M., and M. Muasher. 2018. "Refugee Crises in the Arab World." Carnegie Endowment for International Peace. https://carnegieendowment.org/2018/10/18/refugee-crises-in-arab-world-pub-77522.

Zaiotti, R. 2006. "Dealing with Non-Palestinian Refugees in the Middle East: Policies and Practices in an Uncertain Environment." International Journal of Refugee Law, 18(2): 333–353. Doi: https://doi.org/10.1093/ijrl/eel006

Zakharia, L. and S. Knox. 2014. "The International Aid Community and Local Actors: Experiences and Testimonies from the Ground." Civil Society Knowledge Center, Lebanon Support. https://civilsociety-centre.org/paper/international-aid-community-and-local-actors-experiences-and-testimonies-ground.

Michael Alexander Ulfstjerne

# Ode to Wall

## Introduction

Towards the end of his influential book on Nations and Nationalism Ernest Gellner (1983) invoked the difference between a pre-nationalist landscape and a world of nations and nationalisms by reference to the contrasting painting styles of Kokoschka and Modigliani: the former working by way of interweaving and overlapping shades, where the latter is made up of neat and sharply defined shapes in distinct colours. The stark opposition between a world defined by movement in patches and shreds and one in which difference and rights are chiselled into the soil is defining still for much politics today. Often such opposition comes in irreconcilable terms between those who harbour ideas of free movement in a borderless world and those for whom the nation state is the crux of all things true and safe, a natural extension of culture as such. In her classical text, National Geographic (1992) Anthropologist Liisa Malkki takes Gellner's observation one step further as she considers what implications the 'naturalization' of borders and national identity have for those who fall outside the 'national order of things':

> The naturalization of the links between people and place leads to a vision of displacement as pathological, and this, too, is conceived in botanical terms, as uprootedness. Uprootedness comes to signal a loss of moral and, later, emotional bearings. Since both cultural and national identities are conceived in territorialized terms, uprootedness also threatens to denature and spoil these (Malkki, 1992: 34)

It's not uncommon that scholars of migration, conflict, and globalization find borders, walls, or other forms of territorial enclosure genuinely unsympathetic. And with good reason. Borders restrict movement and mobility. They not only enclose national territories, but the rapid growth of gated communities and slums attest to the expansion of internal borders (Low, 2003; Davis, 2006).

Difference and inequality are organized spatially through building walls (Caldeira, 2000). Such inequality is even more evoked when people move across national borders, attesting to clearly defined hierarchies of mobility (Glick Schiller & Salazar, 2013). Particularly research into topics as conflict, refugees, and migration have long criticized the border as a differential technology that allows some to move while others less fortunate remain stuck in a state of protracted uncertainty. In other words, while the George Clooneys of the world accumulate frequent flyer miles as they traverse borders in a frictionless fashion (Up in the Air, 2009), others cling on the wheels of planes in the meagre hopes of simply arriving somewhere else. By implication, borders quickly translate as the embodiment of populism, xenophobia, neo-nationalist sentiments, fear, and myopia. But what goes amiss in this reading? Such swift conclusions, I will argue in the remains of this chapter, are likely to collapse the social functions of borders or walls altogether.

Against this background what I hope to accomplish here is if not to re-configure physical demarcations as an unlikely ally in times of insecurity and crisis then at least propose a more ambiguous reading of the border. This is not simply to play the Devil's advocate or trade into populist reason, but to take issue with the ways in which uncritical visions of cohabitation, commonality, and frictionless movement across an imagined Kokoshkian topography may at times prove counterproductive. To do so I make two interventions: first, thinking along other kinds of territorial markers, I consider the social function of physical demarcations through the case of refugee housing design; second, I present a brief reflection on the border as architecture. Beyond its' use as a technology of power, the border – I argue – is a site for intense imaginations and contestation.

## Designing borderless spaces

Territorial markers may be important for reasons that are easily forgotten in the current polemics against borders. Allow me here to make a brief aside, shifting the emphasis from the national borders to another kind of bordering practice of a more domestic kind. I do this to provide one example of how the ideological eradication of borders in the name of commonality may be futile, if not outright counterproductive.

Since the so-called refugee crisis of 2015, scores of Scandinavian designers, architects, and entrepreneurs have produced innumerable ways to quick-fix integration and ensure healing through smart housing designs. In most of these designs, we can discern the assumption that common spaces are key to psycho-social welfare and at the same time beneficial to integration, whatever this is taken to mean. A glance back at earlier high tides of refugee reception shows that this tendency is not entirely new. Refugee housing designs for Bosnian refugees who arrived in Scandinavia in the 90s fleeing the War in Bosnia and Herzegovina (1992–1995) were similarly characterized by the inclination to give priority to common spaces (community kitchens, spaces of socializing, etc.) over private or individual family spaces. Interesting here is how such caring design considerations not only prescribes a certain 'cultural geometry' (Murphy, 2013) with little or any recognition of doing so, while seemingly also downplaying the others' need for privacy. The values ascribed to open kitchen areas and ostensibly non-gendered spaces are largely devoid of its interventionist effects, as if cleansed by aesthetic considerations, sometimes even to the extent of overrepresenting such ideologies in architectural and design thinking. Design is, by implication, distinctly political. Even the Scandinavian version. Here, it's interesting to note the importance of domestic boundaries as crucial features of identity management in a Scandinavian context. As shown by Pauline Garvey in her wonderful article, Domestic Boundaries: Privacy, Visibility and the Norwegian Window (2005), privacy is an elusive term and often relates perceptions of 'the social gaze'. In her reflection on issues of privacy and the fondness of 'boundary marking' in Norway, Garvey (2005) observes an interesting tension: 'Numerous physical and social barriers distinguish public from private sphere, and yet the private home does not seem to be contradicted by relatively unhindered domestic visibility' (Garvey, 2005: 161). We see this in the public character of domestic windows: undrawn curtains, window paraphernalia, ornaments, lights. More than simply being a token of securing a domestic space and rendering certain activities invisible to outsiders, privacy is deeply contextual and reveals the importance of a particular 'social gaze' (Garvey, 2005: 161). This becomes strikingly obvious in cases where foreigners or migrants fail to live up to these dispositions often triggering a range of local suspicions and sanctions, even interventions (Garvey, 2005; Larsen, 2011).

One notable example of this from the most recent 'refugee crisis' was the case of the 'Venligbolig' (literally, the friendly home). The name itself was a convenient pun that added a physical form to an amorphously organized solidarity movement (Venligboerne) that had taken action to oppose the Danish government's strict refugee policy with a range of welcoming activities as volunteer driven cafés, help, education activities, etc. In the design solution made by architects Søren Rasmussen (ONV Architects) and Johan Galster (2+1 idébureau) a 35–49m2 Scandinavian wood construction could be transported and lifted into the garden of a typical Danish one-family house (fig. 1.). It was designed to meet the construction and regulatory requirements and to seamlessly connect with the existing water, electricity, and sewage infrastructure. As it conceived of an immediate space for integration with the Danes the concept itself gained a tremendous amount of positive attention when launched. At a first glance it appeared to provide a more holistic and seemingly sympathetic design solution to the housing and integration challenges afforded by the 'crisis'. The refugee families were to settle temporarily in the small wooden homes and could subsequently be introduced to

**Fig. 1:** The 'Venligbolig' refugee housing design solution. The design was made by architects Søren Rasmussen (ONV Architects) and Johan Galster (2+1 idébureau).

both Danish language and customs simply by stepping outside into the garden of a welcoming Danish family. As to the incentives for the Danish families to receive and (out)house refugees the hosts would obtain ownership over the small wooden house upon the end of a 3–5-year refugee housing period and could subsequently re-deploy the structure at their own will: for example, a as guesthouse, 'generation house' (for elderly family members), teenage container, or compile several of them into a club or community centre.

What struck me about the design as well as countless other design ideas was a conspicuous yet ubiquitous lack of clearly defined territorial markers. Where did the Danish one-family house stop, and the friendly home begin? In the architectural rendition we see a large villa on the right-hand side, while on the left side, located on the lawn, is the small neatly designed wood house with large glass panels. Classical privet hedges mark the outer boundaries of the villa ground. Most often privet hedges would be of the type Ligustrum Vulgare (lat.) delivered in the standard sizes of 150 or 180 centimetres. Yet strangely no such demarcation, hedge or line of any kind is set up between the refugees' temporary home and the Danish house. This was a space intended for the purpose of integration. Although celebrated for its ingenuity, the 'Venligbolig' solution was never successfully implemented as a home and never came anywhere near to being a solution of scale.

From earlier ethnographic explorations of different types of refugee housing solutions in the aftermath of the 2015 'crisis'[1] I experienced a similar negation of physical demarcations. In most cases, volunteers or municipal employees would lament the temporary occupants' lacking care for 'common areas' (fælles arealer): rarely occupants would take responsibility for maintaining or cleaning them; at times kitchen utensils would disappear into the private quarters of the occupants. Common areas, moreover, were often a place for daily conflicts and skirmish. Rarely anyone in the municipalities or among the visiting and helping groups of volunteers would question the common spaces themselves: for what were they if not common, benign, and intentionally good? Interestingly, the general neglect of common areas was sharply contrasted with the well-kept and tidy premises of individual quarters. Somehow, these were neat and well taken care of.

What this might suggest is that territorial markers are productive in the sense of generating a feeling of entitlement, of ownership, of self. As Paulina Garvey observes, the domestic boundary is 'an essential feature of identity management' (Garvey, 2005: 161). Moreover, that commonality by design may defeat the purpose entirely. Many families who have made long and perilous journeys are more likely to need their own space at first, and then somewhere down the line we may introduce, or design designated spaces for meeting and learning. 'Please, start with a wall or a fence' has become a catchphrase that I direct towards architectural students and aspiring designers. Often this affords some degree of antipathy and bewilderment. Why would an anthropologist of all people look to the wall or the boundary as an integral part of refugee housing? One place to start could be Frederik Barth's (1969) pioneering work on ethnic boundaries that exactly invites us to reflect critically on the social function of the boundary, not as a static impenetrable line but also as something vital for social interaction and identity formation. Here we may well start with a wall, a privet hedge, a line. Should commonality arise people will surely cross it or come together to break the surface, tear down the fence, or carve out a space to share.

A few years back I encountered such instance of 'reverse construction' in the name of commonality where a group of neighbours in the Belgian city of Ghent decided to undo the walls, hedges, and fences that kept their garden plots apart (Figs. 2, 3). An additional benefit that came from the 'commoning' of the

1 Here I want to acknowledge my collaboration with the non-profit organization 'Emergency Architecture & Human Rights' and anthropologist Zachary Whyte in our joint work on housing designs and refugee settlement processes.

**Fig. 2:** Anti-hedge activity as residents and neighbours establish common playing grounds for children in Ghent, Belgium (author's photo).

once-were-individual plots was to ease the traffic of playing children through the interior of their homes.

The point here is not in any way to diminish the suffering that borders as spaces of governance and exception inflict upon those who risk their lives crossing them) – not in the recent years of heightened migration flows (de Genova, 2017), nor historically. Neither is this to praise the current proliferation of borders, walls and the techniques that govern them. The 'Trump wall' ostensibly aimed to impede illegal crossings in the US-Mexico border region is merely one out of a long line of policy follies that illustrate the flawed assumptions around the governing power of walls. The purpose of my intervention here, then, is primarily to present a brief reflection of the border or wall that is not singularly premised on the idea that all physical or territorial markers are impediments to humanity or solidarity. The conspicuous lack of private space in the case of Danish refugee home designs is paradigmatic for how easy some logics travel from one arena to the next. This, while surely meant well, may found yet other markers or

**Fig. 3:** Establishing common playing grounds for children in Ghent, Belgium (author's photo).

boundaries that are much harder to tear down. Now, from this brief empirical foray into on refugee housing design I move on to consider borders and walls as architectures of power, but also as sites for contestation and imagination.

## Architectures of power and contestation

In his work, Discipline and Punish (1977), the French philosopher Michel Foucault proposed the architectural metaphor of the 'Panopticon' to unravel contemporary processes of power, surveillance, and subject formation in our modern society. Here, Foucault appropriates the English philosopher Jeremy Bentham's design of the 'Inspection House' (also known as the Panopticon). In the design, every inmate is confined in cells arranged in a circular building along an outer wall in a fashion that renders every inmate potentially visible from a central vantage point or tower of inspection. In this way, the Panopticon is premised on the faculty of sight. In a similar fashion, Foucault argues, institutions as prisons, schools, asylums, and factories are structured in a way that renders some things visible (the refugee, inmate, worker, or child) while the power of the 'inspector' works by way of invisibility:

> Hence the major effect of the Panopticon: to induce the inmate a state of conscious and permanent visibility that assures the automatic functioning of power. So to arrange things that the surveillance is permanent in its effects, even if it is discontinuous in its action; that the perfection of power should tend to render its actual exercise unnecessary (Foucault, 1977: 201).

If we consider the border through a Foucauldian optic, it can be seen as a manifestation of a particular form of state authority. While the contemporary political pre-occupation with building walls and securing borders seem far from rendering its 'actual exercise unnecessary', the implementation of recent smart border technologies as surveillance of carriers and routes of migration, the use of digital archives to survey migration populations, and the ever more popular employment of biometrics as retinal scans, iris recognition, facial or voice discernment are well explained by Bentham's panoptic prison design, rendering potentially visible all clandestine and suspect movement. Territorial borders mark the beginnings and ends of 'espace propre' (de Certeau, 1993: 153–154) that in French denotes ownership, cleanliness, and something 'proper'; they define both in-and out-sides. Borders, by implication, help to perform and exercise nationhood and forms of belonging as they materialize as boundaries that contain, regulate, discipline, and sieve populations into those who belong and those who don't. Pointing to the close link between humanitarianism, borders, and migration management Mezzadra and Neilson write:

> Borders are becoming increasingly govern-mentalized or entangled with governmental practices that are bound to the sovereign power of nation-states and also flexibly linked to market technologies and other systems of measurement and control. They are sites where multiple governmental actors come into play (Mezzadra and Neilson, 2013: 176).

In a slightly different reading, walls, physical demarcations, and border architectures are more than simply manifestations of a sovereign power. With reference to the storming of the Parisian Bastille, read as the 'revolt of the mob against the monuments' (Bataille in Hollier, 1989: xi), the late French thinker George Bataille suggested that any architecture of power contains the seed and substance of its own 'de-formation'. The Bastille that had been the crux of penal authority – used as a state prison by the kings of France – was famously overrun and stormed on July 14th, 1789, only to become a powerful symbol of the revolution and the republican movement. Architecture, in this light, is defined by a multiplicity that works beyond its disciplining and authoritarian function. This exposes monuments of power to radical change to the extent of complete annihilation or inversion. Beyond design, walls and borders exert a force but simultaneously incite a variety of transgressions like clandestine crossings or more or less blunt forms of resistance. I distinctly remember the spiteful joy of relieving myself on some monumental, imperial piece of architecture in a non-disclosed European city some years back. On occasions, such multiplicity has been incorporated into architecture itself. As architect Bernard Tschumi (1987) observed in regard to his design of the Park de la Villete that was constructed on the former site of the Parisian slaughterhouses, architecture can also work 'against itself'. The Park itself was designed in a way to disable any overarching or predominant meaning. Three distinct systems of a grid, its lines and surfaces are laid out without reference to a higher order, structure, or synthesis. They collide and everyone is to experience it individual ways. Hailed as a pioneering piece of 'deconstructivist architecture', Tschumi designed la Villete against the very idea of a structure dictating function.[2]

Historically, walls present plentiful examples of Bataille's point: The Berlin wall was infamous for the everyday tactics of breaching it or facilitating flows across: of things, people, imaginations, of desires. As it finally fell, or rather as it was demolished in 1989, its' demise spurred the optimism of a generation. Bits and pieces were adopted into homes as symbols of reunion, solidarity, sold as small parcels of freedom – the refashioning of rubble as critique.

Murals provide another instance of the counterforce that walls and physical demarcations also exert. A case in point is the Wall Museum in Berlin by Checkpoint Charlie (infamous crossing between the former East and West), in turn, combining original remnants of the checkpoint architecture with reconstruction materials and tourist facilities. Other examples include the graffiti of the Intifada (Peteet, 1996); unionist murals in Northern Ireland (Hocking, 2012); anti-US murals of Teheran display only the most recent of a long line of anti-enemy murals, most recently taking more ambiguous and thus less propagandistic forms (Khosravi, 2013). Another well-known example is the English underground stencil artists Banksy's appropriation of the controversial Israeli West Bank barrier. Using only a handful of images, Palestine is rendered as nothing short of the world's largest prison.

---

2 Beyond Tschumi, several other renowned architects have sought to translate deconstruction to architecture including Frank Gehry, Rem Koolhaas, Zaha Hadid, and Peter Eisenman. All of these were among architects who starred in exposition, 'Deconstructivist Architecture', at The Museum of Modern Art's (NYC), June 23–August 30, 1988. A common concern here was to challenge and abandon functionalism.

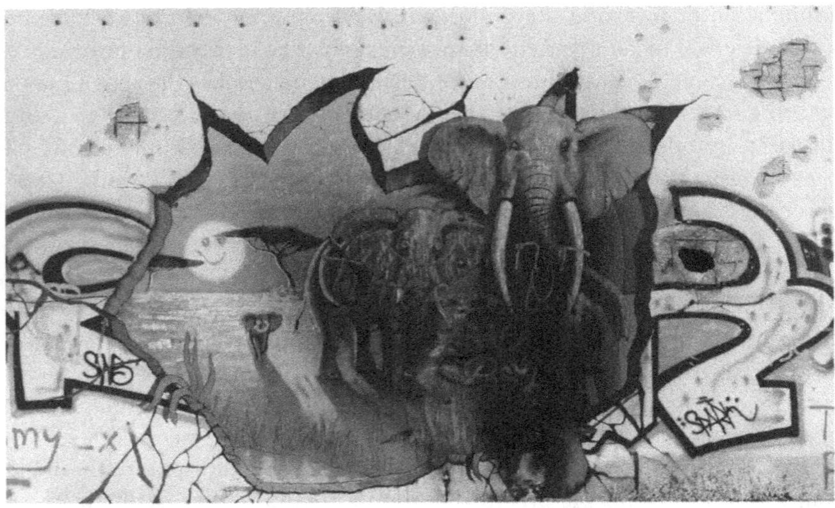

**Fig. 4:** Graffiti inside a war-torn industrial building in the outskirts of Sarajevo, Bosnia 2018 (author's photo).

Walls provide the canvas for graffiti and murals across the world. They display public forms of critique, perform alternating claims to citizenship and solidarity across class and ethnic boundaries, they expose power, and provide spaces for unofficial forms of commemoration. Abandoned buildings, sometimes entire districts, have become the backdrop for a new generation of subversive muralists. In this sense, the wall/border/territorial marker is a place of potential renewal, meetings, and in the final instance – of commensuration of radical difference. This is not necessarily understood as a horizontal, present commensuration between peoples as in Modigliani's painting – but equally of a more temporal sort: a difference between a now and whatever can potentially be. I recall how I was once suddenly abducted into a Safari landscape (Fig. 4) while walking through post-conflict urban architecture in Sarajevo a few years back. Amid the ruins and rubble of an abandoned industrial building left devastated from the 1992–1995 war in Bosnia and Herzegovina (BiH), a local graffiti artist had crafted a soft-lighted sunset savannah with a group of friendly-looking elephants, parading across the otherwise grey, run-down wall.

## An(other) wall is possible

While there is no doubt that borders and walls are raised to divide and separate people and groups, they are also crucial sites for contestation, for potential meetings, for exchanges, for construing commonality in new and unruly ways. They are part of what the authors of this anthology's introduction frame as the relations between displacement and emplacement, but in no simple or singular way. They work as places of both collaboration and struggle. Romeo and Juliet's classical love story was premised on a divide, between names and households. The divide incited the strength to breach it and the tragic demise of the two young lovers served to consolidate the ancient feud between households for generations to come. As Franz Kafka's small essay, The Great Wall of China (2002 [1919]) reminds us, the wall, even those that remain unfinished are intense sites of imagination. These may be premised on constructing nations imagined from its gaps and fissures, but also, as Bataille's revolt against architecture would suggest, they may also attest to 'an otherwise', something that exist at odds with dominant modes of being (Povinelli, 2014).

While Berlin is often celebrated as the city without walls, the time since the demolition of the Berlin Wall has seen a stark proliferation of other walls and enclosures. Borders and border technologies are as popular as ever. This is obvious from the way new 'borderscapes' are assembled across public and private domains (Rajaram & Grundy-Warr, 2007); how some borders travel southward to make up yet other precarious outer-layers of confinement; and in the way new agents and technologies enforce them.

Although initially employed to describe the German efforts to secure their positions during WW2, 'Fortress Europe' (Festung Europa) has acquired another meaning in a post-war context. It is now used as a term to condemn the state of migration policies in the EU, both as concrete border fortifications as in the Spanish North African Enclaves, Ceuta and Melilla, but also as a more general critique of the increased prevalence of anti-immigration sentiments. Borders and the borderlands that emerge at the margins of nation states (Agier, 2016) are more than physical spaces. The crafting of new legal and regulatory boundaries has quickly accompanied refugees and migrants' arrival at the shores of Europe. These may be subtler than barbed wire and concrete walls but inflict no less suffering and anxiety.

There are now more border infrastructures in the world than ever before, both physical and virtual. More than simply be read as to signify the prevalence of paranoid politics and neo-nationalist sentiments this may also alert out attention towards a crisis of sovereignty (Browne, 2018). And just maybe we are closing in

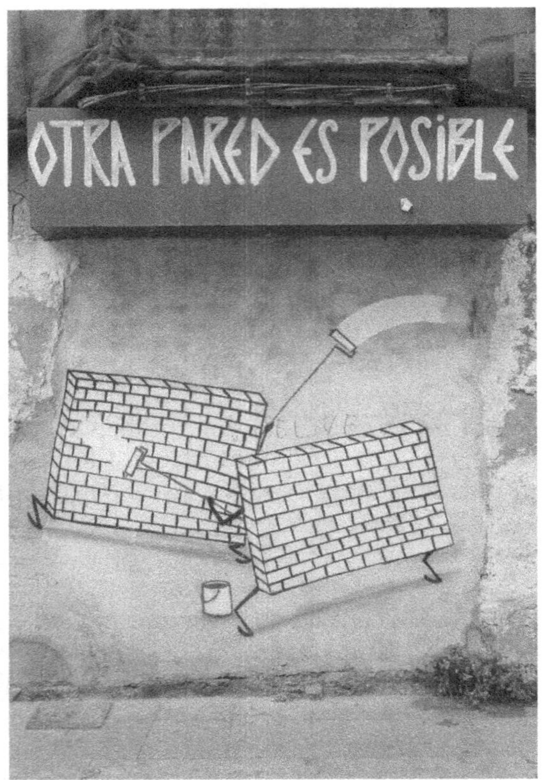


**Fig. 5:** Photo by courtesy of Commons Wikimedia.

on a tipping point of sorts. The way the Bastille once fell, architectures of enclosure and immobility may once again become the canvas of revolutions. Here, however, we must be careful not to descend into faulty ideals. What's beyond the wall is uncertain. It's riddled by chance. With breaking down walls does not necessarily follow a heightened state of commonality. As recent scholarship has shown, walls and borders have multiple meanings (Balibar, 2002), temporalities, functions, materialities. They are elastic, productive and ambiguous (Weizman, 2007; Mezzadra and Neilson, 2013). And some may be more sympathetic than others. And on this note I'll end, just adding a line from one muralist street-artist in the Spanish city of Valencia, otra pared is posible (fig. 5). Another wall is possible.

## Bibliography

Agier, M. (2016). Borderlands: Towards an Anthropology of the Cosmopolitan Condition. Cambridge: Polit Press.

Balibar, É. (2002). Politics and the Other Scene. London: Verso.

Barth, F. (1969). 'Introduction' in Fredrik Barth (ed.), Ethnic Groups and Boundaries: The Social Organisation of Culture Difference. Bergen: Universitetsforlaget; London: Allen & Unwin, pp. 9–38.

Brown, W. (2018). Walled States; Waning Sovereignty. New York: Zone Books.

Caldeira, T. (2000). City of Walls. Crime, Segregation, and Citizenship in São Paulo. Berkeley: University of California Press.

Davis, M. (2006). Planet of Slums. London: Verso.

De Certeau, M. (1993). The Practice of Everyday Life, trans. Steven Rendall. Berkeley: University of California Press.

De Genova, N. (ed.) (2017). The Borders of 'Europe': Autonomy of Migration, Tactics of Bordering. Nicholas De Genova (ed.). Durham, ND: Duke University Press.

Foucault, M. (1977). Discipline and Punish: The Birth of the Prison. London: Allen Lane.

Garvey, P. (2005). 'Domestic Boundaries: Privacy, Visibility and the Norwegian Window.' Journal of Material Culture, 10(2): 157–176.

Gellner, E. (1983). Nations and Nationalism. Ithaca, NY: Cornell University Press.

Glick Schiller, N. & Salazar, N.B. (2013). 'Regimes of Mobility Across the Globe.' Journal of Ethnic and Migration Studies, 39(2): 183–200.

Hocking, B. (2012). 'Beautiful Barriers: Art and Identity along a Belfast "Peace" Wall.' Anthropology Matters, 14(1): 92–117.

Hollier, D. (1989). Against Architecture: The Writings of George Bataille. London; Cambridge: MIT Press.

Kafka, F. (2002 [1919]). The Great Wall of China. London: Penguin Adult.

Khosravi, S. (2013). 'Graffiti in Tehran.' Anthropology Now, 5(1): 1–17.

Larsen, B.R. (2011). 'Drawing Back the Curtains: The Role of Domestic Space in the Social Inclusion and Exclusion of Refugees in Rural Denmark.' Social Analysis, 55(2): 142–158.

Low, S. (2003). Behind the Gates: Life, Security, and the Pursuit of Happiness in Fortress America. New York: Routledge.

Malkki, L. (1992). 'National Geographic: The Rooting of Peoples and the Territorialization of National Identity among Scholars and Refugees.' Cultural Anthropology, 7 (1): 24–44.

Mezzadra, S. & Nelson, N. (2013). The Border as Method, or, The Multiplication of Labor. Durham and London: Duke University Press.

Murphy, K.M. (2013). 'A Cultural Geometry: Designing Political Things in Sweden.' American Ethnologist, 40(1): 118–131.

Peteet, J. (1996). 'The Writing on the Walls: The Graffiti of the Intifada.' Cultural Anthropology, 11(2): 139–159.

Povinelli, E. A. (2014). 'Geontologies of the Otherwise.' Theorizing the Contemporary, Fieldsights, January 13. https://culanth.org/fieldsights/geontologies-of-the-otherwise.

Rajaram, P., & Grundy-Warr C. (Eds.). (2007). Borderscapes: Hidden Geographies and Politics at Territory's Edge. Minneapolis: University of Minnesota Press.

Stoetzer, Bettina. (2019). 'Europe's Other Walls.' Anthropology News, 60(6): 100–106.

Tschumi, B. (1987). Cinégramme Folie: Le Parc de La Vilette. Princeton, NJ.: Princeton Architectural Press.

Weizman, E. (2007). Hollow Land: Israel's Architecture of Occupation. London: Verso.

# Notes on Contributors

**Magnus Andersen**, PhD, is a postdoctoral researcher at the Department of Culture and Learning, Aalborg University, where he is a member of the research group Democracy, Migration and Society. Andersen's research is located in the field of post-operaismo. His research interest is within areas of political economy, labour, migration, and logistics.

**Ahlam Chemlali** is a Ph.D. fellow at DIIS – Danish Institute for International Studies and the Department of Politics and Society, University of Aalborg. Her research examines the politics and practices of border violence as a key phenomenon in contemporary European migration politics. Chemlali explores how the militarisation and externalisation of European border control to North Africa produces the everyday violence of the border and how this shapes gendered experiences.

**Sophia Dörffer Hvalkof** is a former Research Assistant at the Department of Politics and Society, Aalborg University where she was a member of the research group Global Refugee Studies.

**Brigitte Dragsted** is a PhD student at Global Refugee Studies. Her doctoral research focuses on police violence, drawing on ethnographic material from Nairobi, Kenya. Analytically, she is interested in how police violence becomes intimate. In her dissertation, she asks how we might conceive of policing relations as violent intimate relations where police and policed are mutually implicated in spatial, discursive, and bodily registers.

**Dr. Tamirace Fakhoury** is an Associate Professor of Political Science and Global Refugee and Migration Studies at the Global Refugee Studies Research Group (GRS) at the University of Aalborg in Copenhagen. She is also the Scientific advisor to the Kuwait Chair at Sciences Po in Paris (2020–2022). Prior to joining the University of Aalborg, Tamirace was an Associate Professor at the Lebanese American University and the director of the Institute for Social Justice and Conflict Resolution (ISJCR). From 2012 until 2016, she was a visiting Assistant Professor in the summer sessions at the University of California in Berkeley. Her core research and publication areas are: migration and refugee governance in conflict areas; international responses to forced migration; norm contestation in the international system; the European Union's external migration policy; and power-sharing and ethno-sectarian conflicts.

**Steffen Jensen** is Professor at the Department of Politics and Society, University of Aalborg as well as a senior researcher at the Danish Institute Against Torture. He has published extensively on gangs and policing, violence and conflict as well as on human rights and development. His publications include *Gangs, Politics and Dignity in Cape Town* from Chicago and James Currey and *Communal Intimacy and the Violence of Politics: Understanding the war on drugs in the Philippines* forthcoming at Cornell. He is currently involved in several research projects exploring violence and displacement in urban centers across the global north and south.

**Anja Kublitz** is an anthropologist and associate professor at Aalborg University. She has conducted fieldwork among Muslims in Danish housing projects since 2005. Her publications include 'Omar is Dead: Aphasia and the Escalating Radicalization Business', *History and Anthropology* (2021), and 'From Revolutionaries to Muslims: Liminal Becomings across Palestinian Generations in Denmark', *International Journal of Middle East Studies* (2016). She is currently working on a monograph entitled *Life of Catastrophes: Mutable Conflicts among Palestinians in Denmark.*

**Morten Lynge** Madsen is an industrial PhD student at Global Refugee Studies and Plan international Denmark. His doctoral research focuses on young people's individual and collective encounters with authority at the urban margins of Nairobi, Kampala, Addis Ababa and Harare. He is interested in the ways in which violence shapes the relationship between young citizens and authority and affects everyday claims to rights and participation in local governance processes.

**Malayna Raftopoulos** holds a Ph.D. in Latin American studies from the University of Liverpool. She is an Associate Professor in Development Studies and International Relations/Latin American Studies at Aalborg University. She is also an associate research fellow at the Institute of Latin American Studies, University of London, the Human Rights Consortium, University of London, and the Centro Latino Americano de Ecología Social, Uruguay. Her research interests focus on environmental governance, climate change mitigation and adaptation, extractivism and natural resource development and human rights. Her publications include; Provincialising Nature: Multidisciplinary Approaches to the Politics of Nature in Latin America (ILAS, University of London Press);

Natural Resource Development and Human Rights in Latin America: State and Non-State Actors in the Promotion and Opposition to Extractivism Activities (HRC, University of London Press); and Social- Environmental Conflicts, Extractivism and Human Rights in Latin America (Routledge).

**Rieke Schröder** is a PhD fellow at the Department of Politics and Society, Aalborg University. Her research focuses on queer feminist perspectives on migration and displacement. She is a fellow of the German Academic Scholarship Foundation and has received scholarships from the Friedrich-Ebert-Stiftung and the DAAD (German Academic Exchange Service) in the past. She holds a Master of Science in Global Refugee Studies from Aalborg University. She is editor of *The Interdisciplinary Journal of International Studies*, a student driven, Aalborg University based, peer-reviewed journal.

**Asta Smedegaard Nielsen**, PhD, has a background in sociology and media studies, and is currently employed as a postdoctoral researcher at the Department of Politics and Society, Aalborg University. Nielsen's research interest is within the areas of media and migration, critical race and whiteness studies, and affectivity studies. She has published studies of media representations of issues such as terrorism, family migration and the racialization of children.

**Marlene Spanger** is an Associate Professor at the Department of Politics and Society, Aalborg University, Denmark. Spanger's research fields include ethnographic fieldwork and discursive formations within the policy field of prostitution and anti-trafficking, transnational intimacies, and migration with a special attention to labour, gender, sexual and racial issues. She was co-chair of the Working Group: Sex, Money and Society in the COST Action IS1209 'Comparing European Prostitution Policies: Understanding Scales and Cultures of Governance (ProsPol)' (2012-2017). She is the co-author (with May-Len Skilbrei) of the volumes: 'Prostitution Research in Context. Methodology, Representation and Power' (Routledge 2017) and 'Understanding Sex for Sale Meanings and Moralities of Sexual Commerce' (Routledge 2019).

**Anabel Soriano Oliva** is a recent graduate student from the master Development and International Relations: Global Refugees Studies at Aalborg University. With a background in philosophy from the Complutense University of Madrid, she centers her research in political philosophy within a feminist perspective, particularly regarding topics such as the relation between spatiality and identity and the relation between social imaginaries and political action.

**Michael Alexander Ulfstjerne** has a background in anthropology and is currently employed as assistant professor at the Department of Politics and Society, Aalborg University, Denmark. Ulfstjerne's research is located in the intersection between material culture and displacement. His publications cover diverse topics such as architecture, spatial planning, camps, economic booms and busts, and the field of informal economy and alternative currencies.

## Political and Social Change

Edited by Martin Bak Jørgensen and Óscar García Agustín

Volume 1 Martin Bak Jørgensen / Óscar García Agustín (eds.): Politics of Dissent. 2015.

Volume 2 Laura Bang Lindegaard: Congestion. Rationalising Automobility in the Face of Climate Change. 2015.

Volume 3 Ben Dorfman (ed.): Dissent! Refracted. Histories, Aesthetics and Cultures of Dissent. 2016.

Volume 4 Aleksandra Ålund / Carl-Ulrik Schierup / Anders Neergaard (eds.): Reimagineering the Nation. Essays on Twenty-First-Century Sweden. 2017.

Volume 5 Mette Toft Nielsen / Peter Hervik: Women in post-revolutionary Egypt. Can Behaviour Be Controlled? 2017.

Volume 6 Ben Dorfman: 13 Acts of Academic Journalism and Historical Commentary on Human Rights. Opinions, Interventions and the Torsions of Politics. 2017.

Volume 7 Maren Lytje: On the Justice and Justification of Just War. How Does Life Dwell in the State? 2018.

Volume 8 Ben Dorfman: Rights under Trial, Rights Reflections. 13 Further Acts of Academic Journalism and Historical Commentary on Human Rights. 2020.

Volume 9 Trine Lund Thomsen (ed.): Changes and Challenges of Cross-border Mobility within the European Union. 2020.

Volume 10 Rieke Schröder / Anabel Soriano Oliva / Steffen Jensen (eds.): Situating Displacement. Explorations of Global (Im)Mobility 2022.

www.peterlang.com

www.ingramcontent.com/pod-product-compliance
Lightning Source LLC
Chambersburg PA
CBHW031541260326
41914CB00002B/206

* 9 7 8 3 6 3 1 8 4 7 6 0 2 *